Teaching Psychology

A Step By Step Guide

Teaching Psychology

A Step By Step Guide

Sandra Goss Lucas
University of Illinois, Urbana-Champaign

Douglas A. Bernstein
University of South Florida

2005

LAWRENCE ERLBAUM ASSOCIATES, PUBLISHERS
Mahwah, New Jersey　　　　　　　　　　London

Lawrence Erlbaum Associates, Inc., Publishers
10 Industrial Avenue
Mahwah, New Jersey 07430

Cover design by Kathryn Houghtaling Lacey

Library of Congress Cataloging-in-Publication Data

Goss Lucas, Sandra.
Teaching psychology : a step by step guide / Sandra Goss Lucas,
Douglas A. Bernstein.
p. cm.
Includes bibliographical references and index.
ISBN 0-8058-4224-1 (cloth : alk. paper)
ISBN 0-8058-4225-X (pbk. : alk. paper)
1. Psychology—Study and teaching. I. Bernstein, Douglas A. II. Title.
BF77.G67   2004
150'.71—dc22

2004046911
CIP

Books published by Lawrence Erlbaum Associates are printed on acid-
free paper, and their bindings are chosen for strength and durability.

Printed in the United States of America
10 9 8 7 6 5 4 3 2 1

Preface

We came to this book from very different backgrounds, but with a single purpose, namely to share with you what we have learned about teaching psychology, and what others have learned through their research on effective teaching.

Sandy always wanted to be a teacher, and fulfilled that dream by pursuing a teacher education program and earning a teaching certificate in Social Sciences. After completing student-teaching at a junior high school and an internship at a high school, she earned a master's degree in Teaching Social Sciences, then spent the next 6 years teaching psychology at two different community colleges. Married with two small children, her next step was to complete the PhD program in Educational Psychology (with an emphasis on teacher behavior) at Indiana University. Before being admitted to that program, she was told by members of the admissions committee to rewrite her goals statement that, in their view, placed too much emphasis on teaching and not enough on research. She did so, but throughout her graduate career she continued to find opportunities to teach.

Doug came to teaching through a much different route. His first course was introductory psychology, and he was assigned to teach it while he was still a graduate student at Northwestern University. Unlike Sandy, he had absolutely no preparation for teaching, and learned to teach as best he could, mainly through the school of hard knocks, as it were. After completing his doctorate in clinical psychology Doug joined the faculty at the University of Illinois at Urbana-Champaign where, except for a couple of sabbaticals and short leaves, he spent 30 years teaching graduate and undergraduate psychology courses.

In 1984, after Doug was appointed as director of the department's large, multisection introductory psychology program, he was looking for an assistant director, and Sandy applied for the job. Thus began a 20-year partnership that has evolved into a wonderful friendship.

The first thing we did was to revise the structure of the introductory course and reorganize the administrative structure through which it was taught. We each taught our own sections of the course, but part of our reorganization plan took the form of creating a training program for the graduate students who would be teaching most of the other sections. After decades of offering teacher preparation programs and advice to these students, and eventually to all graduate teaching assistants in the department, we realized that we had collected a lot of material that might be of value to new teachers in other psychology departments, too. We found several ways to share bits and pieces of that material with our colleagues. For a number of years, we gave 1-day workshops on the teaching of psychology at various locations around the country. And we continue to give talks on teaching, separately and together, at the Annual National Institute on the Teaching of Psychology, and elsewhere. Then we began to write about teaching. In a chapter in Prieto and Meyers' *The Teaching Assistant Handbook*, Sandy described the orientation program we developed for psychology teaching assistants at Illinois. In 1997, Doug described his views on teaching introductory psychology in a chapter for Robert Sternberg's book, *Teaching Introductory Psychology: Theory and Practice*. And in 2001, Roddy Roediger asked Doug to write a chapter about teaching for the revised edition of *The Compleat Academic*. Doug invited Sandy to be his co-author on that chapter, and while writing it, we realized that what we wanted to say about teaching psychology far exceeded our page limit.

This book is a greatly expanded discussion of the topics in that chapter, and more. It is based on our own teaching experiences, as well as on the research and experience of other psychology faculty whose work we have read and whose advice we have taken. We obviously share a general set of values about teaching psychology, but there are some details of policy and procedure on which we disagree. These occasional disagreements gave us a chance to offer multiple options for dealing with various teaching situations.

We wrote this book mainly with novice psychology teachers in mind, but we know, too, that seasoned teachers—including ourselves—can benefit from exposure to new teaching ideas and techniques, and from occasionally reevaluating their teaching and its effectiveness. We think our own teaching has improved as a result of writing this book, so we hope the book will be valuable to all teachers of psychology, no matter how much teaching experience they have.

You will notice that our presentation focuses on the practical far more than the theoretical. There are already many good books about the educational and psychological theories underlying effective teaching at the postsecondary level, and much of the advice we offer is grounded in some of those theories. But our main goal was to create a "how to" about the teaching of psychology that can be read from beginning to end, but can also serve as a quick reference and source of specific ideas for dealing with a wide range of teaching situations at a moment's notice. It is the kind of book that Doug could have used back in 1966 to help make his first teaching experience easier, less stressful, and more effective.

As you can see in the table of contents, we have organized our material in roughly the order a new teacher might need it. In Chapter 1 we describe some basic principles of effective teaching, the characteristics of today's students, and the expectations placed on today's teachers. Chapter 2 deals with such topics as developing course goals, how to plan a course, write a syllabus, establish a grading system, and choose a textbook. Chapter 3 presents a step by step guide to the first few days of class, from finding and exploring the classroom, to presenting a syllabus, to ending a class session. Chapter 4 focuses on the development of one's teaching style, and on the many options psychology teachers have to express that style in the context of giving lectures, conducting demonstrations, asking and answering questions, leading discussions, and the like. In Chapter 5, we offer advice and suggestions for evaluating student learning and performance via exams, quizzes, and a wide variety of writing assignments. We also provide guidelines for developing and grading each type of evaluation method, and we suggest ways of matching evaluation options—and one's evaluation criteria—to course goals and objectives. Chapter 6 takes up the vital topic of faculty–student relations, and how to manage them. Here you will find advice on how to create a comfortable and inclusive classroom climate, provide academic assistance, protect students' privacy, improve their motivation to learn, write letters of recommendation, and assist students with special needs or problems, as well as how to prevent and manage students' classroom misbehavior, deal with complaints, special requests, excuses, and academic dishonesty, all within the context of the highest standards of teaching ethics. Chapter 7 deals with the technology of teaching psychology, and because our own expertise in this area is limited, it was written in collaboration with Elaine Cassel, our lead consultant, David Daniel, and Missa Eaton. The chapter includes not only a description of the impressive high-tech equipment and methods now available, but also a discussion of how to use that equipment and those methods in the service of one's teaching goals. We point out that technology can enhance or interfere with a classroom presentation and can promote or impair learning; we therefore urge teachers to think carefully about when, and whether high-tech teaching approaches will advance teaching goals. In Chapter 8 we take up the topic of how to evaluate the quality and effectiveness of teaching. We emphasize the importance of establishing a continuing process of self-evaluation, and of relying on colleagues as well as students as sources of evaluative information. Finally, in Chapter 9, we close with a discussion of the need to integrate teaching into the rest of one's academic life, including how to deal with the anxieties and stresses associated with teaching.

In every chapter, we offer checklists and/or other material that we think will be of use to new and experienced teachers alike, including sample lecture notes, sample writing assignments, sample grading criteria, and even forms for dealing with students' excuses and complaints about exam items. To make it easier for you to adapt this material for your own courses, we have placed it on the CD-ROM that accompanies this book. When you see a 💿 icon in the margin of any page, you will know that the material referred to in the nearby text appears on the CD. The CD also contains a wide variety of other material that we did not have space for in the book, but that we thought you would like to have available, such as a rating sheet for choosing a textbook, a generic syllabus template, a student grade-record sheet, a sample statement on academic integrity, examples of writing assignments, examples of collaborative learning assignments, examples of quiz formats, a pool of less-than-perfect test items that you can use to hone your item-writing skills, samples of criterion-based and norm-based course grading systems, and sample letters of recommendation to help you accommodate student requests for such letters.

We hope that you enjoy reading this book as much as we have enjoyed writing it, and we look forward to hearing your comments on our efforts, and your suggestions for improvement. You can reach us at gossluca@uiuc.edu or douglas.bernstein@worldnet.att.net

We would like to thank our colleagues who provided feedback while the manuscript was in preparation. They include Bill Buskist, Auburn University; Steven Meyers, Roosevelt University; Jane Halonen, University of West Florida; and Kathryn Quina, University of Rhode Island.

—Sandra Goss Lucas
—Douglas A. Bernstein

Chapter 1

Introduction

Some Basic Principles of Effective Teaching
The Scholarship of Teaching
Your Role as a Teacher
Some Final Comments

We know a senior professor whose sole preparation for college teaching came during his third year in graduate school when he received a one-sentence letter assigning him to teach introductory psychology the following term. Quite a few important items were left out of this letter. It said nothing about (a) what topics to cover, (b) how to create a syllabus, (c) how to select a textbook, (d) how to prepare lectures and class activities, (e) how to evaluate students' performance, or (f) how to handle student-related problems such as grading complaints, classroom disruptiveness, make-up exam requests, and referrals to the counseling center. He had to learn these things—and everything else that psychology teachers should know about teaching—through trial and error in the classroom. It is no wonder that facing that first class was one of the most frightening experiences of his life (Bernstein, 1983).

This story is not unusual, nor does the teacher preparation picture in psychology seem to be changing much. Recent surveys indicate that despite growing awareness of the challenges and stresses that teaching creates for new teachers, only about 60% of psychology departments in the United States offer their graduate students any kind of teaching training (Buskist et al., 2002; Prieto & Meyers, 2000). That figure might sound substantial, but the extent of the training varies widely. Most often, it takes the form of a one-shot seminar or orientation session presented by the psychology department or a campus faculty development office. Only about 40% of psychology departments offer one- or two-term courses that provide graduate students with didactic and practical training in all aspects of teaching. And the vast majority of those courses are either not required (and therefore not heavily enrolled) or required only of students serving as teaching assistants.

In short, most new teachers of psychology enter their first undergraduate classrooms having spent years as apprentices to expert mentors in research and scholarship, but with little or no formal preparation for their role as a teacher (Buskist et al., 2002; Golde & Dore, 2001; Kennedy, 1997; Mervis, 2001). They are forced to rely on their wits and their guts, along with informal advice, the examples set by their own teachers, and readings on how to survive in the classroom (e.g., Boice, 1996; Brown & Atkins, 1988; Cannon & Newble, 2000; Curzan & Damour, 2000; Cyrs, 1994; Davis, 1993; Flood & Moll, 1990; Forsyth, 2003; Johnson, 1995; Lambert, Tice, & Featherstone, 1996; Magnan, 1990; Markie, 1994; McKeachie, 2001; Meagher & Devine, 1993; Royce, 2000; Sawyer, Prichard, & Hostetler, 2001; Weimer, 1996).

We have spoken to experienced psychology faculty who do not see this situation as all bad. Having survived their own teaching trial by fire, they are content to let academic Darwinism run its course. Unfortunately, when it comes to teaching, it is not just the fittest who survive. Many of the less fit teachers in psychology classrooms today got that way because, having so little information about the teaching process, they got off to a bad start, had bad experiences, and became less and less interested in teaching, let alone in trying to teach better (Boice, 1998b). The results of this process are bad for these teachers' professional development and even worse for their students.

There is plenty of controversy over exactly what constitutes "effective teaching," and exactly how best to teach, but there is also a body of teaching research and some teaching lore, too, that is relatively well accepted and most definitely useful. Our goal in this book is to pass on the results of that research and some of that lore—about how to organize and deliver a lecture, ask stimulating questions, lead discussions, deal with classroom management problems, write exams, and the like. We hope that having this information in mind will help make your first forays into the white water of teaching psychology a lot less stressful, and will help you to become a better teacher sooner. We begin by considering some general principles of effective teaching that, along with research evidence and our own experience, provide a foundation for all the advice and recommendations we offer later.

SOME BASIC PRINCIPLES OF EFFECTIVE TEACHING

The first seven of these principles come from a 1987 article entitled, appropriately enough, "Seven Principles for Good Practice in Undergraduate Education" (Chickering & Gamson, 1987; Chickering & Gamson, 1991). Although focused on undergraduate teaching, these principles can be applied equally well to teaching psychology at any level. Here they are.

Encourage Student–Faculty Contact

Frequent and fruitful contact between students and faculty inside and outside the classroom is important for establishing and maintaining students' motivation and involvement in the learning process. When students know that their teacher cares about their progress, they are more likely to persist at learning tasks, even when the tasks are difficult. Further, the experience of getting to know at least a few teachers as individuals can enhance students' intellectual and emotional commitment to learning.

Encourage Cooperation Among Students

Learning is enhanced when it occurs as part of a team effort. Like effective work, effective learning can often come through social collaboration rather than isolated effort in a competitive atmosphere. Collaborative learning also offers the advantage of helping students develop social responsibility while interacting with others whose ideas and thoughts expand their own thinking and deepen their own understanding.

Encourage Active Learning

"Learning is not a spectator sport" (Chickering & Gamson, 1991, p. 66). Students learn, retain, and understand more course material when they actively engage it—by talking about it, writing about it, questioning it, debating it, applying it, and relating it to what they already know—rather than sitting passively as information washes over them in lectures, videos, or other prepackaged formats.

Give Prompt Feedback

To focus their efforts to learn, students need feedback about what they know and what they don't know. This feedback should be frequent enough to guide students' efforts; it can take the form of pretests on course material as well as all sorts of quizzes, examinations, papers, projects, and other assignments that help students reflect on how far they have come in accomplishing their learning goals and how far they still have to go.

Emphasize "Time on Task"

Laboratory studies indicate that some forms of learning can take place without conscious attention, but in psychology courses there is no substitute for paying attention and devoting time to the learning task. Teachers can play a vital role in promoting adequate "time on task" by focusing most of every class session on the material to be learned, not on trivial or irrelevant discussions. They can also help students learn to use time wisely, both in terms of efficient and effective study skills and in relation to time management in general. Whether this assistance comes through personal advice or referral to campus counseling facilities, it can offer a vital aid to learning for those who need it most.

Communicate High Expectations

Expect a lot from your students and you are likely to get it. A teacher's high expectations can maximize the performance of all students—from those who are bright and motivated to those who are less well prepared or initially less eager to exert themselves. When students experience their teacher's high expectations as realistic, if challenging, their expectations of themselves tend to rise accordingly (see Treisman, 1985).

Respect Diverse Talents and Ways of Learning

Like other people, students differ among themselves in many ways, including what they know, what talents they have, and even their favorite ways to learn. A student who shines during class discussion might be all thumbs in a lab session. Students who are used to dealing on their own with practical matters in the workplace might be less adept at, or patient with, assignments that focus on abstract theories or group problem solving. If possible, give students the opportunity to show their talents and learn in ways that work for them, but don't hesitate to challenge them to learn in new ways that do not come so easily.

The next three principles of effective teaching come from the Center for Teaching Excellence, (formerly the Division of Instructional Development) at the University of Illinois, Urbana-Champaign (Center for Teaching Excellence, 1999).

Be Organized and Prepared

The organization and planning that goes into your psychology course help determine what students will learn and how easily they will learn it. A well-planned and well-organized course also conveys to students that you care about teaching and about them. The perception of a caring teacher, in turn, is associated with higher student ratings of teacher performance.

Communicate Enthusiasm

Effective and highly rated teachers also tend to communicate enthusiasm, even love, for psychology, and for the teaching enterprise. There are many ways to get this message across. Lively lectures, fascinating demonstrations, and other dramatic classroom activities certainly convey enthusiasm for the teaching enterprise, but so do high-quality, carefully chosen presentations and assignments, challenging exams, well-conceived grading systems, and the like. When students sense their teacher's passion for the course is authentic, the effect can be contagious.

Be Fair and Ethical

Fairness and the highest ethical standards—in presenting material, in dealing with students, and in evaluating them—is fundamental to effective, high-quality teaching. A related goal is to assure that students deal fairly with one another in the classroom. Students thrive in learning situations where the teacher's integrity and their confidence in that integrity govern all aspects of the course. High ethical standards should be evident in lectures that make all students feel welcome, in even-handed grading, in unbiased consideration of students' requests, and in the avoidance of even the appearance of impropriety in faculty–student relationships. Discrimination, bias, or self-interested abuse of power have no place in teaching (American Psychological Association, 2002).

THE SCHOLARSHIP OF TEACHING

The basic principles of effective teaching reflect part of what Boyer (1990) called *the scholarship of teaching*. It includes (a) knowledge of the content of psychology courses, (b) understanding and applying pedagogical techniques that are capable of communicating that knowledge to students, and (c) striving to promote the kind of active learning that encourages students to be critical, creative thinkers who will use what they learned in class to their advantage long after graduation, and who will see the value of lifelong education. In other words, effective teaching not only involves transforming and extending knowledge, it pushes teachers in creative new directions (Boyer, 1990).

The Scholarship of Learning

The scholarship of teaching, itself, arises in part from *the scholarship of learning* (Cambridge, 2001), which seeks to apply what scientists in psychology and other disciplines have discovered about the learning process and how teachers can facilitate that process. Many of the teaching techniques we describe in later chapters have evolved from this scholarship of learning.

Psychologists' long-standing involvement in the scholarship of learning can be seen not only in the vast psychological literature on the topic, but also in the fact that learning theorists, from early behaviorists to the cognitive theorists of today, have had a keen interest in how their research can be applied to education. In fact, no discipline has been more involved than psychology in the study of teaching and learning (Huber & Morreale, 2002; Nummedal, Benson, & Chew, 2002):

> Optimal teaching was the promise of the grand learning theories that dominated the early years of psychology as a discipline and the field's most prominent theorists, from Thorndike to Skinner, were concerned about the application of their theories to education.... In addition, the "cognitive revolution" of the 1960s initiated research that led to a better understanding about the ways in which information is processed. Another line of research focused on the cognitive development of college

students and both lines of research continue to ground scholarly work on teaching and learning in psychology. (Huber &
Morreale, 2002, p. 13)

Despite what we have said about the typical psychology graduate
student's marginal preparation for teaching, there is a surprisingly
long history of interest among some psychologists in promoting excellence in the teaching of psychology. For example, the 1899 convention
of the American Psychological Association (APA) included a session
on the teaching of psychology, and the second of APA's special-interest
divisions, formed in 1945, was the division on the Teaching of Psychology (Nummedal et al., 2002). It is now known as the Society for the
Teaching of Psychology (STP). In 1990, the APA created its education
directorate with the charge to encourage research on the teaching of
psychology across all subfields. In the late 1990s, the STP Task Force on
Defining Scholarship in Psychology established evaluative criteria for
the scholarship of teaching. They included a high level of disciplinary
expertise, innovation, replication by others, documentation and exposure to peer review, and significant or impactful content (Nummedal
et al., 2002).

The Scholarship of Teaching and Learning

The result of all this activity in psychology, education, and related disciplines has been the development of a *scholarship of teaching and learning (SoTL)*, an applied research enterprise with the central aim of
improving the quality of teaching and learning in college classrooms
and departments and disseminating it beyond these settings
(DeAngelis, 2003; McKinney, 2003). Through SoTL research, instructors are encouraged to be more critical examiners of their own teaching and to share their findings with other instructors in their discipline
and across disciplines. They are also encouraged to see their teaching
activities as potentially valuable sources of scholarship.

This scholarship can take many forms, ranging from simple critical observation of classroom patterns, to use of classroom data to
try out new classroom interventions, to research that compares
testing methods to see which best fosters learning.... The basic
notion is that the teaching and learning in one's own discipline
or profession is itself a kind of living laboratory, a setting in which
all sorts of intriguing, researchable questions quite specific to the
discipline or profession develop. Since those of us in academia
are engaged in teaching, evaluation and course design all the

time, it becomes a natural and very attractive place to conduct a lot of our research. (DeAngelis, 2003, pp. 54–55)

As an example of SoTL in psychology, consider a problem that almost all psychology instructors encounter, namely students who arrive harboring a whole range of culturally transmitted misconceptions about behavior and mental processes (Nummedal et al., 2002). Do these misconceptions—which typically include the "facts" that schizophrenics have split personalities, that negative reinforcement is a form of punishment, and that people only use 10% of their brain cells—create proactive inhibition that interferes with students' learning of empirically supported conclusions about psychology? One psychology teacher believed that they do, but rather than simply bemoaning this possibility, he chose to contribute to the scholarship of teaching and learning by documenting the degree to which his own students' misconceptions about psychology affected their learning in his classes (Cerbin, 2000). Later, he conducted research into the effects of a problem-based learning intervention aimed at encouraging students to evaluate and revise their preconceptions. His work allowed him to assess the actual severity of a perceived problem, led to a test of methods for dealing with the problem that could be of value to other psychology teachers, and helped to guide his classroom teaching.

SoTL is being encouraged by organizations such as the Carnegie Foundation for the Advancement of Teaching and the American Association for Higher Education. The Carnegie Scholars program brings together faculty from a variety of academic fields to design and conduct research on issues in teaching and learning in their fields. The Carnegie Academy for the Scholarship of Teaching and Learning (CASTL) supports the Teaching Academy Campus Program, which works with institutions of all types to foster and support the scholarship of teaching and learning. CASTL has also reached out to scholarly and professional organizations with small grants and other assistance aimed at helping to increase information sharing about teaching and learning.

For more information about the Carnegie Foundation for the Advancement of Teaching, and about CASTL, visit http://www.carnegiefoundation.org/CASTL/highered/index.htm. For more on SoTL, visit the online home of *The Journal of Scholarship of Teaching and Learning* (http://www.iusb.edu/~josotl/), a publication that offers a wide range of articles on SoTL, along with descriptions of how faculty in various disciplines and institutions have become involved in SoTL projects. A description of SoTL projects in psychology is available (Nummedal et al., 2002), as is an annotated bibliography on the scholarship of teaching and learning in general (Hutchings, Bjork, & Babb, 2002).

YOUR ROLE AS A TEACHER

If you are like many new teachers of psychology, it was your interest in psychology itself, not the prospect of teaching it, that led you to pursue a graduate degree and an academic career. In fact, the realization that teaching is a major part of academic life might have dawned on you only slowly over your years of graduate study, and might have come into focus only as you contemplated a teaching assistantship or were discussing teaching assignments with prospective employers. Yet teaching has always been a part of professors' jobs, and in North America prior to about 1850, it was their only job. Around this time, the European university model, with its emphasis on research and graduate education, began to influence higher education in the United States. Especially at major universities, promotion and tenure came to be based more on research productivity than on the quality of undergraduate teaching or service to the community (Boyer, 1990). During World War II, research became even more firmly embedded in professors' job descriptions as the federal government funded research in many disciplines, including psychology, to aid in the war effort. That funding has continued in varying degrees ever since, as have the research activities of college and university professors. Still, surveys of college and university faculty have found that more than 60% of all higher education faculty, including 21% of faculty at research universities, feel that teaching effectiveness should be the primary criterion for promotion and tenure (Boyer, 1990). This view is reflected in the tenure and promotion policies at some institutions, and teaching effectiveness is included in almost every professor's performance evaluations. So even if your academic interests are focused on a research career, there is good reason to spend the time and effort it takes to improve the effectiveness of your teaching.

What Is the Task?

The teaching task you face as a psychology professor depends mainly on the level, type, traditions, and orientation of the department and institution you have joined. If you are at a major research university, you might be asked to teach only two courses per term, and perhaps only one of these will be at the undergraduate level. You might at first be assigned only one course (perhaps a graduate seminar) so that you can get your bearings and establish your lab or scholarly work. If you are at a large community college, you were probably hired primarily, or exclusively, as a teacher. If you are not expected to engage in research, your teaching assignment might include two or more sections of two or more courses, for a total of four to six classes per term. Obviously, the heavier your teaching assignment, the more courses you have to prepare, the less experience you have in teaching them, and the less support there is to ease the burden, the more daunting and stressful the teaching task is likely to be.

Graduate and Undergraduate Teaching

As already mentioned, we believe that the principles of effective teaching, and most teaching skills, apply equally well at the graduate and undergraduate level. You should be aware, however, that the characteristics and needs of undergraduate and graduate students in psychology differ enough that a slightly different approach is required for each group. Most notably, undergraduates, especially those in their first term at college, tend to need more support and socialization into the culture of higher education than do graduate students (Erickson & Strommer, 1991).

Many undergraduates come to college from a high school culture where the rules and expectations are considerably different from those of the culture they are about to enter. For example, they might have been accustomed to having small classes taught by teachers who knew them personally, and who took time to remind them about upcoming assignments, quizzes, and exams and the need to prepare for them. Further, as college-bound members of their graduating class, they might have become used to being among the "smart" kids and performing well above average without having to exert all the effort of which they are capable. Finally, they might have depended on their parents to get them out of bed and off to class on time, not to mention assuring that they were fed and dressed in clean clothes. Most of these familiar circumstances change in college. Students who live at home might retain some of the perks of childhood, but their college teachers are far less likely to track their progress or question irregular attendance or poor performance. They may be faced for the first time with large lecture sections and find themselves too intimidated to ask questions, even after class. They might have few friends on campus, and they might be distressed by the loss of the well-established social support system and the relatively high social status they enjoyed back home. They might even be getting lost on campus from time to time. In many ways, then, they are starting over. If you will be teaching first-year students, keep in mind that they are in the midst of a stressful life transition. It will be up to you to decide how much to "nurture" these students, but be aware that they might want and need more support and assistance than those who are further along in their undergraduate careers.

By the time they enter a graduate program in psychology, your students will usually have well-honed academic skills, and their academic socialization is usually complete. If you teach at the graduate level, your role will expand to include mentoring as well as instruction. In addition to teaching course content, you will be helping students to conceive, develop, and design research projects; analyze the results of those projects; and clearly communicate those results in scholarly papers and presentations. In fact, a vital part of your role as a teacher of psychology graduate students is to act as a role model for the next generation of researchers. And because many of your graduate students will become faculty members themselves, you will also be a role model for the next generation of teachers.

In short, whether you are teaching at the undergraduate level, the graduate level, or both, the development of effective teaching methods will be important for your career, your sanity, and your academic legacy. Most of the suggestions we offer to help you in this regard relate to teaching undergraduates, but keep in mind that virtually everything we suggest—especially the need to be prepared, organized, enthusiastic, and committed—applies to graduate teaching, too.

Who Is the Audience?

In the 1960s, the typical college student in the United States was a White, middle-class male who was enrolled for full-time study, and whose expenses were paid primarily by his parents. He did not hold a job during the academic year, and he entered college with a B average. He expected to perform at an average level and his main goals probably included developing a meaningful philosophy of life (Astin, Parrott, Korn, & Sax, 1997). This profile has changed dramatically since then (Astin, 1990; Astin et al., 1997; Dey, Astin, & Korn, 1991; Erickson &

Strommer, 1991; Hansen, 1998; Higher Education Research Institute, 2002; Menges & Weimer, 1996; National Center for Education Statistics, 1999, 2001; Sax, Astin, Korn, & Mahoney, 1998, 1999, 2000).

For one thing, more students than ever are taking courses on a part-time basis, usually because financial need forces them to hold a full- or part-time job (Erickson & Strommer, 1991). Today's college students also tend to be older than those of the past. In 1970 less than 28% of undergraduates were over the age of 25, but by 1999, that percentage had increased to 39% (National Center for Education Statistics, 2001). Beginning in 1980, female college students have outnumbered males, and now comprise 58% of all undergraduates (National Center for Education Statistics, 2001). The percentage of college students representing various ethnic minority groups has slowly increased, too. In 1971, 91.4% of new undergraduates were European Americans, 6.3% were African Americans, 0.5% were Asian Americans, and 1.3% were Hispanic Americans. By 1998 the figure for European Americans had dropped to 82.5%, whereas the others had risen to 9.4% for African Americans, 4.0% for Asian Americans, and 4.5% for Hispanic Americans (Astin et al., 1997; Sax et al., 1998). These trends are expected to continue such that, collectively, ethnic minority students will constitute the majority of U.S. college students by the year 2025.

The diversity of college students goes far beyond age, gender, and ethnicity. More students than ever before are entering college with less than adequate academic preparation, and with special needs stemming from disabilities. Even the disabilities are more diverse than ever. In the past, most disabilities involved blindness, deafness, paralysis, or other physical problems that could be accommodated by minor changes in the way classes were conducted. Today's teachers are faced with more and more students with learning disabilities or other cognitive difficulties that might be more difficult to accommodate. One major university recently reported that 65% of students registered with the Division of Rehabilitation Services had been diagnosed with cognitive or psychiatric disabilities (Collins, 2003). (We discuss the impact of diversity in today's students throughout this book because you are likely to encounter it in every class you teach.)

In 1967, almost 83% of incoming students chose "developing a meaningful philosophy of life" as their main goal in college; only 43.8% chose "to be very well-off financially." The size of the group choosing the "philosophy of life" goal declined steadily to just over 39% in 1987, and rose to only 42% in 1997 (Astin et al., 1997). Today, being "very well-off financially" is the main goal of 74.1% of entering college students (Astin et al., 1997).

Surveys of college students also document rising levels of academic disengagement (Sax et al., 1998). Students report being bored in class and missing classes at a much higher rate than did students in the 1960s. They say they work hard for teachers they like, but are more likely to slack off, and even cheat, in the courses of teachers they don't like (Erickson & Strommer, 1991).

Student expectations have also changed dramatically in the last few decades. Those who come to college after having experienced "grade inflation" in high school (Astin et al., 1997) expect their high grades to continue. In fact, like their counterparts in fictional Lake Wobegon, most of today's college students tend to rate themselves as "above average" on both academic and interpersonal criteria, and more of them than ever expect to pursue advanced degrees (Astin et al., 1997). These students tend to be surprised and resentful when the level of effort that once led to As or Bs now earns only Cs or Ds. Students' reactions to grades depend partly on their general orientation toward learning (Dweck, 1986; Gaultney & Cann, 2001; Grant & Dweck, 2003; Svinicki, 1998). Those who have a *mastery orientation* tend to be interested mainly in developing skills and learning course content. They care about good grades, of course, but these students focus mainly on increasing their competence. They seek challenges that foster learning, they persist in the face of difficulty, and they do not attribute errors or failure to a general lack of ability (Dweck & Leggett, 1988; Svinicki, 1998). Students with a *performance orientation* tend to be more interested in grades and in appearing "smart" than in actually acquiring skills and mastering course content. Accordingly, they tend to be less persistent than their mastery-oriented peers in the face of challenges and difficulties. In fact, although these students want to do well on evaluated tasks, their fear of failure and negative evaluation is such that they tend to shy away from challenges (Dweck, 1986). When they perform well on a task, their pride stems mainly from having done better than others rather than from having accomplished something for its own sake (Svinicki, 1998). When they do not perform well, they tend to attribute their failure to their general lack of ability (Dweck & Leggett, 1988; Svinicki, 1998). As described in Chapter 6, these differing learning orientations can have significant implications for teachers' efforts to motivate and evaluate students.

In the 1960s, grades were among students' main worries. Today, students are worried about many other things, too, including how to pay for their college education (Astin et al., 1997). More than 40% expect to work part time while attending college (Erickson & Strommer, 1991), and they face other stressors, too. The percentage of students reporting "being overwhelmed by everything I have to do" and "frequently feel depressed" has risen steadily from 1987 to 1997, especially among females (Astin et al., 1997; Sax et al., 1998). Similarly, a longitudinal study of entering students has found declining levels of emotional health during the first year of college (Sax, Bryant, & Gilmartin, 2003). Perhaps as a result of these stressors, including the need for part-time study, students today are taking longer to complete their bachelor's degrees (Upcraft, 1996).

SOME FINAL COMMENTS

In summary, when teaching undergraduate courses in psychology, you will encounter students who represent a wide range of ethnic backgrounds, abilities and disabilities, interests, motivations, and expectations. Some will be diffident and frightened; others will be overconfident and unrealistically optimistic. Whether they are full- or part-time students, many will be trying to fulfill academic obligations while dealing with a job, financial pressures, family responsibilities, relationship problems, and other stressors. Preparing to deal with the diversity of today's students is one dimension of the task you will face as a psychology professor. In the remainder of this book, we address many others, beginning with what might be your first question: How do I start?

Chapter 2

Preparing Your Courses

How Do I Start?
Choosing a Textbook
Creating a Syllabus
Setting Up a Grading System
Communicating With Your Students
Some Final Comments

We try to teach well, and we know that most of our colleagues do, too. Still, we are constantly amazed at how many students tell us about courses they have taken that were so disorganized as to leave students wondering whether they learned anything other than not to take another class with certain instructors. These students describe courses in which instructors provided no syllabus (leaving students in the dark about reading assignments and even exam dates), took so long to grade and return exams that feedback came too late to be of much help, went off on so many tangents during lectures that relevant material was never covered, and even failed to explain how course grades would be determined. This is a shame, because most of the course organization problems that students complain about, problems that could well interfere with their learning, can be prevented simply by taking the time to prepare a course properly. In fact, one of the main keys to effective teaching lies in careful planning (Center for Teaching Excellence, 1999).

HOW DO I START?

Whether you have several months or only a few days in which to plan and prepare your course, our advice remains the same: Get organized and use the time available to do as much advance work as possible.

Goal Setting

The first step is to establish your goals in teaching the course, be-cause—just as when starting on a long trip—once you know where you want to go, it is easier to plan a route that will get you there. Your teaching goals will reflect both what you want your students to get out of a particular course and the purpose the course is designed to serve in your departmental and institutional curriculum.

To be honest, the main goal of many new teachers is simply to get through the course in one piece. This is understandable, but even experienced teachers might not have thought much about their teaching goals—mainly because it is so easy to ignore them. You can teach year after year without ever explicitly establishing goals that go beyond "doing a good job," "teaching the material," "being fair," or the like.

These are fine goals, in general, but there are many other, more specific teaching goals that might guide the development of your course. One way to begin considering them, and the role they play in your courses, is to complete the Teaching Goals Inventory (TGI), which is available in print (Angelo & Cross, 1993), or online at http://www.uiowa.edu/~centeach/tgi/. The TGI lists 53 skills, abilities, and other student accomplishments, and gives you the opportunity to rate the importance of each of them in each of your courses. If you take the TGI online, you can generate an instant report that summarizes the goals that you rated as "essential," "very important," "important," or "unimportant." You can also compare your responses with those of a sample of 2,800 other faculty members. The TGI can be useful in itself, but it might also stimulate you to think about additional goals that you consider important in your courses.

In any case, once you have used the TGI and your own reflections to clarify what you want your students to get from each course, you will find it much easier to plan your courses accordingly. For example, if you think it is important for your students to develop critical thinking skills, you will probably plan a course that gives them the opportunity to, say, critique and debate the validity of research results. If you value collaborative learning skills, you might plan to have students work in teams to summarize research articles, solve course-related problems, or carry out other projects. If you simply want to assure that students can define the terms and identify the concepts presented in the course, you will probably create exams and class activities that test these skills.

Your teaching goals should also take into account the role each course plays in your department and on your campus. Is it a prerequisite for other courses and, if so, what are they? What courses, if any, are prerequisites for yours? Is your course part of a specialized sequence? Knowing what your students are likely to know when they arrive in your classroom will help you to establish a starting point, and the appropriate level, for your lectures and reading assignments. Knowing what your department or college expects students to know when they finish your course will help you decide what material to cover (and not cover), and what level of detail is appropriate. Are students expected to leave your course with a detailed knowledge of, say, social cognition, with a general appreciation of the major themes in psychology, with improved skill at problem-solving, critical thinking, writing, studying, or what? Your lectures and other class activities would probably touch only on the basics of psychology if you are teaching the introductory course, but would focus on more subtle nuances in a capstone seminar for seniors in the psychology honors program. Answering these goal-related questions will help you to make these and numerous other decisions as you organize your courses.

It is not always easy, especially at the beginning of your teaching career, to keep personal, departmental, and institutional goals in mind as you plan your courses, so don't hesitate to ask for advice from more experienced colleagues who have taught the same courses. These people can help you understand how the course has been taught in the past, what approaches have worked and not worked, the reputation the course has acquired, and the like. Correspond, too, with instructors who teach the same or a similar course on other campuses. There are listservs and e-mail groups dedicated to teaching psychology where discussion of appropriate goals and materials for courses is often illuminating, even to an instructor who has taught a course for a number of years. Among the best of these are *TIPS* (Teaching in the Psychological Sciences; http://www.frostburg.edu/dept/psyc/southerly/tips/instruct.htm) and *Psychteacher* (http://teachpsych.lemoyne.edu/teachpsych/div/psychteacher.html).

Finally, remember that course goals are not set in stone. As you gain experience with a particular course at a particular institution, your goals might change. They might become more ambitious, less ambitious, or just different. In any case, one mark of effective teachers is the ability to adapt to changing curricula, changing campus demands, and other challenges, while adhering to the goals and standards they consider most important.

CHOOSING A TEXTBOOK

Once you have established the goals for your course, the next task is to choose a textbook. If you are free to choose any book(s) you wish, we suggest you begin the selection process by examining the books adopted by colleagues who have taught the course recently. Borrow their copies, or take a look at used copies in the campus bookstore. You can also check out the books being used by faculty at institutions similar to yours by visiting their departments' home pages, then following links to the relevant online syllabi. Use e-mail to ask these instructors for evaluative comments on their books, and perhaps send more general requests for textbook recommendations to the psychology teachers' mailgroups mentioned earlier. When you have created a short list of textbook candidates, contact their publishers' sales representatives (just type in the company name at google.com and follow links to local reps) to ask for an examination copy of each book, along with any ancillary materials that might be available to accompany it. Ancillaries might include an instructor's resource manual, a test item bank, transparencies, PowerPoint presentation slides, CD-ROMs, DVDs, a student study guide, case examples, supplementary readings, and many other items.

Which is the right book for you and your students? Making the selection has been likened to buying cat food. It has to be palatable enough to be enjoyed by the ultimate user, but not to the point of being disgusting to the one who chooses it. The palatability criterion was highlighted by Eble (1988) when he noted that "the first consideration in choosing texts is whether students are likely to read them, work with them, and learn from them" (p. 126). He also advised choosing a book that supports students' independent learning. This means that in addition to holding students' interest, the chosen book should be sufficiently clear, current, and free of major errors so that you can rely on it to provide further details and a broader context for your lectures, and that the students can rely on it to support independent learning, including coverage of important topics not included in lectures, and guides to further reading.

We have found it helpful to use a 5-point scale (ranging from *excellent* through *acceptable* to *unacceptable*) to rate psychology textbooks on each of several criteria, including readability, interest to students, accuracy of content, coverage of content, scholarship, appropriateness of presentation level, and quality of the ancillary package. Other, more detailed textbook rating systems are available elsewhere (e.g., Hemmings & Battersby, 1990). With time and experience, you will no doubt develop your own set of criteria that reflect the textbook characteristics you feel are most important in meeting the goals you have established for your course.

If you wish to use other materials in addition to, or perhaps instead of, a main textbook, there are plenty of options, including sets of readings that can be assembled in a course packet (Davis, 1993). You might also assign students to read information that they can download from the Internet, but be sure that you understand relevant copyright laws and restrictions when assembling published materials (Davis, 1993; Hilton, 2003).

Also be aware of the total amount of reading you are assigning. We do not endorse coddling students or expecting too little of them, but try to make reading assignments that can be accomplished—with comprehension—in the allotted time, and in the context of the students' overall course load (Davis, 1993). Remember, your students will have to do the reading for your course while also satisfying the reading required by instructors in several other courses. Be selective and thoughtful, not only in choosing a textbook, but in choosing what material you assign from the book and from other sources. A comprehensive reading list looks great, and even reasonable, at the beginning of the term, but it will not serve the purpose of promoting student learning if the students never have time to cover what you have assigned, let alone think deeply about it.

Finally, we suggest that you put at least one copy of the textbook and all other readings on reserve at the library. As textbook costs have risen, some students find it more and more difficult to purchase all the books assigned in all their classes, and for them, the library is a vital link to your course. Even those who do buy all their assigned books will find it useful to have access to course readings between classes and at other times when they find themselves with time to study, but without their books.

CREATING A SYLLABUS

Your syllabus or course outline is one of the most important documents you will give to your students. A properly constructed syllabus serves not only as a preview and road map of the course, but as a guide to what your students can expect from you and what you will be expecting of them. Creating a course syllabus is a vital step in course planning because the process requires you to think carefully about many course details—including class projects, exam and term paper dates, make-up exam policies, and the like—that might otherwise slip through the cracks until students ask about them.

A well-constructed syllabus can actually help students learn more from your course (Parkes & Harris, 2002). In addition to telling them about the organization, requirements, and scheduling of the course, its coverage of the grading system can show them how to keep track of their performance. When students understand where they stand, gradewise, as the course goes on, they can make better decisions about reallocating their time, if necessary, to improve their chances of success. A syllabus can even serve an advisory function by clearly describing course prerequisites, the amount of time and effort the course will require, tips for effective studying, and the resources available for students who are having trouble in the course. After reading the syllabus on the first day of class, students can more easily decide whether or not they can (or want to) handle your course's requirements in the context of their other courses and commitments. Those who are not prepared, academically or otherwise, to deal with your course can drop it without penalty, thus preventing problems for themselves and you.

A good syllabus outlines course topics, and can also be used to explain why certain content is included. In introductory psychology, for example, students are often mystified as to why they will be reading about the eye and other sensory systems. The syllabus can provide a rationale for such seeming oddities, and can show how the whole course fits together (Parkes & Harris, 2002).

On most campuses, your syllabus is a legally binding contract between you and your students. It provides the grounds for imposing penalties on students who fail to meet their responsibilities, and for students to file complaints against professors who don't follow announced grading procedures or who otherwise depart substantially from what they promised to do (Parkes & Harris, 2002). Accordingly, consider carefully what you say in your syllabus, say it clearly, and then stick to it. If you must make changes after the course begins, don't just announce them in class: Distribute written notification to all students.

In addition to conveying course information, your syllabus can serve as a model of professional thinking, planning, and writing (Parkes & Harris, 2002). Distributing a syllabus that is well organized, clearly written, and free of grammar and spelling errors will not only give students a good first impression of you and your course, but will help create an expectation of the sort of product you will be expecting from them in their written assignments. Reading your syllabus will also affect your students' perceptions of you as a person (Erikson & Strommer, 1991), so be sure it conveys a firm, but friendly tone that shows you care about your teaching (an attribute consistently associated with good teacher evaluations).

If creating a syllabus sounds daunting, don't despair. You will get the hang of it, and besides, you don't have to start from scratch. Start by taking a look at the syllabi written for courses like yours by colleagues in your department, and on psychology course Web sites around the country. In addition, STP offers Project Syllabus at its Office of Teaching Resources in Psychology (OTRP). Project Syllabus is a collection of syllabi for a variety of psychology classes; you can review them by visiting the OTRP Web site (http://www.teachpsych.org) or by going directly to Project Syllabus at http://www.lemoyne.edu/OTRP/index.html. Your campus's instructional development center can also provide general advice and information on writing a syllabus.

A carefully constructed syllabus that accurately describes your course and how you plan to teach it will be a personal document, a snapshot of your teaching style (Parkes & Harris, 2002). Be sure to include it in your teaching portfolio (Parkes & Harris, 2002; see chapter 8). As a permanent record of the nature of your courses, syllabi are often used in evaluating individual instructors, courses, and even programs (Parkes & Harris, 2002).

A Model Syllabus

The first step in creating your syllabus is to look at a calendar. Mark and count the number of class meetings you have available for lectures or other teaching activities, remembering to subtract standard vacation days such as Thanksgiving or spring break. Note, too, any class meetings that coincide with Kwanzaa, Yom Kippur, Ramadan, or other religious holidays that might not be official vacation days.

(All religious holidays are listed on the Internet at http://www.interfaithcalendar.org.) Usually, campus rules and common sense dictate that you not schedule quizzes, exams, or other graded assignments on those days. Next, mark any calendar dates on which your own commitments will require a guest lecturer to stand in for you. Marking the calendar in these ways gives you an overview of your course and makes it easier to see the optimal placement and spacing of quizzes and exams. It will also help you see whether the submission deadlines for term papers or other projects you might be planning to assign will allow you enough time to grade those assignments in a timely manner.

In deciding what to put in your syllabus, err on the side of including too much rather than too little. The more information about the course you provide, the fewer questions you will have to answer in class—or, at least, the easier it will be to refer questioners to the syllabus. At minimum, your syllabus should provide the following information:

1. The name, number, and title of your course (e.g., Psychology 100, Introduction to Psychology). As noted earlier, you should also include a paragraph or so that describes what the course will cover, and perhaps a rationale for the plan. Some instructors prefer to concentrate on five to seven goals for the semester and state them as measurable outcomes (Barrick, 1998; personal communication, February 12, 2003). For example, "By the end of the course the student will be able to differentiate various types of learning and apply them to appropriate situations." Others prefer to offer a more general overview of course goals, such as this one:

> This course offers an introduction to the more applied areas of psychology, including research methods, developmental psychology, learning and memory, thinking and intelligence testing, health psychology, personality, psychological disorders and their treatment, and social psychology. Throughout the course, you will be encouraged to develop your ability to think critically about psychology and about topics outside of psychology. You will get much more out of the lectures and discussions if you read the assigned book chapters before you come to class.

2. The days, time, and location of class meetings (e.g., MWF, 10 a.m., 101 Psychology Building).

3. Your name, office address, office phone, and e-mail address. The decision about whether to list your home phone number should be based on your individual circumstances, but there are a

couple of reasons why we do so. First, unless home phone numbers are unlisted, students can easily find them in the phone book, through directory assistance, or on the Internet. Second, in the decades during which we have provided our home phone numbers, we can count on one hand the number of inappropriate calls we have received. Most students do not abuse the privilege of having this information. In fact, although the vast majority of your students will never call your home phone number, the fact that you provided it on the syllabus tends to demonstrate your concern for students. This practice also follows the first principle for good practice in undergraduate education, namely encouraging student–faculty contact. Still, remember that students often keep late hours, so if you decide to list your home phone number, indicate the hours during which non-emergency calls will be welcome.

4. The schedule of your office hours. Later in this chapter we offer some suggestions for making office hours part of your overall faculty–student communication plan, but for now we just suggest this rule of thumb: Schedule at least two face-to-face office hours per week per course (you might also want to offer electronic office hours via e-mail). When should these hours be? Take your own schedule into account, of course, but when possible, set up your office hours so they do not match the likely scheduling of your students' other classes. Office hours at 9 a.m. on Monday, Wednesday, and Friday, or Tuesday and Thursday, will make visits impossible for students who have another class at those times. Setting up office hours that include, say, 9 a.m. on Monday and Tuesday might be a better plan. Be aware, too, that office hours in early morning or late afternoon (especially on Friday) will probably not attract many visitors. You might wish to reserve the hour before class as preparation time, but the hour following class is an ideal office hour, as discussions begun in class can continue as you walk with students to your office. Avoid "to be arranged" (TBA) office hours. Students are more likely to stop by your office if you have established fixed times at which you will be available. In fact, many students perceive TBA office hours to mean "don't bother me." Whatever your schedule of formal office hours, be sure to let students know that you are available to meet with them at other times, too. You can easily do this by listing your regular office hours and adding the phrase "and by appointment." Taking this simple step will encourage students to contact you even if they cannot attend your standing office hours.

5. The name(s), office location(s), phone number(s), and office hour(s) of any teaching assistants who will be helping you teach the course, along with a brief statement about what these assistants can and cannot be expected to do.

6. A list of all books, articles, and other readings that will be required or recommended for the course, along with information about whether and where these materials can be found on reserve in the library and where they can be purchased.

7. A list of the topics you plan to cover at each class meeting, along with the book chapters or other readings or assignments that are to be completed before each meeting (see Table 2.1). This is a good place, too, to show the scheduling of all exams and quizzes, and the due dates of any other evaluated work, such as class projects, papers, and the like.

8. A list of any special out-of-class activities, such as field trips, lab visits, or departmental colloquia that are available or required. On some campuses, faculty are actually required to include this information in every course syllabus (Barrick, 1998; personal communication, February 12, 2003).

9. A detailed description of exactly how students' performance in the course will be evaluated. This description should begin with a statement about the number of exams and quizzes in the course, whether they will be essay, multiple-choice, or short-answer for-

TABLE 2.1

Sample Schedule of Class Sessions for an Introductory Psychology Course

Date	Class Lecture and Topic	Assigned Readings
8/28	Introduction	
8/30	Subfields and careers in psychology	Chapter 1
9/4	NO CLASS (Labor Day Holiday)	
9/6	Research methods in psychology	Chapter 2
9/11	Research methods in psychology	Chapter 2
9/13	Human development	Chapter 12
9/18	Human development	Chapter 12
9/20	EXAMINATION 1 (Covers chaps. 1, 2, & 12. Bring pencils and your student ID.)	
9/25	Return and discuss exam	
9/27	Learning	Chapter 6

mat, and how many items will be included on each. Include, too, the number and length of papers or mini-assignments, journal writing, laboratory work, and research or projects to be conducted on the Internet. Due dates for these should be included on the class schedule (see Table 2.1), but it never hurts to include that information here, too. (If you plan to require your students to work on the Web or use other technologies to complete various assignments, assure them that they will be given instructions about using the technology involved, if necessary.)

Next, describe how final grades will be determined. Whether you choose one of the grading systems we discuss later, or some other one, be sure to explain it carefully. The more clearly you do so in your syllabus, the less trouble and confusion you will have to deal with at the end of the term. Tell students how much each exam, quiz, or other assignment will count toward the final grade, whether attendance and class participation will affect the final grade, whether and how missed exams or quizzes can be made up, and how missed deadlines will be handled. In addition, make it clear if students are, or are not, allowed to work together on various out of class assignments (Barrick, 1998; personal communication, February 12, 2003). If there is an optional plus/minus grading system in place at your institution, be sure to tell students whether or not you will be using it.

10. A list of learning resources available to students in the course. This list might include, for example, the schedule, location, and cost of tutoring services; and a reminder about readings, lecture notes, practice exams, or other materials that are accessible on the Internet or on reserve in the library.

11. A statement about accommodations for students with special needs. In our courses, this statement reads as follows: "Any student requiring special accommodations should notify the instructor as soon as possible. All accommodations will follow the procedures stated in the University Code of Policies that can be accessed at http:// www.uiuc.edu/admin_manual/code/ rule_4.html."

12. A comprehensive statement of your teaching philosophy, course policies, pet peeves, and rules of course etiquette. Information about your philosophy of teaching helps to humanize you to your students, and also helps them to understand what to expect in your course. This part of your syllabus might include statements such as "I try to promote critical thinking in my classroom—don't

be shy about stating your views," "I try to treat all students with respect," "Attendance is important to me," "Please enter quietly if you come to class late," "No eating or drinking in class, please," "I hope each of you will visit me at least once during my office hours," and the like. In short, spell out everything you do and do not want to have happen in class, and the consequences of rule violations. Some of your preferences, rules, and policies will be unfamiliar to your students, so don't leave students guessing or finding out the hard way. This section of the syllabus can also be used to orient students to your views about, and campus policies on, issues such as plagiarism and other forms of academic dishonesty. It is helpful to provide Web addresses where students can get further information about campus rules governing academic integrity, exam scheduling, and other issues that are relevant to your course, but that usually go undiscovered—even by some faculty (Barrick, 1998).

Keeping Track of It All

Students sometimes forget what the course syllabus says about when quizzes and exams are scheduled, when paper assignments are due, and the like, but they are not the only ones. In the day-to-day chaos of academic life, it is all too easy for teachers, too, to lose track of the assignments they made, the guest speaker they were to contact, or the quiz they were supposed to have prepared. To minimize the chances that you will forget to complete important course-related tasks on time, we suggest that you create for each course a master list of events and responsibilities, organized by date, to act as a "tickler file" (see Fig. 2.1). We have used master lists for decades, and it is amazing how helpful they can be as one gets older and busier—or just older. A good master list can be a life-saver because if you build into it enough lead time for each task, you will never find yourself copying handouts, writing exams, or organizing demonstrations at the last minute. We review our master lists at the beginning of each week of each term to be sure that we are ready for the days ahead. We keep printed copies at home and at the office, but you can also maintain your master list on calendar programs on your department's server, making it accessible on your desktop, laptop, personal digital assistant (PDA), or mobile phone. It might even be possible for the program to send you e-mail reminders when each task on the master list becomes imminent. Be sure to edit the content of each course's master list as the

SCHEDULE OF DEADLINES FOR PSYCH 100

Fall Semester

June 1
  Request midterm exam room from Office of Facility Planning.

June 30
  Contact publisher to confirm book order.

August 1
  Complete and copy fall syllabus.
  Confirm supply of exam and quiz answer sheets

August 10
  Confirm that textbooks are in the bookstore.

August 20–25
  Meet with teaching assistants to review course plans and
    responsibilities.

August 25
  Arrange for midterm exam proctors.

August 30
  Begin writing midterm exam items for September 12 deadline.
  Collect list of special needs students.

September 10
  Schedule classroom visits by peers.

September 12
  Final draft of midterm exam to department staff for formatting.

September 17
  Distribute and collect formative evaluation instrument from
    students.
  Proofread midterm exams and return to staff for duplication.
  Prepare midterm exam conflict application form.

September 24
  Inform students of location of time and day of midterm exam
    review session.
  Make up midterm answer keys; send copy to exam scoring office.
  Create exam instruction transparency for display in class at
    midterm exam.

October 1
  Edit Psych 100 syllabus for spring semester.
  Order textbook for spring semester.

October 5
  Deadline for submission of midterm exam conflict application
    forms.

(continued)

(continued)

Day After Midterm Exam
 Prepare list of 10 most difficult items based on the item analysis to be discussed when returning exams in class.

Three Days After Midterm Exam
 Administer and hand-score midterm conflict exam.
 Collect and consider students' forms requesting review of disputed exam items.

October 20
 Begin writing final exam items for November 7 deadline.
 Arrange for final exam proctors.

November 1
 Order copies of teaching evaluation forms from Office of Instructional Resources.
 Schedule return classroom visit by peer observer.

November 7
 Final draft of midterm exam to department staff for formatting.

November 15
 Proofread final exams and return to staff for duplication.
 Prepare final exam conflict application form.

November 21
 Hand out final exam conflict request forms.

November 26
 Inform students of time and date of final exam review session.

December 15
 Administer final exam.

December 17
 Compute grades, double-check for accuracy, and submit to records office.

FIG. 2.1. A "master list" of instructor tasks. Here is just a small segment of a list we have used for decades in teaching introductory psychology. Such lists not only help you to remember what you have to do, and when, as you teach each course, but will establish a reputation for organization, preparedness, and caring that can improve your teacher ratings and make you the envy of your colleagues. A good master list can even put you in solid with the administrative staff; if you follow the schedule on the list, you will never have to ask them to copy syllabi, handouts, quizzes, or exams at the last minute.

term proceeds. So if it took you a week, not a day, to write a 20-item quiz for your neuroscience course, adjust the dates on your master list accordingly. The next time you teach that course, any scheduling crunches that appeared last time should not occur again.

SETTING UP A GRADING SYSTEM

Grading is often thought of as the mere process of placing a letter from A through F next to each student's name at the end of the term, but grading should be much more than that (Walvoord & Anderson, 1998). It should be an integral part of your courses and should reflect your goals for each course (Zlokovich, 2001). For example, if you want to promote your students' ability to critically analyze research on the effects of psychotherapy, or learn the names of neurotransmitters and psychoactive drugs, or synthesize information about various theories of motivation, your grading, as well as your teaching, should reflect these goals. Evaluated tasks that demonstrate achievement of critical analysis ability, knowledge of vocabulary, or content integration should count most heavily toward student grades.

Grades constitute the second of two kinds of feedback students receive regarding their progress in meeting the goals you have set for them. The first is *formative feedback*, performance-related information intended to guide students as they develop knowledge and skill in your course. Designed mainly to help students improve their performance, formative feedback is more assessment than evaluation. In contrast, grades constitute *summative feedback*, the final evaluation of a student's performance on a particular assignment or in a particular course. Because grades help establish students' credentials for graduation and admission to further educational and occupational opportunities, students want grades—especially good ones—and, at all but a few institutions, faculty members are required to give them. Assigning grades in a satisfactory way takes some doing, and, as always, some planning (Ory & Ryan, 1993; Walvoord & Anderson, 1998).

The Golden Rules of Grading

There is no "best" grading system, but in this section we describe a few golden rules for assigning grades (Davis, 1993; Ory & Ryan, 1993).

First, grading must be accurate, meaning that course grades must reflect each student's level of competency. Accuracy is best achieved through the development of thoughtful assignments and relevant grading criteria.

Second, grading must be fair, and just as important, it must be perceived as fair by students. Therefore, set up a system that assures students that those who turn in equivalent performances will receive equivalent grades. The system should also make it clear that certain ranges of total scores, or percentages of available points, will result in certain grades. Assuring fairness in your grading system is an important aspect of pursuing fairness in your overall teaching effort, a goal consistent with the final principle of good teaching practice listed in Chapter 1.

Third, grades must be dispensed consistently, meaning that the grading system described at the beginning of the term is not subject to unannounced, unpredictable, or repeated changes. Your syllabus should list each and every category in which points can be earned (tests, quizzes, papers, research projects, class participation, extra credit options, etc.), and how many points can be earned in each category. Assign points only on the basis of these categories, and don't make special arrangements with individual students, even when you wish you could. Don't base grades on how much you like particular students, how hard they are trying, or other factors that cannot be quantified and announced in advance. Similarly, don't base grades on students' improvement during the course; doing so can create a disadvantageous ceiling effect for those who do well to begin with. Avoid basing final grades on just two or three assignments. The more graded components you can include—within the limits dictated by class time and grading time—the more representative of student performance those grades are likely to be (Ory & Ryan, 1993). Additionally, try to schedule graded assignments so that they are distributed relatively evenly throughout the term.

Following these "golden rules" will make it easier to follow a final one, namely that grades must be defensible (Ory & Ryan, 1993). Your grading system should allow you to explain and justify—to students or anyone else who has a right to ask—how and why each student's grade was determined. If you heed these basic rules, you will find teaching less stressful, not only because your students will know what to expect, and thus be less likely to argue about grades, but also because you will be far less vulnerable to charges of capricious grading. As you develop and refine your grading system, use it consistently, and learn to rely on its fairness, you will find that the grading process will become less stressful, allowing you to concentrate on your main task, which is teaching.

Choosing Your Grading System

Whatever you do, be sure to choose your own grading system, don't let it choose you. Trouble awaits the instructor who hopes that appropriate grades will make themselves obvious at the end of the term through natural gaps, or break points, in the final distribution of total points earned by students. Even if the teaching gods could be relied on to provide such gaps, using them to establish grades on an ad hoc basis would meet the definition of capricious grading at most institutions. Ad hoc grading is capricious, first, because you would not be able to explain on the first day of class how grades will be determined. It is capricious, too, because the gaps appearing in a distribution are likely to be caused in large part by random factors and measurement error, not by meaningful differences in achievement. If you were to administer an alternate form of your final exam in developmental psychology, the gaps might appear in different places (Ory & Ryan, 1993). Also, in thinking about your grading scheme, don't try to reinvent the wheel. As with other aspects of teaching, consult with your more experienced colleagues to learn about systems they have used successfully. These consultations will also help familiarize you with the grading system rules or norms that might apply in your department and on your campus.

Norm-Referenced Versus Criterion-Referenced Grading.

Once you have completed your consultations, the next step in setting up your grading system is to decide whether to use a norm-referenced system (also referred to as "grading on a curve"), a criterion-referenced system (also called "absolute" or "standards of excellence" grading), a combination of the two, or a contract or mastery learning system.

Norm-referenced grades can be assigned using a planned distribution, as when students whose total scores fall in the top 10% of the class distribution earn As; those in the next 20% get Bs, those in the next 40% get Cs, those in the next 20% get Ds, and those in the bottom 10% get Fs. Notice that, in this system, all possible grades will be assigned, but the actual number of points associated with each grade will vary from class to class, depending on how well the best students do.

Criterion-referenced grades are assigned individually, regardless of the performance of any other student, or the class as a whole. In the simplest form of criterion-referenced grading, an A is assigned to anyone who earns, say, 90% of the points available in the course, or on a particular assignment. Those earning, say, 80% to 89% of the available points earn a B, and so on. The advantages of criterion-referenced grading are that (a) students are evaluated on an absolute scale determined by the instructor's definition of what constitutes mastery of course material, (b) final grades indicate the degree to which students achieved that mastery, and (c) because students are not competing against each other, they tend to be more cooperative (Ory & Ryan, 1993). Potential disadvantages of criterion-referenced grading include the fact that it can be difficult to determine what criteria are valid in a given course, especially when it is taught for the first time. For example, is it reasonable to expect students to achieve at the 90% level in a cognitive psychophysiology course, given the difficulty of the material? If no one reaches that level, will you be comfortable assigning no As? Answering these questions is easier after you have taught the same course more than once, which is why criterion-referenced grading might not be the best system for new teachers (Ory & Ryan, 1993).

Norm-referenced grading has the advantage of rewarding students whose academic performance is outstanding relative to the class (Ory & Ryan, 1993). It can also prevent grade distortions when, for example, even the best students perform poorly because a test or other assignment was flawed in some way. In such cases, the best of the poor performances would still earn As; under a criterion-based system, everyone might receive an F. Norm-referenced grading can lead to some unfortunate consequences, however, especially when there is little variability in the performance of a particular class. Under such a system, even if all your students earned at least, say, 80% of the points available, some of them would still receive Cs, Ds, and Fs. Even if none of your students scored above 50% on any graded assignment, some of them would still get As, Bs, and Cs. In these (thankfully rare) cases, anyone unfamiliar with the characteristics of the class in question could easily be misled about the meaning of norm-referenced grades (Ory & Ryan, 1993).

Hybrid Grading Systems. To exploit the strengths of both norm-referenced and criterion-referenced systems, consider a *hybrid approach*. For example, you might try a less restrictive norm-referenced system in which each student's performance in a particular class is compared to the performance of the best students in that class. In this system, you could assign an A to anyone who earns at least 90% of the average number of points earned by the top five students; those earning 80% of that average would get a B, and so on. Under such a system, there is no predetermined grade distribution. It is theoretically possible for every student to earn an A, assuming they all do very well in the course.

Our own favorite hybrid system was described by Davis (1993) and developed by Frank Costin for a large, multisection introductory psychology course. In this system, you first compute the mean of the scores earned by the top 10% of all students on any graded assignment, whether it be a quiz, an exam, or total points at the end of the term. (If you have 50 students, for example, you would calculate the mean score of the top 5.) You then use this mean as a benchmark for establishing letter grades. For example, to earn an A, students would have to earn at least 95% of the benchmark; earning a B would require 85% of the benchmark; a C would require 75% of the benchmark, and so on (see Table 2.2). Notice that this hybrid incorporates many of the advantages of both norm-referenced and criterion-referenced grading systems. It allows all students to earn an A if they do well enough; it does not penalize students for poorly designed evaluation instruments; and, because most courses enroll at least a few outstanding students, it typically requires a high absolute level of achievement, not just a high relative standing within the classroom, to earn a high grade. Although this grading system is unfamiliar to many students, we have found that they come to like it better than either strictly criterion-referenced or strictly norm-referenced systems.

Mastery Learning Systems. As an alternative to traditional grading systems, some instructors use a mastery approach to learning. Mastery learning systems gained some popularity in the 1970s, stimulated by B. F. Skinner's work on *programmed learning*. He was horrified by the "lock-step" teaching methods used in his daughter's third-grade mathematics class, and in traditional educational systems as a whole. He did not think it made sense to require all students to learn the same material at the same pace, and to be tested on it on the teacher's schedule and then graded based on the level of performance the students had achieved at some predetermined time (Skinner, 1954). He proposed a system whereby students could "teach

TABLE 2.2

Grading

There are 300 total points available in this course. THERE IS NO EXTRA CREDIT. The 300 points are distributed as follows:

Exams	2@50 points each	100 points
Final Exam	1@ 60 points	60 points
Quizzes	6@15 points each (lowest two can be dropped)	60 points
Mini-assignments		20 points
Writing Assignments		40 points
Subject Pool		20 points
Total Points Possible		300

Grades will be assigned on the basis of a modified curve. Your grade for the course will be calculated as follows:

1. The total number of points for each student is computed.
2. A frequency distribution of these total points is prepared and the scores earned by the upper 10% of the students are determined.
3. The mean of this upper 10% of scores is computed.
4. Grades for the course are then assigned as follows:
   Lower limit of A = 95% of the mean of the upper 10%.
   Lower limit of B = 85% of the mean of the upper 10%.
   Lower limit of C = 75% of the mean of the upper 10%.
   Lower limit of D = 65% of the mean of the upper 10%.

Please note that by using this grading system it is possible for all students in this course to earn an A in the course. This scale is also more generous than a straight 90% = A, 80% = B, 70% = C, 60% = D scale.

After every graded assignment, I will show you the distribution of scores and where your individual score falls in the range. I will also provide you with a midterm grade based on your total points earned by that time in the semester. This information will be provided well before the drop date.

If you have any questions about the grading system, please ask me. A sample grading computation is given to help you understand how grading will be calculated.

(continued)

TABLE 2.2 (*continued*)

PSYCHOLOGY 100 GRADING EXAMPLE (Enrollment: 50 students)

1. Total points earned by each student is calculated at the end of the course.
2. The scores of the top five students (who represent 10% of the 50 students in the class) are listed as follows:
   Student 1: 290 points
   Student 2: 285 points
   Student 3: 281 points
   Student 4: 274 points
   Student 5: 270 points
3. The mean of the top 10% of students is found to be 280, as follows:
   290 + 285 + 281 + 274 + 270 = 1,400
   1,400/5 = 280
4. Grade cutoff scores are computed:
   95% of 280 = 266, so the A range is 266–300
   85% of 280 = 238, so the B range is 238–265
   75% of 280 = 210, so the C range is 210–237
   65% of 280 =182, so the D range is 182–209
   The F range falls at 181 and below
5. Final grades are assigned to students based on these cutoff scores.

Note. This section from a course syllabus explains the hybrid grading system that we have found useful in an introductory psychology course over the past 20 years.

themselves," at their own pace, using a teaching machine that presented increasingly difficult material on a particular topic, and test their growing knowledge and mastery as they read by filling in the blanks in incomplete sentences (Skinner, 1968). Skinner's work on programmed instruction was directly responsible for the development of Keller's *Personalized System of Instruction* (*PSI*), which is still in use today on some campuses around North America (Beard & Hartley, 1984; Keller & Sherman, 1974; Ruskin, 1974). Using PSI, students engage modules of course material one at a time, and at their own pace, then take competency tests when they feel ready. If they can display mastery of one module, they are allowed to proceed to the next one. If not, they can study some more and take a new version of the mastery test. This process is repeated as often as necessary with each module in the course until some level of mastery is demonstrated. In short, the PSI instructor establishes the level of knowledge or skill required to earn each letter grade, and it is up to the students to meet the criteria for whatever grade they wish to achieve. In some PSI systems, students must demonstrate mastery of a certain segment of text material before being admitted to lectures related to that material. This arrangement assures that all students in a lecture have read the material relevant to it.

Needless to say, creating a mastery course involves a lot of work. It requires developing modules of course content and an organized and accessible system for testing and retesting students' knowledge of course material. Accordingly, the mastery approach to teaching, and grading, is not the most popular one available. Still, it does have its benefits (Jacobs & Chase, 1992; Kulik, Kulik, & Bangert-Drowns, 1990; Kulik, Kulik, & Cohen, 1979; Svinicki, Hagen, & Meyer, 1996), and with the advent of today's computerized and online testing capabilities, mastery learning systems are now more feasible than ever (Brooks, Nolan, & Gallagher, 2000).

The Role of Extra Credit in Your Grading System

Regardless of the grading system you choose, you might want to consider offering students the option of earning extra credit points for work that goes beyond the standard requirements of your course. Some instructors make extra credit available for optional writing assignments, research projects, or for performance on pop quizzes. The choice is yours. Some experienced instructors favor extra credit options as a way of helping students overcome or compensate for poor performance on standard graded tasks, or as a way of helping superior students enjoy the fruits of their motivation and ability. Others oppose the idea of extra credit, arguing that it is tantamount to capricious grading, or that it offers an undeserved opportunity for lazy students to save their grades at the last minute, thus rewarding sloth and procrastination. If you like the idea of extra credit, but want it to be more than a life raft tossed out to slackers at the end of the term, consider including extra credit opportunities throughout the course.

As you might expect, students like having extra credit options available (Norcross & Dooley, 1993). As you might not expect, though, these options tend to be exercised mainly by the most able and highly motivated students in a class (Hardy, 2001). Perhaps because they recognize this pattern, most psychology faculty do not offer extra credit options as part of their grading systems (Norcross &

Dooley, 1993). If you decide to buck this trend, be sure that your syllabus includes detailed information about extra credit and how to earn it. Discuss the extra credit options on the first day of class, too, and make sure students understand that extra credit is available to anyone who wants to do extra work. Mentioning, or offering, extra credit only to certain students on an ad hoc basis surely falls into the category of making special deals, which is another way of defining capricious grading.

COMMUNICATING WITH YOUR STUDENTS

Clearly explaining your grading system is just one way of establishing the communication channels that foster good student–faculty contact, the first principle of effective teaching. Another of these channels is opened when you encourage students to ask you questions and discuss course-related problems and issues before, during, and after class, and at other times, too. The traditional format for out-of-class communication is the faculty office hour.

Establishing Office Hours

We have already suggested that you set up two office hours per week, per course, and that you schedule your office hours at convenient times that are least likely to consistently conflict with your students' other classes. However, do more than simply make yourself available. Go out of your way to encourage students to visit you in your office. Remind them that they do not have to have a problem to meet with you, and that, unlike in high school, talking to an instructor is not "brown-nosing." Give them an agenda for an office visit by suggesting, perhaps, that office hours are good times to discuss questions they have about lectures, prospects for careers in psychology, and the like. If your class is small enough, give a writing assignment early in the course, then ask each student to meet with you to discuss possible topics. Invite students who performed below average on the first graded assignment to stop by to discuss their understanding of the material and possible ways of improving their performance.

Above all, be in your office during your office hours. If you must be gone for a few minutes, be sure to leave a note on your door telling visitors when you expect to be back. If you have to cancel an office hour session, leave a note about that, too, and if possible, notify your classes via e-mail. Failure to appear at scheduled office hours is often mentioned by students as being among their pet peeves about faculty, and can contribute to negative teaching evaluations. Therefore, when scheduling your office hours, don't forget to make them convenient for yourself as well as the majority of your students.

When a student is in your office, we suggest that you leave the door at least partly open, unless the student requests that you close it before discussing a private matter. This simple step provides an important measure of comfort and protection for you and your students.

Contact Via E-Mail

Electronic office hours are becoming increasingly popular supplements to face-to-face office meetings. Using e-mail, students can contact you at their convenience from wherever they have access to the Internet. Using the same access, you can offer virtual consultation from wherever you are. E-mail also gives you the luxury of responding at your convenience, and after you have had time to formulate thoughtful replies. Students appreciate knowing that you are available online, and this knowledge makes them more likely to ask a quick question about a homework problem or a writing assignment than if they had to wait for a scheduled office hour. Further, some of your more reticent students will feel freer to ask their questions and to present their ideas via e-mail in a way they might not have done in class or during an office visit (McKeage, 2001).

E-mail is not a panacea, however. When students are experiencing an academic problem, or if they need information about where to turn for a personal problem, they might want to talk to you in person. Also, because e-mail does not allow students and teachers to see or hear each other, online communication can result in misunderstandings. Finally, the apparent remoteness of e-mail sometimes leads people to make ill-advised comments that would not have occurred in person. So although students are receptive to virtual office hours (McKeage, 2001), a mixture of electronic and face-to-face communication is probably ideal.

The fact that most students check their e-mail several times a day (Askew, 1998) makes it feasible to set up a class mailgroup through which you can communicate with all your students at once, and through which your students can communicate with each other. An active mailgroup offers a good way for you to remind students of an upcoming deadline that appears on their syllabus, to answer a question that came up after a class, or to steer students to Web sites or other sources of information you have recently discovered. One instructor we know e-mails "virtual lectures" to her students following class sessions at which she ran out of time to present important material.

SOME FINAL COMMENTS

In this chapter we have offered advice on setting goals for your course, choosing a textbook, developing your syllabus, grading your students, and communicating with them about it all. Once you have done all these things, it is time to think about the next question you have to address, namely, what you should do during the first few days of class to get your course off on the right foot. This is the subject of the next chapter.

Chapter 3

The First Few Days of Class

Exploring Your Classroom
Establishing Yourself as a Teacher
Presenting Your Syllabus
Learning Your Students' Names
Setting the Stage for Group Work
Ending the First Class
Some Final Comments

You have established goals for teaching your course, selected your textbook, set up your grading system, and created your syllabus. It is now time to prepare for the first few days of class. These will be important days because the way you present yourself and the way you use your time during those first few classes will tell your students a lot about what they can expect from you and your course, and about what will be expected of them. In other words, the first few days of class tend to set the tone for the rest of the term.

If you feel some anxiety on the first day of class, remember that your discomfort is normal, and it stems partly from fear of the unknown, including the fact that you are meeting a group of strangers. Once you and your students get to know each other and begin to form a working relationship over the first few class sessions, you will probably find that teaching becomes much less stressful, and a lot more enjoyable and productive. Luckily, there are some things you can do both before and during the first class meeting to hasten this process.

EXPLORING YOUR CLASSROOM

At least a week before the new term begins, visit each classroom in which you will be teaching and familiarize yourself with its layout and systems. Pay attention to all the details. If the room is normally locked, be sure you have a key. Locate the switches and controls for lighting, projection screens, temperature, and other aspects of the classroom environment that you will need to control during class. Does everything work properly? Is there a podium or table for your notes and other teaching materials and equipment? If not, contact the appropriate campus office to report malfunctions or request items you will need.

If the room is equipped with an overhead projector, slide projector, audio- or videocassette player, or computer-based teaching station, be sure you know how these items operate, where spare projector bulbs are located, and how to replace bulbs if they burn out during class. If you are not sure about any of these things, ask about them in your department or at the campus office that services instructional equipment. That office can probably also provide information on how to get keys or combinations for equipment that is in locked storage in your classroom. If you will be bringing your own projector, laptop computer, or other equipment, locate electrical outlets for plugging it in, and any connections you will need to gain access to a campus computer network. If you will need to use window shades to darken the room during audiovisual presentations, be sure they work properly; if they don't, ask the appropriate campus or departmental office to correct the problem before classes begin.

If you plan to use a chalkboard, dry-erase board, or flip chart, confirm that there is chalk or felt-tipped pens, and just in case, plan to bring your own supply. Finally, be sure that there is enough seating in the room to accommodate the number of students enrolled in your class.

Consider, too, how well the room's seating accommodations fit your instructional style (Chism & Bickford, 2002). For example, many psychology teachers feel that, in small classes, a circular seating arrangement is the most conducive to student–faculty communication, especially if the teacher occupies a different seat during each class period (Billson & Tiberius, 1998). If you plan to create a seating circle, be sure that your classroom's chairs can be arranged this way. Even if you are only planning to have small-group discussions from time to time, figure out how you will set up chairs during these activities, especially if the seats in your classroom are connected or maybe even attached to the floor.

ESTABLISHING YOURSELF AS A TEACHER

It has been suggested that students arrive on the first day of class with four questions in mind: Will this class meet my needs? Is the teacher competent? Will the teacher be fair? Will the teacher care about me? (Ericksen, 1974; Scholl-Buckwald, 1985). They might have other questions and concerns, too, but it is vital to begin to address these four, through word and deed, during the first class session. That session provides your first opportunity to shape students' perceptions of you as a teacher, to establish your rules for the course, and to illustrate the kind of classroom environment you want to create.

Suppose you decide to "make friends" with your students by making the first day of class a short day. You distribute your syllabus, go over the grading system, make a reading assignment, and let the students leave after half an hour. What message would you be sending about yourself, your course, and your approach to teaching? Although you might not have intended to create this impression, students might well get the idea that you don't consider class time to be particularly valuable, that you might not care much about teaching (or them), that they can expect you to do most of the talking, and that they should sit passively and listen. Once those perceptions and expectations have coalesced over the first several classes, they are unlikely to change much (Emmer, Everston, & Anderson, 1979).

Managing Students' Expectations

Here are some tips for using verbal and nonverbal behavior to establish a more desirable set of student expectations on the first day of class.

Arrive Early. Get to class early, and bring with you all of the materials that you will need, including enough copies of the syllabus for everyone, and sample copies of the reading materials you will be assigning. Be prepared to tell students where they can get these reading materials, and which items are on reserve in the library (Davis, 1993). Put your name, and the name and number of your course, on the chalkboard, overhead projector, or computer screen. These simple things send the message that you care enough about your teaching to show up on time, fully prepared (Scholl-Buckwald, 1985).

Be Friendly.   While waiting for class to begin, greet and make small talk with students as they enter the room. This is another simple step, but one that begins the process of establishing mutual respect, and the good faculty–student contact that serves as the first principle of good practice in teaching (Billson & Tiberius, 1998; Boice, 1998).

Be Human.   When it is time to begin the class, introduce yourself, say a few words about your background, your academic and scholarly activities, and maybe even your hobbies and other outside interests. Be sure to tell students why you are interested in teaching this course. Remember that enthusiasm for course material, and for teaching in general, is a characteristic typically associated with instructors who are rated as effective by students and peers (Andersen, 1986; Billson & Tiberius, 1998; Davis, 1993; Eble, 1988; Murray, 1997; Scholl-Buckwald, 1985; Timpson & Bendel-Simso, 1996). Telling students a little about yourself also helps to establish you as a person as well as a teacher.

Invite Contact.   Let your students know how you would prefer them to address you—as Dr., Mr., Miss, Mrs., Ms., Professor, Doug, Sandy, or whatever. If you don't have a preference, tell them that, too, and give them some options. Above all, be sure to remove any doubt or ambiguity about this small but important matter. Some students, especially those beginning their first year of college, will avoid contact with teachers, even if they need help, simply because they were not sure about the proper form of address.

Express Interest in Students.   After introducing yourself, get some information about your students. The simplest way to do this is to distribute index cards on which students can write their name, their major, their e-mail address, the psychology courses they have taken, and topics they want to learn about in your class. Reading these cards after the first class will give you a better idea of who your students are, how well they are prepared, and the range of their interests. Spend a few minutes at the next class session discussing some of the interests expressed—and some of the inevitable funny responses you got. Taking time to do this provides yet another way to show your commitment to teaching and your interest in students.

To create even more faculty–student contact, and a more intimate classroom atmosphere, ask your students to introduce themselves. In a class of 50 or less, have students give their name (you can check attendance as they do so), any nickname or abbreviated name they prefer, their class standing (sophomore, junior, etc.), and perhaps why they have chosen this class. One of us typically asks students to "tell us one reason you are glad to be in class today." In larger classes, you can simply ask students to introduce themselves to those seated nearby.

If you plan to include various kinds of group activities in your course, you might set the stage through more elaborate introduction methods. Some instructors ask pairs of students to interview each other for a few minutes during class, or in a longer conversation outside of class, and then introduce their partner to the class (Scholl-Buckwald, 1985).

You can also use various "ice-breaker" activities to help students become more comfortable with each other, and with you, on the first day of class (e.g., Billison & Tiberius, 1998; Davis, 1993; Scholl-Buckwald, 1985). One instructor asks students to form groups of three or four to write a course-related question they would like the instructor to answer. The instructor then collects the cards, responds to some, and saves the rest for later in the course. This method not only helps students to meet each other, but promotes the second principle of good practice in teaching, namely encouraging cooperative learning among students (Erickson & Strommer, 1991). Other instructors use related methods, such as asking the small groups to respond to a course-related question such as "Which psychologist would you most like to have dinner with, and why?" or "What do you think psychologists do all day?"

Another option is to provide a list of attributes and ask students to mingle to find other students with those attributes. They could search, for example, for others who have taken introductory psychology in high school, are majoring in psychology, have a sibling under the age of 10, slept at least 8 hours last night, or ate breakfast this morning. If you list attributes such as "lives in ____ hall" or "prefers to study early in the morning," the commonalities students find might even help you to create study groups. You could even simply ask students to raise their hands if they fit these descriptions, then have students with raised hands pair up to discuss other things they might have in common. These and other ice-breakers and first-day activities can be found in *Successful Beginnings for College Teaching: Engaging Your Students From the First Day* (McGlynn, 2001).

PRESENTING YOUR SYLLABUS

Once introductions are accomplished, distribute your syllabus (see chapter 2 for ideas on syllabus construction). As you do so, remember that your students are seeing it for the first time. It contains a lot of information, and the students will not be able to absorb it all at once. Plan to highlight the most important elements of the syllabus in class, but encourage your students to use the document as a reference when they have questions about the course and its requirements.

Be sure that you duplicate more copies of the syllabus than you have students. During the first week of the term, students will probably be adding your course to their schedule, so you will need to have extra syllabi for those who enroll after the first day. Also, some students will inevitably lose their syllabus during the term, so it pays to have extra copies on hand. If you don't want to offer replacement syllabi, post the syllabus on your class Web site, if you have one, so that students can print out a new copy for themselves whenever they wish.

Start your discussion of the syllabus by listing your course goals. This strategy offers a natural lead-in to how class time will be spent (Davis, 1993). For example, if one of your main goals is to promote critical thinking about abnormal psychology, or teamwork in problem solving, highlight the fact that the assigned readings are designed to support classroom activities that involve analysis of the validity of psychiatric diagnoses or small-group problem-solving tasks. In this connection, be sure to let students know if the reading assignments are to be completed before or after the class session covering that topic. Some students, especially first-year students, will be unsure about this matter, so state your preference explicitly in your introduction, as well as in the syllabus.

Students will be particularly interested in how they will be graded in your course, so be sure to discuss the number and types of graded assignments there will be and how final grades will be determined. Use visual aids, such as a sample of the grade calculation procedure, to help get this information across (see Table 2.2 in chapter 2).

Encourage Instructor–Student Interactions

Reviewing the syllabus offers a perfect opportunity to continue demonstrating your commitment to the first principle of good practice in teaching, promoting student–teacher interaction. When you get to the part of the syllabus that lists your office address, make it clear that you are interested in meeting with your students. Make it easy for them to find you by giving some details and landmarks that will help students locate your office. Encourage them to stop by to ask questions or simply to introduce themselves. Point out your schedule of office hours, but tell students that you will be happy to arrange additional meeting times by appointment. This is also a good time to highlight your e-mail address and to give students an idea of how long it will normally take to get a reply to their e-mail messages. Let them know, for example, if you don't read e-mail after 10 p.m., or over weekends. If you offer online office hours explain how students can take advantage of them.

Describe aspects of your time schedule that will affect students' access to you. For example, if you have another class immediately before or after this one, explain why you will seem too rushed to chat when you arrive and depart. Otherwise, students might get the false impression that you are not interested in them. Finally, if you have listed your home phone number on the syllabus, now is the time to point out that you also listed the hours (e.g., 9 a.m. to 11 p.m.) during which your students can call it. If you explain the reasons for these rules—that you go to bed early, or that you live with small children or an ailing parent—students are unlikely to abuse the privilege of having your home number.

Describe the Workload

Be honest with your students about the amount of work that will be required in your class. Assure them that it can all be accomplished, but don't underplay the effort that will be necessary to succeed in the course. Most students will rise to the challenge (Timpson & Bendel-Simso, 1996), but those who can't or don't wish to handle the workload are better off dropping your course before it is too late.

This is also a good time to emphasize how important it is to read all the assigned material, and to do so on the schedule outlined in the syllabus. Not every student will follow this advice, but it is worth offering, and worth repeating from time to time throughout the term. When students fail to complete assigned readings, it might be because of time constraints, or even laziness, but sometimes it is because they are having trouble comprehending the material, or because they see no connection between the reading and what is going on in class. In one case we know of, a student asked his professor what the readings had to do with the lectures and was told that there really was no connection and that there was no need to buy or read the assigned textbook (Satterlee & Lau, 2003). Whatever you might think of that arrangement, the fact is that it would have been better for the professor to reveal this information on the first day of class.

If you are like most psychology professors, you will expect your students to read what you assign, so be explicit about how and when to complete the reading assignments. This is especially important when teaching first-year undergraduates. On the first day of class, display a copy of each of the required books, articles, and other assigned materials; note that the schedule for reading them is in the syllabus; and mention where the materials can be purchased and where they can be found in the library or other location. Offering this information not only demonstrates that you care about your students, but also makes it more likely that your students will have the correct materials on hand when they need them. Tell the students, too, a little bit about the texts and other readings you have chosen and how they relate to your course outline and your course goals (Boyd, 2003; Eble, 1988).

Unless you are the world's fastest talker and your students are the world's best note-takers, you won't have time in class to lecture about all the important information that is covered in the textbook. Mention this and point out that, as a result, your students will be responsible for doing a lot of learning on their own. It is vital for students to understand this, especially if you plan to test them on material that is not covered in lecture.

To help students get the most out of their psychology textbook and recognize material that is likely to be covered on quizzes and exams, explain the meaning of pedagogical features such as boldface print, italicized or highlighted text, critical thinking exercises, chapter summaries, self-tests, review tables, and the like (Boyd, 2003). This orientation can be especially important for first-year students and those whose academic preparation has been less than ideal. If they don't know what to look for in their readings, some of these students might not recognize the importance of pedagogical features, and might fail to make use of them as they read and study.

Go Over the Ground Rules

Spend some time, too, on the course guidelines and expectations listed in the syllabus. Tell students, for example, that attendance matters, that they should raise a hand and be recognized before speaking, that eating or drinking is not permitted in class, that you hate it when students start packing up to leave before you have finished a lecture, or whatever other rules and regulations regarding student behavior are especially important to you. Mention, too, the rules that will govern your behavior. For instance, we always tell our students that we will start each class on time and that we will never extend a class beyond its scheduled ending time. (This information helps get students to class early, and assures them they will not have to rush to their next class.)

In laying out ground rules for your course, be explicit. Do not assume that students will already know these rules, even the ones that seem intuitively obvious to you. Your rules might be utterly new to some students, especially those who have operated under different rules (or few rules) in other college classes, or in high school. So after describing your rules and preferences orally, remind students that this information is presented in more detail in the syllabus, and tell them that you would appreciate it if they would take some time to become familiar with them.

Ask for Questions

Once you have covered the course basics listed in the syllabus, be sure to ask for questions. Do so in a way that lets students know that you expect them to have questions and that you are happy to answer them. Murmuring "Any questions?" as you gather your materials to leave the room is not the best way to get this message across. Instead, say something like "OK, I know I have hit you with a lot of information. What questions do you have for me?" If no one immediately asks a question, take some time to scan the classroom. This, too, demonstrates that you really want students to respond. Be sure to wait long enough for students to work up the nerve to raise their hands (believe it or not, some students will be more nervous about addressing you in class than you are about addressing them). If no questions are forthcoming, have a few in mind to get the ball rolling. You could say, for example, "You might be wondering if the exams are cumulative (or whether attendance is mandatory, or what to do if you have to leave class early, or how to choose a paper topic, or where the lab is)." Then give the answers in a friendly way. In short, if you want your students to feel free to ask questions throughout the course, offer them genuine opportunities to do so on the first day, and then reward them when they respond.

Another way to stimulate syllabus-related questions is to ask students to form small groups, give each group an index card, and ask them to list on it their questions about the course and its requirements (Erickson & Strommer, 1991). After a few minutes, collect the cards and answer the questions.

LEARNING YOUR STUDENTS' NAMES

There are four main reasons why we think it is important to learn as many of your students' names as possible as early in the term as possible (Billson & Tiberius, 1998; Davis, 1993; Erickson & Strommer, 1991; Leamnson, 1999). First, it is less stressful to teach people you know rather than a group of strangers. Second, your effort to learn names—even if you don't learn them all—clearly demonstrates that you care about them as people, an attribute that is likely to improve your teaching ratings. Third, learning names can help your students feel less anonymous and less disconnected from their instructors. Being seen as an individual, not a number, can be especially important to first-year students, who might be finding themselves in relatively large classes for the first time. Finally, feeling a closer connection to faculty can help students to do better in their classes, and it certainly makes them more likely to seek help and advice when they need it (Erickson & Strommer, 1991; Leamnson, 1999). Learning students' names can be a daunting task, especially in large classes, but there are some ways to make it easier.

Collect Flash Cards

One psychology instructor we know asks each of her 200 students to paste a photo of themselves to the back of the 3 × 5 information card she hands out on the first day of class. She carries these cards with her for the next couple of weeks, using them as flash cards to test herself as she learns students' names at odd times, such as while riding the bus, while waiting for meetings to begin, and even just before bed. (To assure that she gets these cards back on the second day of class, she makes it a course requirement to turn them in, and gives points for doing so!)

Create a Context

Another instructor capitalizes on the principles of cognitive psychology to create a context for remembering students' names (Bailey, 2002). He finds that the more information he gathers about students, the easier it is to remember their names. Accordingly, he asks students to include on their information cards such items as the names of their pets, or something about themselves that they consider "cool" or unique. He also creates location cues by asking students to sit in the same seats throughout the term. Further, as students ask or answer questions or make comments during class, he jots down information on their cards—such as hair color or voice characteristics. He then engages in elaborative rehearsal, creating a "funny, weird, or meaningful association with some information about each student" (Bailey, 2002, p. 184). He organizes the cards in an order that duplicates the students' location in the classroom, and even uses chunking by creating a story that links the students in each row. Finally, he tests his memory by trying to fill in the correct names on a blank seating chart. Eventually, he can call on students by name in class, and as they turn in assignments or enter the room.

Practice, Practice, Practice

In relatively small classes, you can practice learning names simply by calling the roll each day. We tell our students that the roll call is done only so we can learn their names, and that there is no penalty for missing class, but we find that taking attendance actually seems to boost attendance. Whether you call the roll or find other excuses to use your students' names, you will find that practice eventually helps you to remember many more names than you thought you would. Don't be afraid to make mistakes. Tell your students that you want to get to know their names, that you will try to call them by name, and that you would appreciate it if they correct you when you make errors. They will not be insulted if you call them by the wrong name, and they will help you to get it right.

SETTING THE STAGE FOR GROUP WORK

If you plan to ask your students to work together in groups or teams, either in class or outside of class, set the stage for collaborative learning by assigning students to their working groups during the first few days of class. By creating the groups yourself rather than allowing students to do so, you can assure that each group is as diverse as possible in terms of gender, ethnicity, and year of study. By establishing these groups early in the term, you create the opportunity for students to form a supportive network of classmates from the beginning. Students who are in the same work group for class discussions might end up in the same study group when the time comes to prepare for quizzes and exams.

Forming working groups is easy. On the first or second day of class, send around a sign-up sheet and ask everyone to fill in their name, year in school, campus phone number, e-mail address, and campus address. (If you have already handed out information index cards, this step is unnecessary.) Later, you can assign students to groups based on gender, ethnicity (if you know it), seniority, and address (those who live close to one another might be more likely to meet outside of class). At the next class, announce the composition of the groups you have formed. Then ask the members of each group to get together during that session to work on a problem or answer a question, and make a group report to the class. A few sessions before your first quiz or exam, give the work groups a few minutes in class to arrange a time and place to get together to study.

Having students work together periodically in class and encouraging them to study together outside of class not only helps them to get to know, like, and depend on one another, but also helps create a friendlier and more supportive classroom environment for you as their teacher. We discuss group learning activities in more detail in Chapter 4.

ENDING THE FIRST CLASS

There is a lot of administrative work to do on the first day of class, but as we mentioned earlier, it is important to cover some course content, as well (Scholl-Buckwald, 1985). Depending on how much time you have available before the end of the class period, you can begin your first lecture, or pose some questions for students to answer (perhaps in small groups), or maybe even administer a short quiz designed to test students' knowledge of, or misconceptions about, the content of your psychology course. In our introductory psychology courses, we often hand out a brief true–false test with items that seem quite easy and obvious (e.g., "schizophrenia is a form of multiple personality" or "it is easier to get help in a crowd"), but that all represent common misconceptions about behavior and mental processes. Students are surprised and curious when the quiz is scored in class and they discover that many of the things they thought they knew about behavior and mental processes turn out to be wrong. This experience helps to motivate students to begin their reading, and to come back to the next class.

Whatever option you choose, it is good to give students a taste of the course material to come, so that they leave that first class with something to think about. Don't forget to remind students of their reading assignment for the next class, as well as any other homework you have set for them—including the return of information cards or other material you have asked for.

Bringing class to an organized conclusion is important for every session, not just the first one. As the end of class approaches, don't just let time run out. Reserve a few minutes to summarize the main points you have covered and to say a few words about the material you will address the next time (Billson & Tiberius, 1998). You might even consider using the final 2 minutes to have your students jot down and turn in their reactions to the day's lecture. This little exercise not only shows that you care what your students think, it also provides you with immediate feedback on how the class went (McKeachie, 1986).

SOME FINAL COMMENTS

Just as you will do on the first day of class, this chapter has presented too much material for you to absorb all at once. We hope the summary and Checklist 3.1 will serve as a useful reminder when you meet your new class for the first time. The checklist also includes items discussed in Chapter 2 that are especially relevant to keep in mind on the first day of class. You might want to make a copy of this checklist and bring it with you to class.

Checklist 3.1
Some Points to Remember
About the First Day of Class

Before the first class meeting:

1. Become thoroughly familiar with the required resources (textbook, study guide, etc.) so that you can easily answer questions about them.
2. Visit your classroom before the term begins to check on its physical layout and characteristics. Is the room kept locked and, if so, how do you get a key? Where are the light switches? Are there enough student chairs and desks? Is there an instructor desk, podium, and overhead projector? If you are going to use an overhead, where do you plug it in? Will you need an extension cord? If you will use a chalkboard, is there chalk available, or do you need to bring your own? If you will need to darken the room to make overheads, PowerPoint,

or videos more visible, are there shades at the windows—and do they work? Is any of the audiovisual or computer equipment locked in cabinets or closets for which you will need keys or lock combinations? Is there any missing or broken equipment?

3. Write a syllabus that includes:
   a. The course number and title.
   b. When and where the course meets.
   c. Your name, office address, office phone number, e-mail address, and office hours. (If you decide to provide your home phone number, include rules for its use (e.g., "Please do not call me at home after 10 p.m.")
   d. A list of all required and recommended readings and resources.
   e. A brief statement of course goals and a description of what the course will cover.
   f. A description of all evaluation procedures, including exactly how the final grade is computed and an explanation of every graded component.
   g. A course outline that includes (a) a list of all lecture and discussion topics and associated readings or other assignments, and (b) the dates of all quizzes, exams, and other important course events, as well as deadlines for papers and other assignments.
   h. A summary of your policies about making up missed exams or quizzes, and how late papers will be dealt with. (Remember that the syllabus is a legally binding contract between you and your students. It specifies the rules, expectations, and responsibilities that will guide their behavior, and yours, during the course. Think carefully about what you say in your syllabus, and seek advice from more experienced colleagues if you are in doubt.)

4. Plan a course content "teaser" for the first day of class—a question, a group project, a problem, or a dilemma for students to deal with that will help them begin to think about the material to be covered in the course.

Some First Day Dos And Don'ts

DO:

1. Arrive early with all of the materials that you will need. Write the course name and number and your name on the overhead or blackboard.

2. Chat with students as they enter the classroom before class starts. Treat your students with respect.
3. Introduce yourself. Tell your students a little about your background, interests, and so on. Tell them how they should address you: first name, Mr./Ms., Dr., Professor, and so on.
4. Distribute your syllabus and go over the important points, including course ground rules. After covering the basics, ask for questions, then scan the room as you give the class plenty of time to work up the courage to speak. If no questions are raised immediately, be ready with some of your own. For example, "Is the final exam cumulative?" "What do you do if you are sick on the day your first reaction paper is due?" or "Whom should you contact if you have to miss a lab (or class session, experiment, paper deadline, etc.)?"
5. Encourage students to come to your office hours with additional questions, or just to get acquainted.
6. If you want to create an early active learning experience, do a course-related demonstration or set up a brief group activity. For example:
   a. Assign students to small groups and give them 5 minutes to agree on a course-related question that they would like the instructor to answer and then write that question on an index card you have provided.
   b. Present a problem or case study for students to solve or analyze.
   c. Ask students to tell you what topics they are most interested in learning about in the course. List these topics on the board or overhead projector, and note which topics will be covered in which course content areas.
   d. Ask students to write a paragraph about what they hope and expect to get out of your course.

DON'T

1. Arrive late and ignore students.
2. Distribute the syllabus and dismiss class.
3. Let students sit through the entire class without giving them the opportunity to meet even one other student in the class.

The first day of class is a challenge, but once it is over, you will soon realize that the rest of the term remains, and you have a lot of psychology to cover. How can you present that material in the most effective way, and in a manner that matches your teaching style? These are some of the questions we consider in the next chapter.

Developing Your Teaching Style

When Brookfield (1990) described teaching as "the educational equivalent of white-water rafting" (p. 2), he was referring to the emotional ups and downs that college faculty typically experience. Most veteran psychology teachers know exactly what he meant. We have all had days when our classroom is alive with the excitement of effective teaching and eager learning, as well as days when planned demonstrations and activities don't work, when students are mystified by even the most carefully crafted lectures, and when the process of

55

handing back exams turns ugly. Actually, we would take Brookfield's metaphor a step further, because for most new psychology faculty, teaching is the equivalent of white-water rafting without a guide. As mentioned in Chapter 1, unlike our colleagues in elementary and secondary education, psychology faculty enter the classroom with little or no training in the theory and practice of teaching. We tend to teach by default, doing the best we can, and often following the examples (good and bad) set by our own teachers. The results can be mixed, at best. As one observer bluntly put it, "Many faculty are not effective in the classroom because they don't know what they are doing or why" (Weimer, 1988, p. 49).

This condition need not be permanent, however, nor are certain faculty doomed to swirl forever in the rapids. True, psychology faculty whose personalities include conscientiousness, extraversion, and openness might find it especially easy to do well in the classroom, but with enough planning, practice, and effort, virtually anyone who wants to become an effective teacher, or a more effective teacher, can do so. In this chapter we briefly describe some of the most notable characteristics of effective teachers, and then consider some of the specific teaching methods and behaviors that contribute to their effectiveness—and that can contribute to yours, too.

SOME CHARACTERISTICS OF EFFECTIVE TEACHERS

In 1997, Murray conducted a meta-analysis of research on the relationship between teachers' instructional activities (the process of teaching) and the educational changes that appear in students (the outcomes of teaching). He found three aspects of teacher behavior to be positively correlated with student learning: enthusiasm, clarity, and the ability to have good rapport with students (Murray, 1997). Similar features of effective teaching have been identified by other researchers (Feldman, 1998; Junn, 1994; Lowman, 1998; Marsh & Roche, 1997; McKeachie, 2001; Teven & McCroskey, 1996).

For example, after reviewing research on undergraduate students' evaluations of teachers, Lowman (1998) proposed two main dimensions of effective teaching. The first, called *intellectual excitement*, includes clarity of communication and positive emotional impact on students. Teachers who are strong on this dimension are described not only as "knowing the material," but as being able to see it from various perspectives, to organize and present it from a novice learner's perspective, and to explain the material in ways that all students can understand. These teachers also use voice inflections, gestures, and movement to transform teaching into a type of performing art that elicits strong positive emotions in their students. Lowman's second dimension, called *interpersonal rapport*, includes the ability to engender students' respect, but without creating anxiety, anger, or resentment. Lowman suggested that behaviors related to the interpersonal rapport dimension tend to appear both in class and out of class, whereas behaviors associated with the intellectual excitement dimension tend to appear mainly in the classroom.

Feldman (1998) identified a set of behaviors that teachers as well as students consider important to a teacher's classroom effectiveness: (a) sensitivity to, and concern with, students and their progress; (b) preparation for and organization of the course; (c) content knowledge; and (d) enthusiasm for the subject matter and for teaching itself. Seldin (1999a) summarized the characteristics of effective teachers as follows:

> Treating students with respect; providing the relevance of information to be learned; using active, hands-on student learning; varying instructional methods; providing frequent feedback to students on their performance; offering real-world, practical examples; drawing inferences from models and using analogies; providing clear expectations for assignments; creating a class environment which is comfortable for students; communicating to the level of their students; presenting themselves in class as "real people"; using feedback from students and others to assess and improve their teaching; reflecting on their own classroom performance in order to improve it. (p. 3)

People who display these characteristics have obviously developed a teaching style that is comfortable for them and their students, and that serves to promote many of the principles of good practice in teaching we described in Chapter 1. Yet if you watch effective teachers in action, you will find that there are many variations on this basic style. In other words, effective teachers don't follow a pre-established script; they have found their own unique way to pursue the principles of effective teaching within the framework of their own personalities.

Is teaching effectiveness affected by a teacher's gender? Overall, no. Students' ratings of teaching effectiveness are about the same for male and female teachers (Cashin, 1995; Centra & Gaubatz, 2000). Although the characteristics of effective teachers apply to both genders, men and women might have to find slightly different ways of communicating those characteristics to students. For example, students might perceive female teachers to be a more accessible and a bit less threatening than male teachers, which might make it easier for females to convey their caring (Centra & Gaubatz, 2000; Goss, 1983). Accordingly, men might have to go out of their way to remind students about, say, their availability via office hours or on e-mail. At the same time, female teachers might find that they have to do a little more than male teachers, especially at the beginning of a new term, to establish themselves as knowledgeable authority figures. One study found, for example, that college students tended to think of female instructors as "teachers," whereas they labeled male instructors as "professors" (Miller & Chamberlin, 2000). To counteract the possible operation of such cognitive biases, many experienced female members of the psychology faculty make sure to use their academic title (e.g., Dr., Professor) or preferred form of address (Ms., Mrs., Miss) on their syllabus, their Web site, and handouts, quizzes, and any other material they distribute to students. They might also dress for class a bit more formally than their male counterparts, and find ways early on to mention their educational background and the nature of their scholarly work.

In general, then, you don't have to conform to someone else's ideal of a "good teacher" to be an effective teacher. As you begin to develop your own teaching style, don't feel obligated to emulate a favorite teacher—unless that person's style and your own are truly alike. In the long run it is best to simply be yourself. If you have a humorous streak, don't try to suppress it in the classroom. However, if you don't normally make wry comments and engage in witty repartee, don't try to be a comedian in class. The truth is that students tend to like and respect teachers who display almost any interpersonal style as long as that style is authentic and as long as it is clear that the teacher cares about them, and about teaching the course. By the same token, they tend to dislike even the flashiest, funniest, or most scholarly style if it is seen as phony.

Being genuine is an essential part of developing your teaching style, but it is not sufficient in and of itself to guarantee success in teaching psychology. Similarly, although it is vital to care about your teaching and your students, you still have to find appropriate ways to communicate that caring. An important key to effective teaching, then, is to translate your motivation and good intentions into good practice. This means learning or honing a variety of more specific skills that can help you to be an effective teacher (Junn, 1994;

Lowman, 1998; McKeachie, 2001). In the pages to follow, we offer our advice on how to (a) create interesting lectures, (b) promote active learning, (c) conduct memorable demonstrations, (d) ask and answer questions efficiently, (e) stimulate class discussions, (f) incorporate student presentations, (g) provide opportunities for cooperative learning, (h) use illustrative case examples, (i) arrange service-learning experiences, and (j) encourage students to think critically about psychology and life in general.

EFFECTIVE LECTURING

If you are like most psychology teachers, and certainly like most new teachers, you will spend a lot of class time giving lectures. As former students, we all know that lectures can be boring, but most of us know, too, that when properly organized and delivered, lectures can also be an effective, even inspiring, teaching instrument. A good lecturer can give an engaging and memorable presentation on anything from neuroanatomy or color vision to cognitive dissonance or decision making (Ashcroft & Foreman-Peck, 1994). Some teachers seem to be born to lecture and they do well at it almost from the beginning. For the rest of us, becoming an effective lecturer takes a lot of planning, a lot of practice, and a willingness to learn and change on the basis of feedback and experience. We don't have a simple prescription that will guarantee your success as a lecturer, but we can offer some tips and guidelines for preparing and delivering effective lectures.

Planning Your Lectures

First, decide what content you want to cover in a particular lecture and then prepare a set of notes on that material.

Writing Lecture Notes. Some teachers like to write out their notes in complete sentences. Here is an example from a lecture on the structure of the brain:

> The forebrain controls the most complex aspects of behavior and mental life. It folds back over and completely covers the rest of the brain. The outer surface of the forebrain is called the cerebral cortex. Two structures in the forebrain, the hypothalamus and the thalamus, help operate basic drives, emotion, and sensation. The thalamus acts as a relay station for pain and sense-organ signals (except smell) from the body to the upper

levels of the brain. The thalamus also processes and makes sense of these signals. The hypothalamus lies under the thalamus (hypo means "under") and helps regulate hunger, thirst, and sex drives. The hypothalamus is connected to the autonomic nervous system and to other parts of the brain. Damage to parts of the hypothalamus upsets normal appetite, thirst, and sexual behavior.

Narrative notes like these can be a life-saver early in your teaching career, especially if you feel the need for a lot of help in remembering the details of course content. Unfortunately, narrative notes can create a tendency to read them aloud, so unless you are an accomplished dramatic actor, the result can sound stilted and might create a boring and uncomfortable experience for your students and for you, too. As an alternative to writing a complete lecture script, consider organizing your notes as an outline that contains enough information to remind you what you want to say, but that is not as constraining as a full-blown narrative. As shown in Fig. 4.1, this outline can include asides, examples, and cases that you might want to mention. We have used such outlines for decades in presenting our own lectures, and we have found them not only useful, but flexible. For example, when we come across new examples, research studies, or cases that are relevant to a particular lecture, we simply jot down a note about them in the margin of the outline and incorporate them into our presentation the next time we deliver that lecture. If the additions work well, we then alter our computer file and reprint the outline with the new material in its proper place.

As a result, our lecture outlines have become more elaborate over the years, but you can also decide to reduce the level of detail in your outline as you become more experienced and confident. We know of psychology teachers who have become so exceptionally familiar with their course content that they rely entirely on a brief list of topics to remind them of their planned lecture sequence; all the details, cases, and examples are fixed in memory and require only minimal retrieval cues. So their lecture notes look like this:

The Central Nervous System
Spinal Cord
Hindbrain
Midbrain
Forebrain

I. Major Structures of the Brain

A. Brain consists of hindbrain, midbrain, and forebrain.
  1. Subdivisions do not have clear-cut borders.
  2. Interconnected by fiber tracts.

B. *Hindbrain* a continuation of the spinal cord.
  1. *Medulla* involved in basic life functions (e.g., blood pressure, heart rate, breathing).
    a. *Reticular formation*; web of neurons threading throughout the hindbrain and into the midbrain that
      i. help alert and arouse other brain areas. (Note: If the fibers from the reticular system are disconnected from the rest of the brain, coma results.)
  2. *Cerebellum* allows the eyes to track a moving target accurately.
    a. Coordinates fine motor movements
    b. May also store a memory code for well-rehearsed movements.

  Note: Hearing slightly delayed feedback from one's own speech, as when people call in to talk shows and hear their own words coming from the radio, disrupts the cerebellum's role in creating fluency. If callers do not eliminate this delayed feedback by turning down their radios, they might begin to stutter.

C. *Midbrain* is a small structure that relays information from the eyes, ears, and skin and controls certain types of automatic behaviors.
  1. The midbrain's *substantia nigra*, and its connections to the forebrain's *striatum*, permit the smooth initiation of movement.

  Note: These connections, which are damaged in Parkinson's disease, use dopamine as a neurotransmitter.

D. *Forebrain* is largest part of the brain and actually folds back over itself and completely covers the other parts. Has several structures within it.
  1. The *thalamus* processes inputs from sense organs (including pain), and then relays sensory information to other appropriate forebrain areas.
  2. The tiny *hypothalamus* (under the thalamus) helps regulate hunger, thirst, and sex drives.
    a. Influences both the autonomic and endocrine systems
    b. Contains the *suprachiasmatic nucleus*, the brain's "clock" that sets biological rhythms for the body's functioning.

  Note: This might be the part of our body responsible for our peak time of alertness—"morning people" and "night people." *(continued)*

(continued)

3. *Amygdala* involved in linking stimuli from two sensory modalities and in fear and other emotions.
    a. Its activity is altered in people suffering from posttraumatic stress disorder.
4. *Hippocampus*; critical for the ability to form new memories.
    a. Memories are not stored in the hippocampus but are transferred elsewhere.

Note: Mention case of H.M.: Damage to his hippocampus prevented him from forming new long-term memories.

FIG. 4.1. A sample of lecture notes in outline form.

Assuming that, like us, you have not reached that level of lecturing skill, we suggest that you overprepare each lecture outline. By this we mean that you write the outline so that it includes more material than you can possibly cover in one class period. Overpreparation might seem unnecessary at the time you are doing it, but it has two advantages. First, it assures that you will not run out of content even if nervousness causes you to speak faster than normal, or if you decide to skip parts of a lecture that, in light of how the class is going, now seem too complex, too simple, or not likely to work as well as you had expected. Second, overpreparation gives you a head start on your lecture for the following class session.

Remember, though, that the fact that you have prepared a lot of lecture material doesn't obligate you to cover all of it in any particular session (Zakrajsek, 1998), or even to cover it at all. There will inevitably be some topics that you will have to leave out of your lectures, or that you will have time only to touch on, if you are going to keep reasonably close to the schedule of topics, reading assignments, and exams and quizzes advertised in your syllabus. We don't worry too much about leaving a topic without fully addressing it, because we believe that although students learn a lot from lectures, they don't learn from lectures alone. They also learn—and are responsible for learning—from their assigned reading, from talking to teachers and fellow students, and from computer labs, class projects, papers, and other activities. So don't rush your lectures in an effort to cover everything you wish you could cover. If you do, you will be exhausted, and your students will be overwhelmed.

To make future lecture planning easier, keep track of where you had to stop at the end of each class session. This simple procedure creates a record of your intended, and actual, pace of progress through the course. You can then use this information to plan the same lecture the next time you teach the course, or when delivering it in another section of the course. You can keep these records by making a note in the margin of your lecture notes, by marking the lecture topic outline in your copy of the syllabus, or as one of us does, by keeping a running log of the topics covered in each lecture.

Keeping Students Interested. When planning your lectures, remember that there are limits on your students' attention span and information-processing capacity. Traditional wisdom and our own experience suggests, for example, that student attention is usually highest during the first 10 minutes of a lecture, after which it tends to wane unless something is done to recapture it (McKeachie, 1999). In fact, some research suggests that the average student can absorb only about three to five major points in any particular lecture (Lowman, 1995). Accordingly, the most effective lecturers plan lectures that concentrate on those few major points (Tozer, 1992), presenting information about each of them in several ways to maximize the chances that everyone understands the material. This might mean, for example, presenting and giving applied examples of three main theories of prejudice rather than trying to describe in detail every theory listed in the textbook.

Further, organize your lectures so that they periodically refresh your students' interest and attention. Perhaps the best way to do this is to divide each class period into four to five segments of 10 to 15 minutes each, depending on the length of your time slot. Then plan something for each segment that is likely to be especially interesting, surprising, or engaging. That "something" might involve one of the active learning methods described in more detail in the next section; or it might simply be an unusual way to introduce a new topic or subtopic—perhaps by telling a story, posing a problem, framing a dilemma, describing a mystery, or asking a question. For example, reading an excerpt from the case of "H.M." or showing a "Mr. Short-Term Memory" sketch from *Saturday Night Live* are just two attention-getting ways of introducing a lecture segment on the formation of long-term memories.

By organizing your lecture outline into related but discrete, potentially stand-alone segments, it should be possible to introduce each segment in an engaging way, complete it, and move on to the next segment in time to recapture your students' attention if it is fading a bit. Another advantage of a segmented lecture outline is that it allows you to quickly change the sequence in which you cover various topics (assuming it makes sense to do so) based on the questions students are asking, and how they are responding to the material. For example, suppose that your well-organized summary of biological, psychodynamic, cognitive-behavioral, and humanistic models of psychopathology has fallen flat, and as has happened to all of us at one time or another, your students' faces have lost all expression. Don't panic. You can decide on the spot to play that taped interview of a mental patient now rather than later, and ask the class to consider how each theoretical model would explain this person's condition. By inserting high-interest content sooner than you had planned you will have re-engaged the class. Having such flexibility built into your lecture outline can pay big dividends in terms of helping you keep your students attentive and involved.

Delivering Your Lecture

Easily perceived stimuli also help hold students' attention, so when it is time to walk into the classroom and deliver your carefully planned lecture, remember that the first step in keeping your students with you, mentally, is to be a clear presence, physically.

Being Seen and Heard. As you lecture, be sure that all your students can see you. We strongly recommend that you lecture while standing, and that you assure that the podium—or wherever you will be spending most of your class time—is visible from every seat. If an injury or disability requires that you lecture sitting down, try to position yourself on a platform or other elevated location, especially in classrooms where seats are not arranged on risers. In these flat classrooms, students in the back might be especially likely to lose focus if you let yourself become no more than a disembodied voice.

We suggest, too, that you move around the room a bit as you lecture, perhaps even walking among the students if you are comfortable doing so. Take a few pages of lecture notes with you so that you won't be moored to the podium and forced to return to it every few seconds, like a yo-yo. A certain amount of movement—along with whatever characteristic hand gestures you might use while speaking—creates visual variety that helps hold your students' attention, but don't overdo it. Students tend to find it distracting, even annoying, when teachers pace frantically or engage in certain other repetitive actions such as endlessly capping and uncapping a pen. (See chapter 8 for some tips on getting evaluative feedback on your lecturing style.)

Whether you are in motion or simply standing at a podium, you can increase your students' attentiveness by constantly scanning the room and making eye contact with everyone from time to time. Some students will look back at you with more interest than others, so there is a natural tendency to spend more time looking at those who are "with you." However, if you can resist letting your scanning pattern be shaped by this kind of operant reinforcement, you will find that even the less involved students will stay at least marginally interested if you use your eyes to let them know that you are talking to them, too.

Be sure, also, that all your students can hear what you are saying. If you are teaching in a large classroom, or if you have a soft voice, you might need to use a microphone. (As described in chapter 3, you should determine this need while you are exploring your classroom and its facilities before the new term begins.) Once you are sure it is audible, use your voice to attract attention. Speaking too softly, or too quickly, or speaking in a monotone are sure-fire ways to lose students' interest. You might even put some of them to sleep. If you are not sure how you sound in the classroom, record yourself as you deliver a mock lecture, then listen to it and try to be objective about the volume, clarity, and quality of your voice (ask a friend or colleague to comment on the tape, too). If you are not happy with what you hear, work on speaking louder, more distinctly, and with more variations in pitch to help keep students interested and awake (McKeachie, 2001).

Incorporate Audiovisual Material. Audiovisual material helps hold students' attention, too, so use it whenever possible. If you are describing the results of the Milgram experiments, or the structure of the eye, or various categories of memory, for example, don't depend on your words alone to keep students riveted. Show a video clip from Milgram's original study, present a CD-ROM image of eye anatomy, or a transparency or PowerPoint slide listing the memory components you plan to cover. You might also want to present some of this material on handouts on which students can take notes as you lecture.

Define Your Terms. Remember, too, that it is easy for your students to lose interest if they don't understand the vocabulary you are using. In addition to speaking audibly, clearly and in an organized way, be sure to define and display the spelling of every psychological term that is likely to be unfamiliar to students. There are a lot more of these unfamiliar terms than you might think. If you are like most psychology teachers, you have come to adopt a specialized vocabulary that is easily understood by your colleagues but that could mystify, confuse, or mislead the average student, especially those taking their first psychology course. For students new to psychology, the course-specific meaning of terms such as *reinforcement, correlation, fMRI, attribution,* and perhaps even *cognition* will probably require some explanation, and terms such as *priming, retroactive interference,* and *interposition* surely will! Even in upper division and graduate courses, there will undoubtedly be terms that students will be encountering for the first time. The more often you use such terms without defining and displaying them, the harder it is for students to follow the thread of your narrative, and the easier it is for them to lose interest in the lecture.

Ask for Feedback. How will you know if students don't immediately understand the terms you use? If you have previously invited students to raise a hand when they don't understand something in your lecture, a few might actually do so and ask for a definition or a spelling, but most will not. If you wonder whether students have understood a particular term, be on the safe side and take a moment to define and spell it. Be proactive in heading off misunderstanding and confusion about other things, too. Pause now and then to ask if anything you have said so far—including new terms—is unclear. You can gauge how often to do this partly on the basis of students' facial expressions and posture. When you see a few frowns, furrowed brows, or heads resting on palms, some students are probably confused or are losing interest, so that would be a good time to stop and ask for some more explicit feedback. (We say "when" you see these signs because even the most effective and experienced teachers have a few students who are likely to be bored, fall asleep, or leave class early; don't be too hard on yourself when you see these things in your own classroom—unless the entire class leaves!)

Don't just ask the perfunctory "Are there any questions?" question, however. Show your students you truly care how the lecture is going. Ask something like "OK, what terms have I used that you don't understand?" or "What questions do you have at this point?" or "Is all this making sense to you?" or "Am I going too fast? Too slow?" Instead or in addition, you might use one of the active learning methods described later to assess your students' understanding of the previous few minutes of the lecture.

Give Plenty of Examples. In addition to defining and spelling key terms, concepts, principles, and phenomena, be sure to illustrate them with at least one, and preferably several, examples or analogies. For example, when presenting material on homeostasis, give a couple of examples of homeostatic processes, such as the body's efforts to maintain constant levels of temperature or blood sugar. Then, to make the concept even clearer, you could point out that the homeostatic process is similar to the action of a thermostat-and-furnace system that maintains constant temperature in a house. By including lots of examples, analogies, metaphors, and similes, you not only hold your students' attention, you make the material easier to understand. This is particularly true if the examples, analogies, metaphors, and similes are vivid, offbeat, funny, and relevant to students' life experiences (Center for Teaching Excellence, 1999; Tozer, 1992; Zakrajsek, 1998). One instructor we know told his students about a line of ants marching along his kitchen floor, and used the image as an amazingly memorable example of the common fate principle of perceptual organization. The instructor's resource manuals that accompany most psychology textbooks usually offer excellent examples that you can sprinkle into your lectures to clarify and enliven even the most difficult concepts. Many former students have told us that it was our "weird" examples that stuck in their minds and helped them to understand and remember important material, and retrieve the information on exams.

Emphasize Linkages. It is easier for students to pay attention to what you are saying if they can easily see how the topic of each lecture segment fits into the rest of the lecture, and into the rest of the course. Help them to see the "big picture" by creating a brief overview of each day's lecture that you can display at the beginning of class. If you put this overview on a blackboard, a second overhead or computer screen, or a handout, students can easily refer to it throughout the session. The overview need be no more than a version of your lecture outline that contains only the main topic headings. See Chapter 6 for a discussion of how such *advance organizers* can be used to help students link new information to what they have already learned.

Emphasize these linkages in your lectures, too. Point out how each new topic you discuss is related to those covered in previous lectures, or to topics yet to come. To take just one example, a lecture on brain chemistry is likely to be a lot more interesting to the average student if you describe its role in creating the effects of drugs we might use everyday (e.g., alcohol and caffeine), drugs we are not supposed to use (e.g., marijuana and cocaine), and drugs aimed at treating mental disorders ranging from hyperactivity to schizophrenia. Using these kinds of linking transitions in every class session can help students to perceive your lecture—and your course—as a coherent whole rather than a laundry list of unrelated topics.

Practice, Practice, Practice.   We would all like our lectures to come across to students as smooth, fascinating, spontaneous stories, full of memorable examples and elegant transitions, delivered by a professor who uses notes as a reminder, not a script. Approximating this ideal takes years of experience, but even one dry-run presentation of each lecture can improve your classroom presentations considerably. You can use as your audience a video camera, a tape recorder, a willing friend or relative, or even a sympathetic pet! If you tape the lecture, review the tape and focus on any mannerisms, vocal patterns, dysfluencies (e.g., uhmmms and ahs), or repetitious words or phrases (e.g., "ya' know?" or "OK?") that might be distracting or annoying to listeners. Then try the lecture again and see if you can improve on the things you didn't like the first time. You might never get yourself to stop saying "OK?" but the practice won't have been wasted: You will be amazed at how much easier it is to give a lecture in class when it is not the first time you tried it. (See chapter 8 for more on evaluating your teaching style.)

Ending Your Lecture

As you lecture, keep track of the time, and in the last 5 minutes of the class period, bring your lecture to an end in an organized way by summarizing its key points, or asking the students to do so. Don't hesitate to generate some curiosity about your next lecture by offering a "teaser" about something it will contain. When students hear that "Next time, we'll find out how many of you are colorblind," or "On Friday you'll have a chance to figure out which parenting style you grew up with," you can be sure a lot of them will be in class.

In other words, organize the end of the lecture as carefully as you organize the rest of it. Otherwise, you will be in the middle of presenting important material just as the class ends, when few students are likely to be paying much attention. They watch the time, too, and many will already have started packing up to leave. You can minimize this tendency, and the noise it creates, by nipping it in the bud. The first time you encounter the beginnings of anticipatory departure behavior (ADB), get everyone's attention and explain that ADB is annoying to you and disruptive to other students. Explain, too, that there is no need for ADB because you promise never to continue lecturing beyond the end of class period. Gentle reminders about this plan in the next class or two are usually all it takes to eliminate the problem.

PROMOTING ACTIVE LEARNING

The traditional teaching model, in which a professor lectures while students take notes, has a long and distinguished history and is likely to be with us for a long time to come. However, as most of us know from our own student days, passively listening to lectures, even well-presented ones, can get boring after a while. So as mentioned earlier, we suggest that you supplement your lectures with lots of opportunities for *active learning*, which means that students (a) do something other than watching and listening, (b) work on skill development rather than just try to absorb information, (c) are required to engage in higher order thinking about course material (e.g., "What does it mean?" rather than just "What am I supposed to remember?"), and (d) have a chance to explore the ways in which course material relates to their own attitudes and values (Bonwell & Eison, 1991). You can promote active learning in a virtually endless number of ways. For example, you can assign small-group problem-solving tasks; set up classroom debates; ask students to write and discuss "one-minute essays" about a particular topic (e.g., "What do you think Milgram's obedience studies say about human beings?"); let students use a "thumbs up" or "thumbs down" sign to indicate agreement or disagreement with lecture content; and give a multiple-choice question based on the main point of the previous 15 minutes of your lecture (Heward, 1997).

Students tend to enjoy active learning experiences, and show special interest in courses that incorporate them (Moran, 2000; Murray, 2000). Active learning methods help students to go beyond memorizing isolated facts, think more deeply about course material, consider how new material relates to what they already know, and apply what they have learned to new and different situations. This kind of more elaborate thinking about course material also makes it easier to remember that material. Studies of students in elementary schools, high schools, community colleges, and universities have found that active learning methods are followed by better test performance and greater class participation as compared with passive instructional techniques (e.g., Brelsford, 1993; Chu, 1994; Hake, 1998; Kellum, Carr, & Dozier, 2001; Kerr & Payne, 1994; Meyers & Jones, 1993).

Some active learning techniques, such as a "one-minute essay," are easy to use and don't take much class time. Others, such as in-class debates or role-playing activities, are more time consuming and might be more difficult to organize and carry off successfully. Our advice is to start slowly, trying out short, easy active learning methods at first, then progressing to more elaborate ones as you gain experience and confidence in using them.

We present some ideas for active learning methods later in this chapter, but there are other valuable sources, as well, including the instructor's resource manuals that accompany most major psychology textbooks, and a number of activities handbooks for psychology (see Table 4.1). There are other, more detailed presentations on active learning and we recommend that you consult them, too (e.g., Bonwell & Eison, 1991; Meyers & Jones, 1993; Silberman, 1996).

Remember that active learning techniques need not replace more traditional teaching approaches. Instead, as suggested earlier, you can use them to create variety and a change of pace—for your students and yourself—so that every class session features portions in which students become participants, not spectators (Shulman, 2003). In accordance with the segmented lecture format discussed earlier, some instructors organize their lectures into 10-minute "lecturettes" (Jenkins, 1992), each of which is separated from the next by some kind of active learning experience, such as a few minutes of small-group or individual work on some problem or task. As the students work, the teacher walks around the classroom, answering questions, making comments, and the like, before reconvening the whole group for the next lecturette.

TABLE 4.1

Some Sources of Ideas for Promoting Active Learning in Your Classroom

Benjamin, L., & Lowman, K. (Eds.). (1981). *Activities handbook for the teaching of psychology* (Vol. 1). Washington, DC: American Psychological Association.

Makosky, V., Whittemore, L., & Rogers, A. (1987). *Activities handbook for the teaching of psychology* (Vol. 2). Washington, DC: American Psychological Association.

Makosky, V., Sileo, C., Whittemore, L., Landry, C., & Skutley, M. (Eds.). (1990). *Activities handbook for the teaching of psychology* (Vol. 3). Washington, DC: American Psychological Association.

Benjamin, L., Nodine, B., Ernst, R., & Blair Broeker, C. (Eds.). (1999). *Activities handbook for the teaching of psychology* (Vol. 4). Washington, DC: American Psychological Association.

Ware, M., & Johnson, R. (Eds.). (2000). *Handbook of demonstrations and activities in the teaching of psychology: Vol. 1. Introductory, statistics, research methods, and history* (2nd ed.). Mahwah, NJ: Lawrence Erlbaum Associates.

Ware, M., & Johnson, R. (Eds.). (2000). *Handbook of demonstrations and activities in the teaching of psychology: Vol. 2. Physiological-comparative, perception, learning, cognitive, and developmental* (2nd ed.). Mahwah, NJ: Lawrence Erlbaum Associates.

Ware, M., & Johnson, R. (Eds.). (2000). *Handbook of demonstrations and activities in the teaching of psychology: Vol. 3. Personality, abnormal, clinical-counseling, and social* (2nd ed.). Mahwah, NJ: Lawrence Erlbaum Associates.

Teaching of Psychology, the official journal of Division 2 of the American Psychological Association, the Society for the Teaching of Psychology (Web site at http://www.ithaca.edu/beins/top/top.htm; the Society's Web site is at http://teachpsych.org).

Buffington, P. (1996). *Cheap psychological tricks: What to do when hard work, honesty, and perseverance fail.* Atlanta, GA: Peachtree.

Slife, B. (2001). *Taking sides: Clashing views on controversial psychological issues.* Guilford, CT: Dushkin/McGraw-Hill.

"Teaching Tips" is a regular column featured in *The Observer*, the official newsletter of the American Psychological Society.

Psychwatch is a publication of Psychwatch, Inc. (http://www.psychwatch.com).

CONDUCTING MEMORABLE DEMONSTRATIONS

Like lectures themselves, classroom demonstrations have long been used as part of traditional classroom teaching. Demonstrations offer a particularly useful way to illustrate a wide variety of psychological concepts, principles, and phenomena. For example, a video of children failing a conservation task can make the principle of conservation come alive for students, just as playing a taped interview with a hospitalized patient can give bipolar disorder a human voice. Although demonstrations can be vivid and dramatic, they do not automatically promote active learning. Many demonstrations, such as those just mentioned, are fascinating, but because they leave students in the role of passive observers, they might not be as memorable as they could be.

With some creative adjustments, however, almost any demonstration can become an active learning opportunity for students. In fact, of all the active learning activities available for use in the psychology classroom, we think that demonstrations are the easiest and most enjoyable—for both students and faculty. Consider that taped interview with a mental patient. Instead of telling students that they are about to hear someone who has been diagnosed as bipolar, you could preview the tape by asking students to decide, based on their *DSM–IV* handout, which diagnosis they think the patient should receive, and why. At the end of the tape, the class can "vote" on a diagnosis, and in the following discussion, students can describe the specific behaviors that led to their decision. Compared to simply playing the tape, this procedure is virtually guaranteed to produce deeper cognitive processing of the interview content, and more elaborate consideration of what it conveyed. Similarly, if you are lecturing on compliance, you could demonstrate its power by asking a student to make a funny face or take off a shoe. But how much more memorable it would be if you asked the entire class to stand, turn in a circle, jump up and down, or engage in some other pointless activity! This version of the demonstration is not only more memorable for having given everyone a personal experience with compliance, but makes it impossible for anyone to think "I wouldn't have done that."

In short, we suggest that you not only take every opportunity to spice up your lectures with demonstrations, but that you choose demonstrations—or revise them—so that students become active participants instead of passive observers. There are many more such opportunities to use active learning demonstrations than you might think. The instructor's resource manuals and Web sites associated with many psychology textbooks are filled with ideas and detailed instructions for conducting active learning demonstrations. Many of the items listed as sources for active learning in Table 4.1 are also excellent sources of active classroom demonstrations. More general tips for using active learning demonstrations can also be found in journals such as *College Teaching*, *The Teaching Professor*, and *The National Teaching & Learning Forum*. Finally, don't forget to ask your more experienced colleagues to tell you about the active learning demonstrations that they have found useful.

A word of caution, however: Always practice every planned demonstration before you try it in class for the first time. Even procedures that seem simple and foolproof on paper can be complex and tricky in practice, and it is much less costly (and embarrassing) to discover this in the company of friends and colleagues than to squander time and a teaching opportunity in the classroom. This point was underscored some years ago when an introductory psychology teacher we know tried to present an unusually vivid demonstration of the application of operant conditioning principles, particularly stimulus control. The plan was for a police officer from the local canine unit to bring his dog to class and put the animal through its paces, including obeying commands to "attack" and "stop." Unfortunately, the officer's work schedule left no opportunity to rehearse the demonstration. So when the officer stood on one side of the stage of our colleague's lecture hall and commanded his dog to attack a student "suspect" who had volunteered to stand on the other side of the stage wearing an arm protector, there was, shall we say, a chance for unforseen complications. The plan was for the officer to give the "stop" command before the dog reached the "suspect," and though the dog tried to stop, he slid across the polished hardwood stage, reached the frightened student and began to gnaw violently on the arm protector until he was called off. A dry run of this demonstration would have revealed the slippery floor problem; as it was, the demonstration was memorable, but not for the right reasons.

ANSWERING AND ASKING QUESTIONS

Another easy and obvious way to promote active learning in the classroom is to ask students questions and to encourage them to ask questions of you. Yet in the average college classroom, regardless of course level or section size, less than 4% of class time is devoted to the important process of asking and answering course-related questions (Weimer, 1989). This pattern is probably due partly to the fact that many teachers, certainly many psychology teachers, are focused on covering a certain amount of material in each class session, which creates a tendency not to interrupt lectures by asking students any questions. Further, these teachers' verbal and nonverbal behavior tends to send the message that they don't have time to stop for questions from their students, either. Even those who do pose questions, and who invite students to ask questions, might not generate the kind of lively exchange they are after. Usually, the problem lies in how they question their students and how they respond when students question them. In this section, we highlight some ways in which you can handle both of these processes in ways that can enliven the classroom atmosphere and help students learn.

Answering Students' Questions

The way you deal with your students' questions can solidify or undermine your relationship with them. If you respond with impatient or perfunctory answers, students will get the message that you don't care much about their learning, and that they shouldn't ask any more questions. Assuming that this is not what you want to convey, we suggest that you let students know, on the first day of class and frequently throughout the term, that you are happy to answer their questions. Then, when someone raises a hand to ask a question, recognize the person (calling the student by name, if possible) and listen carefully to the entire question to be sure you understand it. Don't interrupt with an answer that presumes you know what the student is getting at; you might end up answering the wrong question!

Provide verbal and nonverbal reinforcement during the question. Establish eye contact, nod with understanding as the question is being asked, and perhaps move closer to where the student is sitting so as to hear better. Don't look at your notes or fiddle with the computer or gaze out the window. Let the student, and the rest of the class, know that the question has your full attention (Goodwin, Sharp, Cloutier, Diamond, & Dalgaard, 1981).

Next, repeat or paraphrase the question. This step is crucial not only to assure that you have understood the question, but especially in larger classrooms, that everyone else has heard and understood it, too. Students will lose interest in the proceedings if you are answering questions—or responding to comments—that they did not hear.

Like listening to one end of a phone conversation, this experience can be frustrating and annoying.

If the question is particularly interesting or thoughtful or common, say so, and let the class know you are glad it was asked. Finally, if you can answer the question, do so. When you are finished, ask if the answer was clear, and offer students the opportunity to ask follow-up questions.

Be prepared, too, for questions you can't answer. All psychology teachers get such questions, and how you respond when you are stumped can be just as important to good student–faculty relations as when you have a ready answer. Above all, relax. Your students do not expect you to have a full and complete answer to every possible question about every aspect of psychological knowledge, especially if you are at the beginning of your teaching career. Stay calm, don't demean students for stumping you, and don't try to make up an answer. If you do, your students will eventually see through the pretense and lose respect for you. (One of us had a professor whose students occasionally entertained themselves in class by asking questions about nonexistent psychological theories, just to listen to the answers he would fabricate.) We suggest that, instead, you deal with tough questions in four steps.

First, admit that you don't know the answer (or don't have much of an answer), and reinforce the questioner for asking the question. We typically say something like "Wow, that's a great question. I don't think I know the answer to that one." Second, ask if anyone else has any idea what the answer might be. This step conveys respect for your students, in that it suggests that someone in the room might know more about a particular topic than you do. (In some cases, this might actually be true!) Third, promise to do some research on the question and report back to the class at the next session, via e-mail, or perhaps on the course Web site. Fourth, keep your promise. Post the results of your research on your Web site or begin the next class with a summary of what you have found. Your students will appreciate your efforts more than you can imagine.

You might also want to respond to particularly intriguing questions with the suggestion that the entire class should seek answers, too. However, we advise against making this a formal assignment because students tend to perceive such assignments as punishment for asking questions. The result might be the development of a group norm in which few students ask questions, and those who do are censured by the rest of the class.

Asking Questions

We have suggested that you pose questions during your lectures—beginning on Day 1—as a way of creating variety and promoting active learning, but what if no one responds? If this possibility is a worry, you can minimize the problem by phrasing your questions clearly and carefully and then giving your students enough time to (a) come up with their answers and (b) work up the courage to raise a hand. Like teachers in general, most psychology faculty tend to allow only a second or two of "wait time" before answering their own question. Waiting any longer creates what seems to them to be an awkward silence. However, such a short wait time can be counterproductive. It implicitly tells students that you don't really expect them to answer your questions, and eventually they might not even try (Andersen, 1986). If you give students about 5 seconds to think about your questions—maybe 6 or 7 seconds for especially profound or complex questions—they are far less likely to view your questions as rhetorical and far more likely to come up with good answers (Tobin, 1987). Even some of your "slower" students might participate more, simply because you have given them sufficient time to think of an answer.

While silently counting off the seconds during the waiting period, let your students know you want to hear from them. Scan the room with a hopeful look on your face, making eye contact all around. If no hands go up, be ready to call on those whose facial expression indicates they might want to reply. (Say something like, "Margo, you look as though you might want to answer this one.") If you have no takers after 7 to 10 seconds, it is probably time to rephrase or simplify the question.

Sometimes it is the way we pose a question that makes it so hard to answer. Questions that are clear and straightforward tend to draw the quickest and most interesting replies. So ask "How might we apply Bandura's ideas about modeling to teach social skills to retarded children?" rather than "What do you think of Bandura's idea about modeling?" In other words, give your students a clue about the focus of your question rather than asking them to figure out what you are driving at. If you ask "What is the most telling criticism of evolutionary theories of human social behavior?" the students have to guess what you think it is. If you want them to think about the issue, ask something like "What do you see as the biggest problem with using evolutionary theory to explain human social behavior?"

Overall, the more questions you sprinkle throughout the lecture, the more carefully you phrase them, and the more patient (up to a point) you are in waiting for answers, the more responsive your students are likely to be. It will not take many class sessions of such questioning techniques before your students will be comfortable with your questions and willing to answer them.

STIMULATING CLASS DISCUSSIONS

Whether in the service of active learning or just keeping class sessions lively and varied, you might sometimes want to offer students the opportunity to discuss course-related topics with you, and among themselves. Many students feel more connected to the course when they are given these opportunities, and discussions also help students think about, recognize, and express views about course material that might otherwise have gone unexamined (Timpson & Bendel-Simso, 1996). As with other classroom skills, learning how to encourage and moderate spontaneous discussions of course material takes some practice. When you want to be sure a discussion takes place during a particular class session, you will also have to plan for it. Here are a few guidelines for setting up and conducting successful class discussions; additional advice is contained in other sources (e.g., Brookfield & Preskill, 1999; Davis, 1993; Forsyth, 2003; McKeachie, 2001; Neff & Weimer, 1989).

First, if you decide in advance that a class discussion of some topic would be useful, let your students know about it at the previous class session, and remind them about the required prediscussion readings, Internet research, or other assignments that they should complete. (If planned discussions are a main feature of your course, you should list the dates of each in your syllabus, along with any associated preparation work.) Completing these assignments will make it much easier for students to participate in, and get the most out of, the upcoming discussion. You might also hand out a list of questions or issues that will frame the discussion scheduled for the next class. Reading through this list allows students to begin considering their views on the discussion topic, and to see the relevance of what they are being asked to do in preparation. Some instructors even ask students to organize their thoughts in a "one-minute paper" or other brief in-class writing assignment immediately before the discussion begins. This strategy has been called *writing to learn* (Erickson & Strommer, 1991).

It goes without saying, of course, that when it comes to scheduled discussions, you should be way ahead of your students (Cashin & McKnight, 1989; Ewen, 1989). Develop a plan for jump-starting the discussion. In abnormal psychology, for example, you could present an audio- or videotaped segment of a case study that students have already read about, and then invite them to discuss possible causal factors, the accuracy of diagnosis, various treatment options, the client's prognosis, and the like. As described later, case analysis can also be used in many other psychology courses, including sensation and perception, developmental, personality, social, forensic, industrial/organizational, and the like. Another way of stimulating lively discussion is to ask students to engage in a short role-play in which they illustrate some course-related topic such as a particular personality trait, interview method, leadership style, parenting practice, or whatever. As yet another effective discussion starter, ask a provocative question or describe an extreme position about some course-related topic (e.g., "What would happen if we outlawed all tests of mental ability for college admission?" or "What would you say to a state governor who proposed that people should have to take parenting classes and get a license before they could legally have children?"). Students are usually eager to respond to such hypothetical questions (Davis, 1993).

In fact, discussion starters like these might be so successful that your main problem will be to assure that the discussion remains focused and productive. To prevent a discussion from degenerating into an academic version of the *Jerry Springer Show*, let your students know about whatever rules you intend to apply, such as that students must raise their hands and be recognized by you before speaking. If the topic under discussion is highly emotionally charged, you should also warn everyone that there is no place in your class for racist, sexist, homophobic, or other *ad hominem* remarks. You should always be prepared to intervene to put a stop to any such remarks, but try to do so in a constructive way. Unless the remark is simply too extreme to tolerate, we suggest that you not directly punish the offending student. Instead, try to use the incident to move the discussion forward. For example, you might say to the class, "You know, X probably wasn't aware of it, but that comment was actually a pretty good example of the kind of (say) homophobia that makes life more difficult for gays and lesbians. Given the prevalence of those views, what do you think it says about sexual orientation as a choice versus a biological predisposition?"

Whether a discussion was planned or arose in response to something you or a student said in class, encourage all your students to participate by rewarding those who speak first. Maintain eye contact and nod your head as they talk, rephrase what they have said so that the entire class can hear, and then ask the class to react to what they say. Now and then, you might also want to offer interim summaries of what has been said so far as a way to generate further comments and reactions (Cashin & McKnight, 1989; Ewen, 1989). Once things get rolling, though, don't feel obligated to respond to every student's comment—or at least leave plenty of wait time before doing so. If you don't dominate the situation, your students will eventually begin to talk directly to each other. If you seek to fill brief silences with a minilecture, your students will soon get the message that this is entirely your show, and the discussion might dry up (Brookfield & Preskill, 1999; Cashin & McKnight, 1989; Ewen, 1989).

As one teacher put it, your ideal role in a discussion is to

> discretely employ initiating, leading, clarifying, and probing questions rather than authoritative statements or rhetorical questions to guide the flow of the discussion toward its intended purposes and to enhance the value of the experience for members.... [You also should] generate a non-evaluative, non-threatening environment conducive to a free and open interchange of ideas. (Fisch, 2001, p. 6)

In other words, challenge your students during discussions, but don't make them feel threatened (Cashin & McKnight, 1989).

We have talked about organizing discussion sessions for the class as a whole, but it might sometimes be easier to get all students involved if discussions take place, or at least begin, in smaller groups (Erickson & Strommer, 1991). For example, you can ask students to spend some time discussing a topic, question, case, or issue in groups of three to six, and then ask a representative from each group to summarize for the entire class that group's answer, position, or conclusions. You can then invite reactions from other groups via individual comments or their own representatives' reports, which might support or conflict with what has already been said.

When it is time to end the discussion, bring it to a close a few minutes before the end of the class period. This will give you time to summarize the most important points raised, to clear up any misconceptions or misinformation that might have been created, and to suggest additional reading or Web-based research that will help students follow up on what they have learned.

ASSIGNING STUDENT PRESENTATIONS

Many psychology teachers presume that they are the main source of knowledge in the classroom, but there are many ways in which students can also learn on their own, and from each other. Some of these are described later in the section on cooperative learning, but here we emphasize the value of class presentations by students. These presentations not only serve as an alternative source of course information, but stimulate students to delve deeper into a topic than they might otherwise have done. After all, one of the best ways to learn about a topic in psychology is to prepare a lecture on it! Student presenters also get practice and develop skill at public speaking in a relatively nonthreatening atmosphere (Ashcroft & Foreman-Peck, 1994).

The main hazard when scheduling student presentations is the same one that haunts the scheduling of guest lectures by faculty colleagues, namely that the presentations might be poorly organized and boring. To help your students do the best job possible, you might want to provide a set of grading standards similar to the paper-grading rubrics discussed in Chapter 5. If you distribute the rubric when you announce the student presentation assignments, it will be more likely to create the kinds of presentations you are after. One such rubric told students that their presentations would be evaluated on five dimensions: length, content, delivery style, audience involvement, and use of audiovisuals. The handout describing the rubric provided specific illustrations of exemplary, minimally acceptable, and unacceptable presentations. On the audience involvement dimension, for example, an unacceptable performance was defined as "put class members to sleep," whereas an exemplary performance was defined as "related the topic to the students' lives and used concrete examples, stories, quotes, and questions to involve the audience" (Wilson, 1999, p. 3). With this detailed rubric in mind, students created highly organized presentations, some of which included audience interaction segments and audiovisual aids that energized the class and kept everyone involved.

You can allow students considerable latitude in their choice of presentation topics, or you can create a *structured academic controversy* in the classroom by asking everyone to summarize their views and conclusions about a particular course-related theme or issue, such as the possibility of recovered memories or the value of bilingual education. Because some of these presentations will inevitably include conflicting views, they serve as stimuli for discussions about which view seems to have the best supporting evidence, what additional information might be needed before drawing final conclusions, and the like. You might even assign students to obtain that additional information, and to present it at a later class session (Johnson, Johnson, & Smith, 1996, 2000). In any event, structured academic controversies offer excellent opportunities to promote the kinds of critical thinking skills about psychology that we describe later in this chapter.

There are also far less structured ways to arrange student presentations. In her large introductory psychology class, one teacher spends the first 5 minutes of a class session describing three concepts that the students have read about in their textbook (Bleske-Rechek, 2001). She then assigns one third of the class to address each concept by forming small groups and spending 25 minutes coming up with a real-life situation that illustrates or demonstrates that concept. Each team then presents its results to the class. Instead of using a complex grading rubric, this instructor simply gives credit for student participation; the presentations themselves are ungraded. She reports that students put a lot of work into their presentations and many of them are excellent.

CREATING OPPORTUNITIES FOR COOPERATIVE LEARNING

Small-group activities that lead to class presentations are but one example of collaborative and cooperative learning activities. *Collaborative learning* is a general term referring to group learning experiences that can range from peer tutoring and student–faculty research projects to short-term group work in class. *Cooperative learning* is a subtype of collaborative learning, and refers more specifically to activities in which 2 to 15 students work together toward a common goal (Cooper, Robinson, & McKinney, 1994; Halpern, 2000).

Here, we focus on the creation of cooperative learning groups, the collaborative learning format most commonly used by psychology faculty (Millis & Cottell, 1998). These groups can be formal or informal. *Formal* cooperative learning groups spend all or part of an academic term working on an experiment, a survey, or some other long-term research or writing project. *Informal* cooperative learning groups come together for shorter periods, sometimes for just a few minutes, to work together on a relatively simple assignment (Johnson, Johnson, & Smith, 1998).

To be most successful, cooperative learning groups should have two main attributes. First, they should create *positive interdependence*, meaning that the students must work together to do well on their assignment. This feature helps to promote an atmosphere in which there is no incentive for group members to compete with each other. Second, the groups should promote *individual accountability*, meaning that each member's contribution to the group's effort must be measurable. This second attribute minimizes the phenomenon known as *social loafing*.

It is also a good idea to constitute the groups so that they include members of both genders, and are as heterogeneous as possible on ethnicity and other demographic variables (Halpern, 2000; Johnson, Johnson, & Smith, 1991; Millis & Cottell, 1998). When set up properly, cooperative learning groups give students the opportunity to address course material in a new and interesting way while providing valuable experience at working with others to achieve success. These groups also help students to develop the leadership, communication, and other social skills needed to function effectively in the context of a team. In this regard, encourage your students to discuss among themselves how the group is working (or not working), the nature of any problems they might be encountering, and how they can overcome those problems (Brown, 2000; Cooper et al., 1994; Halpern, 2000; Johnson, Johnson, & Smith, 1991, 1998a, 1998b; Millis & Cottell, 1998; Smith & MacGregor, 1998).

The effectiveness of cooperative learning in psychology classrooms is supported by hundreds of studies indicating that this teaching format results in higher achievement and more positive and supportive relationships among students than does competitive or individualistic learning (Fullilove & Treisman, 1990; Johnson et al., 1991, 1998a). A number of factors have been proposed to explain the apparent value of cooperative learning. For example, some students find it easier to learn when discussing course material with peers than when listening to a professor's lecture. Peers speak the same generational language, they are less threatening to each other in terms of power and status, and they might be more willing to reveal to one another what they don't understand. A supportive peer group atmosphere also offers a safe opportunity for students to check the validity of what they think they know, and to be corrected and taught by fellow students whose knowledge is more extensive.

These benefits do not magically appear simply because, like Linda Richman on *Saturday Night Live*, you ask students to "talk among yourselves" (Halpern, 2000; Johnson et al., 1991). To get the most from cooperative learning activities, you'll have to take an active role in planning and overseeing them. Here are some tips for doing so (Cooper et al., 1994).

First, if you are new to cooperative learning methods, start slowly. Make these methods just a small part of the total grade. For example, as described in Chapter 3, one of us typically sets up study groups on the second day of class and then asks these groups to get together that day to work on a simple, but graded, statistical problem. These same groups reconvene from time to time during the term to work on other graded assignments in class. Each group also makes a presentation to the class in which they summarize and analyze a classic study in psychology, and for which group members receive a grade based on their part of the presentation.

Second, no matter how simple or complex the task you assign to groups, be sure to introduce it clearly. All too often, instructors describe cooperative learning assignments in class only to be inundated afterward with requests to clarify the assignment. Worse, some groups do not realize that they misunderstood the assignment and work hard to complete the wrong task. To minimize both problems, we suggest that you describe each cooperative learning assignment in a handout so that everyone understands precisely what they are to do, how they are to do it, what the product should be, and when the work is to be handed in or presented (Jenkins, 1992; see Fig. 4.2).

Third, although some instructors see cooperative learning activities—especially those that occur during a class session—as an opportunity to take a break, the truth is that successful cooperative learning activities actually intensify student–faculty contact. As your groups work on their tasks, you should offer support by strolling around the room, answering procedural questions, monitoring progress, and keeping everyone on task (Halpern, 2000). Your hands-on involvement with cooperative learning groups intensifies the students' time on task, increases their motivation, gives them more immediate feedback on progress, and provides a model for how to think about course material (Halpern, 2000).

Other sources provide further information on setting up effective cooperative learning activities and managing the problems that can arise from them (Brown, 2000). One of the biggest of these problems is student resistance to the cooperative learning enterprise. For one thing, engaging in cooperative learning requires students to change their classroom role from passive observer to active participant. The

GROUP ASSIGNMENT #10: PERSONALITY THEORIES

After completing this assignment you should be better able to distin-guish among the four major theories of personality and understand some of the positive and negative aspects of each. By completing this assignment as a group, you will be exposed to a more in-depth analysis of each theory. Here is how to complete the assignment:

1. First, as a group, identify a famous person, a cartoon character, a prominent person on campus, or someone else that most people in class will know. (2 minutes)

2. Decide, as a group, which theory of personality (psychodynamic, humanistic, trait, social-cognitive) will be used to develop a personal-ity profile of the selected person. Be sure to discuss the pros and cons of each theory before deciding on the one you will use. (10 minutes)

3. Develop a personality profile of the person you chose. For exam-ple, if you chose to write a profile of Madonna using a psychody-namic theory of personality, you might want to describe the roles of id, ego, and superego in guiding her behavior. If you chose to de-scribe her using trait theory, you might include comments about where she falls on the introversion–extraversion dimension, or on the Big Five dimensions, of openness, conscientiousness, and so on. (5 minutes)

4. Choose someone to speak for your group, preferably someone who has not been the spokesperson in previous group assignments.

5. When your group is called on in class, read your personality pro-file and ask the class to guess whom you are describing. When lis-tening to other group's profiles, ask yourself which personality theory they have applied, and how accurately they have applied it.

FIG. 4.2.   A sample handout for a cooperative learning assignment. This is an ex-ample of the kind of handout you can distribute in class to help your students better understand, and more effectively complete, cooperative learning projects.

same is true of other active learning methods, but cooperative learn-ing groups also require students to prepare more extensively for cer-tain classes, and makes attendance at those classes less a personal choice than a community need. Moreover, participation in coopera-tive learning groups makes it difficult or impossible for some students to stay in the class background, as shyness or lack of interest might or-dinarily lead them to do.

Cooperative learning activities also require students to abandon the idea that they are in competition with their peers; instead, they are expected to work with others for mutual benefit. Some highly competitive students find this aspect of cooperative learning especially distasteful. Although some students easily take to the idea of peer-to-peer learning and teaching, those who hold more traditional views of the teacher as the only source of knowledge in a course might find it difficult to accept the cooperative learning format as promoting real learning (MacGregor, 1990). With all this in mind, be sure that, in addition to carefully explaining to students what they are to do in each cooperative learning assignment, you describe the value of cooperative learning in general, and why students are being asked to work in a group on this assignment. Let them know you understand that, for some, this will be a new and possibly jarring experience, but ask them to withhold judgment until they have tried working in a group format for a while.

Jigsaw

A special version of cooperative learning, called *jigsaw*, was developed by Elliot Aronson (1978) and later embellished by others (K. Smith, 2000). Its original purpose was to reduce racial prejudice by arranging for Black and White students in newly integrated elementary school classrooms to work together and get to know one another as individuals. In a jigsaw exercise, each member of a small work group gathers information that is needed by the entire group to solve a problem or complete some other task. As an "expert" in one particular area, each group member spends some time presenting information to the rest of the group, as well as listening as other members make their presentations. This arrangement makes every member of the group equally valuable, so the group's work cannot be dominated by a couple of students. Further, even the quieter students must actively participate for the group to succeed.

Jigsaw can be applied in college psychology courses, too. We know of one instructor, for example, who uses a modified jigsaw technique. She assigns each of several student groups to research a different psychological disorder. One student in each group is responsible for learning about the prevalence of the disorder, another gathers information about its symptoms, others focus on the causal factors suggested by various theories of psychopathology, and still others review the nature and results of various treatment methods. Each person summarizes the resulting information for the group, after which everyone works together to write a short paper about the disorder, which is then presented to the class. In another version of jigsaw, each group member chooses to read a different journal article from a list of classic studies in psychology. After each person becomes familiar with the study's design, participant selection process, procedures, results, conclusions, and relevance, the group meets to decide which of the articles will become the focus of its presentation to the class. Next, the group decides which of its members will be responsible for presenting a particular aspect of the study, such as (a) an introduction and summary; (b) possible design flaws, limitations, or ethical concerns; (c) how the study relates to material covered in class or in the textbook; (d) its importance for understanding psychology; and (e) the main points the class should remember about the study. After the students have worked on their individual segments of the presentation, the group meets again to discuss what each person plans to say, to exchange constructive criticism about those plans, and to make final decisions about how the classroom presentation should be organized. For more information about using jigsaw, visit www.jigsaw.org.

USING CASE EXAMPLES

Professors of business, law, medicine, and other professions have long used case examples as a main vehicle for helping their students learn and understand the implications of course material. Reading, analyzing, and discussing cases creates opportunities for students to engage in active learning and—when allowed to work in groups—in cooperative learning as well. Faculty in psychology use case studies, too, especially to illustrate material in personality and abnormal psychology courses, but cases are now also finding their place in many other courses. One introductory psychology instructor we know has incorporated case studies as an integral part of his class presentations on topics ranging from research methods and biological processes to learning, memory, and social psychology (Hendersen, 2002a). Some of these cases are really just standard lecture examples that he has expanded into "case-lets" or "mini case studies." However, because they allow students to actively engage the example rather than just hearing about it in a lecture, these case studies can help make even large lecture sections more interactive (Hendersen, 2003).

Indeed, most psychology instructors use case studies to promote discussion of what a case illustrates, what it means, how representative it is, and what conclusions can (and cannot) be drawn from it. Some instructors read cases in class, then ask students to discuss them in a general session or in small groups. Others distribute a case study handout in one class session, and ask students to be ready to discuss it at the next class. Some also include a list of study questions to help students think about the case, and might even require students to submit a memo summarizing their analysis of the case (Silverman & Welty, 1990). The memos can be collected and graded; doing so encourages students to spend the time necessary to read and analyze each case (Leonard, Mitchell, Myers, & Love, 2002). You will probably find that the more you ask students to do with cases, the more likely they will all have something to say when the cases are discussed in class.

To prepare yourself for these discussions, think about the case and recognize that you might have to summarize and synthesize differing interpretations of it. In fact, because students' views of a case can be so diverse, discussing cases in class has been described as "like bringing a scattered group of parachutists into contact from all the random places they have landed" (Boehrer & Linsky, 1990, p. 52). As with any class discussion, remember to encourage all your students to participate. You can do this in relation to cases by asking open-ended questions, and questions that do not have just one right answer. Although you might begin by asking the class, say, how many employees worked at the factory described in a case study, if your ultimate goal is to help students understand differences among leadership styles, it might be more productive to ask questions such as, "Which of the supervisors did the maintenance staff like best, and why?" In other words, your questions should be designed to stimulate exploration of the meaning of the case, not just to demonstrate an ability to recall its facts (Silverman & Welty, 1990).

In deciding whether to use a case study activity at a particular point in your course, ask yourself, first, what the goal of the activity will be. Is it to familiarize students with a particular concept, principle, or phenomenon, to explore the causes of some phenomenon, or what? Once you have decided what student competencies you want to promote, it will be easier to decide on the structure and details of the case study activity (Leonard et al., 2002). For example, if your goal is to help students to think more deeply about theories of prejudice, you might ask them to read about the background of someone who has been convicted of a hate crime and then perhaps write about the biological, cognitive, and social factors that might have contributed to the person's attitudes and behaviors. If the goal is simply to underscore differences in parenting styles, you could read transcripts of interviews with parents, then ask the class to say whether the parents are permissive, authoritarian, or authoritative, and why.

Select cases that seem most appropriate for meeting your objectives. You will find such cases included in the instructor's resource manuals that accompany various psychology textbooks, and in many other sources, as well—including scholarly publications, newspaper articles, films, books, and, of course, the Internet (see Table 4.2). If no appropriate case studies are available, you might consider developing your own. For example, to help him conclude his introductory psychology course, the professor mentioned earlier created his own case study for use on the last day of class. It presents a science fiction writer's view of what psychology courses will look like in 50 years. The professor uses it to show students that psychology is a dynamic,

TABLE 4.2
A Sampling of Sources for Useful Case Studies

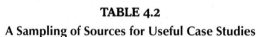

Web sites

The National Center for Case Study Teaching in Science Case Collection: Psychology (ublib.buffalo.edu/libraries/projects/cases/ubcase.htm#psychology)

The Social Science Information Gateway (SOSIG; http://www.rdn.ac.uk/casestudies/sosig)

Books and journals

Dziegielewski, S. (2002). *DSM–IV–TR in action.* New York: Wiley.

Meyer, R. (2003). *Case studies in abnormal behavior* (6th ed.). Boston: Pearson Education.

Oltmanns, T., Neale, J., & Davison, G. (2004). *Case studies in abnormal psychology* (6th ed.). New York: Wiley.

Rosenthal, D. (2002). The case method—A joint venture in learning: A message from the editor. *Journal on Excellence in College Teaching, 13,* 1–141. (This entire issue is devoted to using the case method in college classrooms.)

Sacks, O. (1970). *The man who mistook his wife for a hat and other clinical tales.* New York: Harper & Row.

Sacks, O. (1996). *An anthropologist on Mars: Seven paradoxical tales.* New York: Vintage Books.

Schreiber, N., & Miller, J. M. (2004). *Developing critical thinking through case studies.* New York: Prentice Hall.

Note. If you are interested in discussing and exchanging case studies with Robert Hendersen, you can reach him via e-mail at hendersr@gvsu.edu constantly changing discipline. He also uses the case as a spring-board for a class discussion about whether the discipline of psychology as we know it today will even exist in 50 years, and if so, what questions will have been answered and what questions will remain or emerge. Finally, to demonstrate how quickly psychology changes, he reads now-outdated information about human behavior and mental processes, as presented in 50-year-old introductory psychology textbooks (Hendersen, 2002a).

You can create fictional cases from your imagination or from bits and pieces of real cases. (If you do fabricate any cases, or alter the details of real ones, be sure to let your students know about it. Case examples need not be real to be realistic, or to illustrate and help students understand course material, but it is vital that students know whether they are reading about real examples, composites created from real examples, or fictional accounts that typify real phenomena.) Be sure also that the cases you choose (or create) are short enough and sufficiently focused to permit your students to read and analyze them in the class time allotted. Finally, the cases should be written at a level that is appropriate for your students; that is, challenging, but not too complex (Leonard et al., 2002).

Finding, creating, and using case studies in class can require a lot of time and energy, but the results can be well worth the effort. Faculty who have done so report a wide range of benefits, such as helping students to identify and think about problems, evaluate possible solutions, and appreciate general principles that can be applied in other situations. Dealing with cases also enlivens the classroom atmosphere and enhances students' involvement with course material and with each other, all of which is especially valuable in large classes (Boehrer & Linsky, 1990; Hendersen, 2002a; Silverman & Welty, 1990).

ARRANGING FOR SERVICE-LEARNING

Service-learning is an approach to teaching that integrates community service with academic study to enrich learning, teach civic responsibility, and strengthen communities (Fiske, 2001; National Service-Learning Clearinghouse, 2003). Among the advantages attributed to service-learning are that it allows students to learn by joining theory with experience and thought with action; to see the relevance of an academic subject in the real world; to do important and necessary work while increasing civic involvement; and to encounter a richer context for learning—including cross-cultural experiences and preparation for careers (Cooper, 2003). As in other disciplines, service-learning is becoming an ever more common component of psychology courses, largely because of its value in helping students experience the real-world context in which psychological principles and phenomena appear (Enos & Troppe, 1996). For example, in a psychology of aging course, one instructor arranged for students to visit homebound elderly people. He found that the service-learning experience resulted in far more positive attitudes toward the elderly and a more thoughtful orientation toward the students' own aging process (Marchese, 1997).

Service-learning can be used as a small component of your course, or it can be one of its core aspects. To be effective, though, service-learning components must be integrated into the rest of the course in ways that help promote your course goals. This integration includes establishing criteria for the grading of students' performance in the service-learning component of the course.

If you plan to include a service-learning component in your course, be aware that there are many time-consuming logistical problems to address, including making the community contacts necessary to create service-learning placements, and finding the time to supervise the students who occupy them (Hardy & Schaen, 2000). Arrangements must be made, too, for transporting students to and from their placements, assuring their safety, and insuring against liability claims in the event of accident or injury. In short, creating service-learning opportunities is a lot of work, and if you are new to teaching, it might be wise for you to postpone your efforts to include a service-learning component in your own courses. However, don't forget that the option exists, or that service-learning placements can create some of the most important and memorable aspects of a student's course experience. You can find more information, resources, tips, and useful links relating to the use of service-learning in books (e.g., Bringle & Duffy, 1998), or at Web sites such as that of the UCLA Clearinghouse for Service-Learning (http:// www.gseis.ucla.edu/slc/) or the *Michigan Journal of Community Service-Learning* (www.umich.edu/~mjesl/).

ENCOURAGING CRITICAL THINKING

It is almost always possible to use lectures, class discussions, demonstrations, case studies, student presentations, and service-learning experiences to encourage your students to think critically about psychology, and about life in general. Wade (1988) defined *critical thinking* as the process of assessing claims and making judgments on the basis of well-supported evidence. Expanding on that definition, Halpern (2002) described critical thinking as

> the use of those cognitive skills or strategies that increases the probability of a desirable outcome. It is purposeful, reasoned, and goal directed. It is the kind of thinking involved in solving problems, formulating inferences, calculating likelihoods, and making decisions. Critical thinkers use these skills appropriately, without prompting, and usually with conscious intent in a variety of settings. That is, they are predisposed to think critically. When we think critically, we evaluate the outcomes of our thought processes—how good a decision is or how well a problem is solved. Critical thinking also involves evaluating the thinking process—the reasoning that went into the conclusion we have arrived at or the kinds of factors considered in making a decision. (p. 93)

A list of the critical thinking skills that Halpern (2002) had in mind are presented in Table 4.3.

Students in your courses might already be familiar with the concept of critical thinking, and might also recognize the importance of employing critical thinking skills. However, as Halpern (2002) pointed out, just because people know how to think critically doesn't mean they will do so. Using critical thinking skills on a daily basis takes time, practice, and the motivation to exert the added effort required. With their focus on various aspects of the behavior and mental processes that govern all human affairs, psychology courses are particularly appropriate venues for helping students to refine and practice their critical thinking skills. As a psychology teacher, you can be an active agent in motivating them to do so. There are many ways in which you can encourage and reward critical thinking as you teach, but as with other aspects of effective teaching, they will take some thought and some planning.

Consider classroom demonstrations. We have already suggested the importance of conducting demonstrations to create opportunities for active learning, but you can also turn many of them into critical thinking exercises as well. To take just one example, suppose that, in a course on sensation and perception or introductory psychology, you plan to demonstrate the opponent processes involved in the visual system. A standard method for doing so is to spin a spiral pattern to generate after-images that create the sensation of movement in the opposite direction (Holland, 1965). (If you spin the spiral to cre-

TABLE 4.3

Halpern's (2002) Taxonomy of Critical Thinking Skills

These skills not only help students to better understand, evaluate, and apply what they learn in psychology courses, but also help them make more informed and logical decisions as consumers, employees, and citizens.

1. *Verbal reasoning skills*. These are the skills needed to comprehend and defend against the persuasive techniques embedded in everyday language. They include, for example, the ability to recognize that an individual's thoughts determine the language they use to express them.

2. *Argument analysis skills*. These include the ability to identify conclusions, recognize variations in the quality of reasoning in support of an argument, and determine the overall strength of an argument.

3. *Hypothesis testing skills*. These include the ability to accumulate observations, formulate hypotheses, and evaluate and use evidence to decide if it confirms or disconfirms those hypotheses.

4. *Skills for understanding likelihood and uncertainty*. These include, for example, understanding the meaning of statistical summaries, and how statistics can be used to both represent and misrepresent facts. These skills also include the ability to recognize the importance of base rates in evaluating hypotheses, and to understand and appreciate the impact of cognitive biases about probability, gains and losses, and the like on judgments and decision-making processes.

5. *Decision-making and problem-solving skills*. These include the ability to properly define and represent problem statements; identify possible goals; generate, select, and try alternative solutions; and choose the best alternative given the purpose of the problem-solving or decision-making task.

ate the appearance of inward movement, the afterimage creates the impression that objects in the visual field are moving outward, or expanding.) By definition, this is an active learning experience, but there are a number of ways in which you can make it an opportunity for critical thinking, too. For one thing, you can ask the class to predict—on the basis of lectures and readings—what they will experience, and why, when they look at your face after seeing the spinning display. To make correct predictions, the students will have to recall what they have learned about feature detectors in the visual cortex, then apply that knowledge to a new situation. Another option requires the help of an assistant and two spirals, each located in opposite corners of the classroom. Ask each half of the class to look at a different spiral, and then spin the spirals in opposite directions so that one of them creates the impression of inward movement, and the other shows apparent outward movement. Afterward, when all the students look at your face, half of them will see it appear to expand and the other half will see it appear to shrink. Now ask everyone to describe their differing experience, and then figure out what must have happened, and why.

You can also incorporate critical thinking elements into almost any other aspect of your courses. As already mentioned in relation to students' "diagnoses" of psychiatric patients, case studies can not only illustrate a phenomenon, but can stimulate students to think critically about them. You might also use descriptions of, say, people with symptoms of neurological damage or impairment. After reading about each case, students could be assigned to hypothesize which brain areas are affected and whether the problem is likely to have been caused by brain damage or drugs and, if the latter, which drugs might be involved.

You can even use the course textbook as a vehicle for critical thinking. We know of an instructor who asks his students to choose a page of the text that is of particular interest, and to read one or more of the scholarly references cited on that page. The students then decide if the evidence in those references warranted the assertions made in the book. If not, the students are to rewrite the page as they think it should appear, given the evidence available. It is unlikely that many authors of psychology textbooks anticipate that their books will be used in this way, but many texts, especially those for the introductory course, incorporate a variety of other features designed to promote critical thinking. In the book we know best, each chapter contains a "Thinking Critically" feature that invites students to ask themselves five questions about a particular chapter-relevant topic or issue: What am I being asked to believe or accept? What evidence is available to support the assertion? Are there alternative ways of interpreting the evidence? What additional evidence would help to evaluate the alternatives? What conclusions are most reasonable? (Bernstein & Nash, 2005; Bernstein et al., 2003). Other books offer other similar features, all of which can be used to reinforce your message about the importance of critical thinking. There are also excellent books that focus specifically on promoting critical thinking in every aspect of your teaching (e.g., Halpern, 2002, 2003).

TEACHING STYLE AND CLASS SIZE

The teaching methods you learn and the teaching style you develop can serve you well in any psychology classroom, but you might have to adjust them to accommodate classes of differing size (Cramer, 1999; Gibbs, 1992; Smith & MacGregor, 1998). The conversational tone and the small-font transparencies (or even hand-held photos) that work well with 12 senior psychology majors seated at a seminar table might not hold the attention of the 300 introductory psychology students you address from the stage of an auditorium. There, you will probably need a podium, a laser pointer, a wireless microphone, large diameter chalk, and large-font overheads or PowerPoint slides.

The prospect of teaching a large class might also tempt you to change the structure of your course, perhaps spending more time on lecturing and less time on classroom demonstrations and other activities. This is understandable. Many instructors, especially newer ones, feel disconnected from their students in large classes. It is more difficult (maybe impossible) to learn and remember all the students' names or to keep track of how well each of them is doing. Many psychology faculty are overwhelmed by the demands of teaching large classes and uncomfortable in a role that makes them feel more like a performer than a teacher (Ward & Jenkins, 1992). The fact that larger classes tend to be noisier, more crowded and hectic, and less conducive to student–teacher chats before and after class can intensify a teacher's (and students') sense of isolation from the educational process. Under these circumstances, it is no wonder that many faculty tend to arrive at the last minute, deliver a lecture, and allow (even encourage) students to listen passively.

Still, it is possible even in large classes to teach effectively and to promote active learning and critical thinking using specialized versions of the lectures, demonstrations, discussions, presentations, and other methods we have described in this chapter. To meet the challenges and compensate for the suboptimal conditions presented by larger classes, however, planning and organization are, as always, the keys to success.

For example, make sure the sound system in the room works properly and be ready to scan all your students' faces for signs of understanding or confusion. If you fail to include every corner of the room (and possibly the balcony), students in "forgotten" areas are more likely to lose interest. Remember that students in a large, crowded room might be more hesitant than usual to raise their hands, so when you pause in your lecture to ask for questions, you might have to build in a little extra wait time, or draw out the students in other ways. We tend to do this by saying something like, "OK, I know you have some questions about what I have been talking about—what are they?" or "Who's got a question but has been afraid to ask it in such a big room?" When students do ask questions, plan ways to amplify the rewards for doing so. For example, leave the podium and approach the student so that the interaction becomes more personal and friendly. Stroll around the room as further questions occur or as a discussion develops. Needless to say, it is absolutely essential to repeat every student's question, answer, and comment so that the entire class can hear it and follow the thread of events. If you follow these simple steps, your students—who have cut their teeth on audience participation talk shows on television—should have little or no trouble accepting the idea that their teacher is walking among them with a microphone. In fact, our experience suggests that there is no reason why student–teacher interactions can't be as easy and as lively in large classes as they are small ones.

Fruitful interactions among students can also take place in big classrooms. Even if theater-style chairs are fixed to the floor, you can ask students to turn to each other to discuss course content in small groups. You can also use the "think–pair–share" technique, in which you pause after completing a lecture segment and use the overhead or computer display to pose a lecture-related problem or multiple-choice question. Then ask your students to choose the answer they think is correct and to compare their answer—and the reasoning behind it—with that of the person next to them. This consultation process will help more students understand why the correct answer is correct when you reveal it. The think–pair–share method also helps students in a large lecture hall to remain more attentive, and might even improve their subsequent exam performance (Ruhl, Hughes, & Schloss, 1987).

Other adjustments to large classes revolve around administrative rather than educational problems. For example, when distributing a handout in a large class, you will have to wait quite a while to confirm that everyone has a copy. Only then can you begin to refer to the handout in your lecture. To minimize the delay, develop a standard strategy for distributing material, perhaps placing a table near the entrance where students can pick up the day's handouts as they arrive. If you don't have teaching assistants, recruit student volunteers to help you quickly get material to the entire class.

You will also have to think about how to collect quizzes and exams as your students complete them, and about how students will retrieve their graded work on the days you hand it back for the vital process of feedback and discussion. Will there be a box in which students should deposit exam forms, test booklets, and answer sheets? Will you have graded exams stacked in alphabetical order for students to collect when you call the first letter of their last name? These are the systems that we have found useful in classes of up to 750, but they must be set up carefully to keep students from seeing each other's results (see chapter 6, where we discuss this and other legal and ethical issues in teaching). One colleague advocates stationing teaching assistants in various parts of the classroom where they hand back exams to students whose last names are in particular segments of the alphabet (Lowman, 1987). Whatever alternative you choose, if you have never taught a large class before, seek advice about your collection-and-return system from a more experienced colleague before making your final decisions. Remember that no matter how carefully you plan and organize your system for returning exams and quizzes, the scene will probably be somewhat chaotic and will probably take 10 to 20 minutes the first time you implement it. Once students learn the system, though, the process will become routine and will take less class time. This is especially true once students learn to come to class on time when graded assignments are being returned.

Further advice on how to adjust your teaching style and procedures to accommodate large classes are available, and we recommend them to you (e.g., Davis, 1993; Gibbs & Jenkins, 1992; MacGregor, 2000; Weimer, 1987).

THE LAST DAY OF CLASS

After all your planning and all your effort, after many weeks of good and not-so-good classroom experiences, you will inevitably find yourself teaching the last class of the term. When you get there, you might find the experience to be bittersweet. You and your students will be sad to see the course end, especially if it has gone well, but also happy to have successfully completed yet another academic term and ready for some relaxation. For many psychology faculty, the last day of class comes and goes without ceremony, yet it provides an opportunity to bring the student–teacher experience to a close in a way that students appreciate and enjoy (Eggleston & Smith, 2001; Maier & Panitz, 1996).

For example, you can spend some time on the last day of class summarizing the course content, reviewing the course syllabus, and discussing which course goals were and were not met. You might also ask students to create concept maps illustrating major aspects of course content and showing how they are interrelated. The last day is also a good time for students to turn in and reflect on the course portfolios they might have assembled during the term (Maier & Panitz, 1996). Consider also the possibility of providing a small memento of the course (Eggleston & Smith, 2001). In a small class, these could be certificates of achievement that include a personal note for each student or an acknowledgment of some aspect of his or her accomplishments in the course. In a large class, the mementos could be "fortunes" containing a reminder of an important idea or lesson from the course or of something that happened in class. Or perhaps just put some words of wisdom on the blackboard, overhead projector, or computer screen for the entire class to read.

Some psychology faculty ask students to spend some time on the last day of class writing a letter that describes some of what they have learned from the course. To help them organize their thoughts, you might ask the students a question such as "What is psychology?" or "Which studies or ideas do you think have been most important in shaping the development of _____ (e.g., biological, cognitive, social, clinical) psychology." As we mentioned earlier in this chapter, one professor ends his course by asking students what they think psychology will look like in 50 years (Hendersen, 2002a). If you administered a pretest at the beginning of the course to assess what your students thought they knew about psychology or one of its subfields, you might also spend part of the last class session reviewing their responses to that test and discussing how their ideas have changed since the first day of class (Eggleston & Smith, 2001). You could even invite your current students to pass on their views of and experiences in your course by writing a letter to the students who will take the course next term. You can either read these letters as part of your efforts to improve your teaching, or perhaps just seal them and hand them out to your next class (Maier & Panitz, 1996).

One of us uses a more general version of this idea in the small honors section of introductory psychology that she teaches each fall to students who are fresh out of high school. At the end of the following spring semester, she sends these students an e-mail message asking them to tell her what they wish they had known about coming to college, but that no one told them. By passing that information on to new first-year students, she helps establish rapport with them, but a side benefit of this exercise is that it serves to maintain rapport with her former students, too. Indeed, remember to take time on the last day of class to invite your students to stay in touch with you throughout their college years, and beyond. If nothing else, ask them to write you a letter at the end of the following term to identify the one thing they learned in your course that they have found useful since the course ended. Hearing from your students on an ongoing basis is not only interesting in and of itself, but can inform your decisions about what to emphasize in your classes. It also serves as a constant reminder that the things you do in those classes now continue to affect your students in the long run.

SOME FINAL COMMENTS

No matter how diligently you follow our advice—and the advice of others—in developing your teaching style and planning your teaching methods, some classes will inevitably go better than others, and you will be reminded again and again of the white water rafting metaphor with which we opened this chapter. As one observer put it, "you must quietly accept that failure is part of the process." (Walck, 1997, p. 476). Still, we hope that the advice contained in this chapter will help to maximize your good teaching days and minimize the not-so-good ones.

Whether we consider a class to be a good one or a bad one depends largely on our students' reactions to us and to our teaching efforts, which includes the quizzes, exams, papers, and other graded assignments we use to evaluate their performance in our courses. Deciding on which of these assignments to choose, and how to create them, is the topic of the next chapter.

Chapter 5

Evaluating
Student Learning

Some Guidelines for Assessing Student Learning
Tests and Quizzes
Written Assignments
**Applying the Psychology of Learning to Student
    Evaluation**
Some Final Comments

If you have any teaching experience at all, you probably know that most students are at least as interested in how their learning will be evaluated—and especially how their grades will be determined—as they are in what the course has to offer them. In fact, students' intense interest in, and emotional involvement with, your evaluation of their learning can make the evaluative process quite stressful, especially for less experienced faculty (Eble, 1988). For most psychology teachers, the greatest challenge associated with evaluation is to develop quizzes, tests, writing assignments, and other performance measures that assess learning in a manner that they, and their students, see as reliable, valid, and fair. They don't want to be seen as pushovers when it comes to evaluation and grading, but neither do they want to establish standards that are impossibly high. Some psychology faculty are also uncomfortable about taking on the role of an "examiner" who sets standards by which other people are to be judged (Ebel, 1965). Yet this is precisely what your departmental executive officers, your colleagues, and your students expect you to do. In this chapter we consider some alternatives for evaluating student learning and we offer some ideas for evaluation procedures that can actually enhance that learning.

SOME GUIDELINES FOR ASSESSING STUDENT LEARNING

Let's begin by considering seven guidelines for evaluating college students (Suskie, 2000) that grew out of the American Association for Higher Education's Principles for Good Practice in Assessing Student Learning (Astin et al., 2003). These guidelines can help you to make decisions about how and when to evaluate your students.

1. *Your learning goals should be clearly stated and shared with your students.* Tell your students what learning goals are most important to you, and what skills you want them to acquire. Explain how achieving these goals and skills can promote students' own long-term educational goals and spell out your reasons for assessing their learning in the way that you do. This orienting information helps students understand and accept the importance of classroom assessment (McKeachie, 2002).

2. *Your evaluation methods should be clearly linked to the goals and skills you emphasize.* As discussed in Chapter 2, if you tell students you want to promote their critical thinking skills, you should be assigning "thought papers," analytical essay exams, or comprehension-oriented multiple-choice tests rather than instruments that focus on the definition of key terms. If teaching definitions or vocabulary is a major goal, key-term tests might be ideal (Clegg, 1994; Erickson & Strommer, 1991; Jacobs & Chase, 1992; Ory & Ryan, 1993). Matching assessment instruments to learning goals is not as easy as it sounds, partly because when you are in the thick of creating exams, quizzes, and other evaluative measures, concern over getting the material to the copy center on time might distract you from focusing on whether your test items are linked to the goals and skills you described as important on the first day of class. Even if you do keep these linkages in mind, time pressure might force you to lower your standards somewhat. In one study, the vast majority of the questions that faculty thought would require their students to use complex cognitive skills actually required no more than the recall of names, terms, or other specific facts (Erickson & Strommer, 1991). Later in this chapter we describe methods to help you solve this problem.

3. *Use many measurements and many kinds of measures.* Overall, the more evaluative components that make up a final grade, and the more varied they are, the more valid that final grade is likely to be (Jacobs & Chase, 1992; McKeachie, 2002; Ory & Ryan, 1993). Teachers who assign final grades based on, say, a midterm and final exam or a term paper and a final exam, are not gathering enough evaluative information to reliably assess student learning or to assign valid grades. Further, evaluations based entirely on multiple-choice exams or entirely on writing assignments might not give all students a chance to demonstrate the full extent of their knowledge (Anderson, 2001; Clegg, 1994).

4. *Help students to do their best on evaluative tasks.* For example, when assigning group projects, specify the outcomes you expect (A short written summary? An in-class presentation?), and let students review projects that have received high (or low) grades in the past. If you plan to give multiple-choice tests, offer students tips on how to take those tests, show and discuss sample questions in class, and perhaps provide past quizzes and exams to help students practice their test-taking skills.

5. *Express confidence in your students.* As in every other aspect of teaching, encouraging your students to try hard and expressing confidence in their ability to accomplish their learning goals can help motivate them to do so.

6. *Don't let evaluation discourage cooperation.* Competition for grades is inevitable, and can be motivating, but be sure that your evaluation system does not create such intense competition that it discourages students from helping each other or working together.

7. *Evaluate your evaluation system.* If a disproportionately large number of students do poorly on your quizzes, exams, and other assessment instruments, ask yourself why this happened. Did the problem lie in the assessment instrument, with its linkage to your learning goals, with the way you taught the material, or perhaps with the students? Addressing these questions can be extremely helpful as you develop your teaching style and your evaluative systems.

Let's now consider some of the specific student evaluation methods you might wish to use in your courses.

TESTS AND QUIZZES

The most commonly employed option for evaluating student performance is, of course, the written test, and its briefer cousin, the written quiz. These can be constructed in essay, short-answer, or multiple-choice format.

Essay and Short-Answer Tests

Essay and short-answer tests can be constructed relatively quickly, provide an assessment of students' writing ability, and can easily set tasks that require high level analysis of course material (Jacobs & Chase, 1992). Essay test items can be written in the form of restricted response questions and extended response questions. *Restricted response* questions are especially useful for measuring students' ability to interpret and apply course information in a specific domain (Gronlund & Linn, 1990; Linn & Gronlund, 2000). An example might be: "Discuss three ways in which classical and operant conditioning differ, and give an example of each difference." *Extended response* questions are broader and provide students with fewer guidelines; for example, "Compare the personality theories of Freud, Jung, and Adler." Many psychology faculty prefer restricted response questions because their relatively limited scope makes it is possible to include more of them in a particular exam. Posing several restricted response questions allows for a broader sampling of course content on each exam.

Writing Essay and Short-Answer Test Items. Here are some tips for writing essay and short-answer test questions (Gronlund & Linn, 1990; Linn & Gronlund, 2000; see Table 5.1):

1. Phrase each question to be as clear as possible. For instance, "Describe at least two benefits and two disadvantages associated with electroconvulsive shock therapy" is clearer than "What do you think of electroconvulsive shock therapy?"

2. Write enough questions to assess learning goals in several topic areas, but not so many that students won't have enough time to write high-quality answers.

3. Include information on the exam form about how much time students should devote to each question, or at least list the number of points each question is worth (Jacobs & Chase, 1992; Ory & Ryan, 1993). This information helps students develop a plan for making the best use of the time allowed to write the exam.

4. If you want students to study the widest range of course content, require them to answer all essay items on your test. Allowing

TABLE 5.1

Some Sample Essay Questions

1. *Compare and contrast X and Y in regard to given qualities.* Example: How would the James–Lang and Cannon–Bard theories of emotion explain the experience of fear?

2. *Present arguments for and against an issue.* Example: What are the advantages and disadvantages of bilingual education?

3. *Illustrate how a principle explains facts.* Example: How does arousal theory explain the fact that having an audience present can sometimes improve and sometimes disrupt a person's ability to perform a behavior?

4. *Illustrate cause and effect.* Example: Describe the evidence you would require to confirm that differing styles of parenting cause differences in children's personalities.

5. *Describe an application of a rule or principle.* Example: How would you take advantage of context-dependent memory to help you do your best on your next psychology exam?

6. *Draw new inferences from data.* Example: What potential weaknesses in the U.S. court system are suggested by research on the nature and limitations of human memory?

7. *Describe how the elements comprising a situation, event, or mechanism are interrelated.* Example: Describe an example of how genetic and environmental factors might combine to influence the development of a shy, fearful, or aggressive personality.

8. *Analyze a situation, event, or mechanism into its component parts.* Example: List at least four factors that might be responsible for the appearance of schizophrenia, and how each of these factors might contribute to the disorder.

Note. These items illustrate some of the many formats you can use in writing essay exam items (Jacobs & Chase, 1992). Whatever formats you choose, be sure to have a colleague, and especially a nonexpert, read each item to be sure its meaning is clear.

them to choose a subset of items means that students are taking different tests, making it more difficult to compare their performance (Jacobs & Chase, 1992; Ory & Ryan, 1993). If you do let students choose a subset of essay items, make it a large subset—five out of six, for example (Jacobs & Chase, 1992; Ory & Ryan, 1993). Allowing too much choice (e.g., two out of six), might lead students to focus their reading and studying on just a few major concepts in each section of the course and ignore the rest.

Scoring Essay and Short-Answer Tests. Essay tests can be scored using analytical or global quality methods (Ory & Ryan, 1993). In the *global quality* scheme, you assign a score to each student based on either the overall quality of the answer relative to other students' answers or in relation to your own subjective set of criteria (Ory & Ryan, 1993). A weakness of this approach is that it might be difficult or impossible for you to precisely describe your grading criteria, thus making it difficult to justify your grades when students inquire or complain about them. The *analytical method* results in grades that are usually easier to defend, because you first write an "ideal answer" to each essay question. These ideal answers serve as scoring rubrics that contain specific, pre-established features that have predetermined point values. So if a question asks students to evaluate the *DSM–IV* as a means of diagnosing mental disorder, you can compare each essay to your ideal answer and award points—up to the maximum score—based on which, or how many, expected elements appear (e.g., two points for each strength or weakness correctly named). The grade assigned to the test as a whole is based on the total number of points earned (Linn & Gronlund, 2000; Ory & Ryan, 1993).

No matter which approach you choose in scoring essays and short answers, be sure to decide—and tell your class—how you will deal with the irrelevant information that some students throw into their essays in the hope that you will allow quantity to compensate for quality. Will you ignore that irrelevant information or deduct points for being forced to read it? (Some psychology faculty choose the former option early in their careers, but change their minds after a few years of searching for responsive answers among pages of "filler" material.) In addition, decide and describe how you will deal with features of essays or short answers—such as poor spelling, grammar, or handwriting—that might be irrelevant to the learning goals of your course but can affect students' ability to reach their long-term career goals.

When the time comes to read a set of essay exams, find a quiet place to work that will be relatively free of distractions, and don't try to grade the entire set in one sitting. Know the limits of your ability to concentrate, and when you identify signs of fatigue, impatience, or "scanning" instead of reading, stop, take a break, or do something else for a while. Distributing the grading task over several sessions will minimize the chance that stress responses will have influenced your grading decisions. As you read, be sure to write comments in the margin that will help the student understand the basis for your scoring of each answer. Don't forget to jot a note of praise for particularly good answers. If your class is too large to allow you to write individual comments on short-answer tests, be sure to make a list of the most common errors and discuss them with your students in class (see chapter 6).

When grading essay exams containing more than one item, score all students' answers to the first question before going on to the next one. This arrangement is especially important if you are using a global quality scoring method. Reading all responses to the same question makes it easier to compare students' performance, and minimizes the development of halo effects in which your reaction to a student's answer to one item might affect your scoring of that student's later answers. To reduce the development of halo effects caused by reading students' responses in the same order time after time, shuffle the stack of exams every time you finish reading all the answers to a given item. Finally, conceal the students' names on the cover sheet of the exam (or have students identify themselves by a code number). If you don't know whose responses you are reading, it is less likely that your scoring of those responses will be biased by positive or negative expectations or impressions of particular individuals.

If you have not previously administered essay or short-answer tests, you will soon discover that reading them carefully and grading them systematically takes an enormous amount of time. Therefore, before deciding to write essay or short-answer tests, estimate how much time it will take to grade each question, increase that estimate to be on the safe side, and multiply the result by the number of students you expect to enroll in your class. Then multiply that figure by the number of tests to be given during the course, and decide whether the resulting time commitment is realistic in light of your other academic and personal responsibilities.

Multiple-Choice Tests

If the time required for grading essay or short-answer tests is likely to be unmanageable, consider using a multiple-choice format for some or most of your student performance evaluations. Multiple-choice tests can be quickly scored by an optical scanner, and, with the proper computer networking facilities, the results can be electronically downloaded into an instructor's computer-based grading roster. In addition, the difficulty level and other information about each multiple-choice item's performance can be assessed by item analysis programs available through many campuses' exam scoring services.

Although multiple-choice tests can be graded quickly, they take a long time to write, and as described later, even more time to write well (Jacobs & Chase, 1992; Ory & Ryan, 1993). One way to spread out the workload is to write two or three multiple-choice items immediately after each class period, when the material, and students' reactions to it, are fresh in your mind (Ebel, 1965; Erickson & Strommer, 1991; Jacobs & Chase, 1992; Ory & Ryan, 1993). This strategy helps assure that all of the important material covered in class is also covered on the exam. It might also result in better quality items that are more closely linked to your learning goals, because you will be concentrating more intensely on each item's wording, clarity, accuracy, and level than might be the case during a last-minute item-writing marathon. You can also use the printed, electronic, or online banks of multiple-choice items that are available through the publisher of your textbook, but remember that the quality of these test item banks is often uneven. Many of them can be edited, though, so you can fix the items you don't like to make them fit your course, thus giving you more time to write fresh items to cover material that you covered in class, but that might not be in the textbook.

Writing Multiple-Choice Items. Here are some useful guidelines for writing multiple-choice items (Erickson & Strommer, 1991; Linn & Gronlund, 2000; Ory, 2003):

1. Each item should have one, and only one, correct or clearly best answer. This simple rule is easy to state, but devilishly difficult to follow, mainly because it is so easy to miss double meanings and slight errors of phrasing that make two alternative answers plausible. In fact, it is often only when a student asks for clarification of an item, or argues with its scoring, that it dawns on you that the item is not as good as you thought it was. It is virtually impossible to avoid writing a few potentially ambiguous multiple- choice items on every exam or quiz, but careful proofreading—by you and at least one other person—can go a long way toward catching and fixing these items before they reach your students. (See chapter 6 for ideas about fair handling of students' complaints about "bad" exam items.)

2. The item stem should be meaningful in itself, should contain as much of the item's content as possible, and should be free of irrelevant material. Example A is better than Example B:

Example A

William James pioneered the _____ approach to psychology.

   a. functionalist
   b. psychodynamic
   c. humanistic
   d. behavioral

Example B

William James, of Harvard University, was one of America's earliest psychologists and the brother of the famous author, Henry James. He

   a. pioneered the functionalist school in psychology.
   b. developed introspection to measure consciousness.
   c. was concerned with perceptual principles.
   d. was the founder of the behaviorist approach.

3. Avoid using negatives in the item stem unless you feel they are necessary for assessing particular aspects of student learning. Negative phrasing tends to make items seem more complicated and, especially under the stressful conditions of an exam, students can easily become confused about what the question is actually asking (Erickson & Strommer, 1991). If and when you do use negative wording, be sure to capitalize or italicize the negative word. Example A is better than Example B:

Example A

Which of the following is NOT a neurotransmitter?

   a. serotonin
   b. dopamine
   c. GABA
   d. rhodopsin

Example B

Which of the following isn't a neurotransmitter?

   a. serotonin
   b. dopamine
   c. GABA
   d. rhodopsin

4. All response alternatives should be plausible, but different enough from the correct alternative to demonstrate students' learning of concepts, principles, applications, and the like. There-

fore, if the correct response to an item is "negative reinforcement," good alternatives might be "punishment," "positive reinforcement," and "differential reinforcement." In other words, the incorrect responses should come from the same pool of knowledge as the correct response, but unless you are trying to create an extremely difficult item or to pose a "trick" question (which we do not recommend), be sure that the incorrect choices are not so similar to the correct one that even your best students might miss the distinction. Although it is tempting to include implausible, funny, or ridiculous alternatives just to break the tension of the exam, remember that using too many of these, or using them too often, can make the exam results less meaningful than you might wish.

   5. All response alternatives should be grammatically consistent with the item stem so as not to eliminate some of them from consideration or give away the correct answer. Example A is better than Example B, which disqualifies two response alternatives on grammatical grounds alone:

Example A
Cameron has learned to need a certain drug in order to feel confident. He is _____ this drug.
   a. tolerant of
   b. addicted to
   c. psychologically dependent on
   d. physically dependent on

Example B
Cameron has learned to need a certain drug in order to feel confident. He is _____ on this drug.
   a. tolerant
   b. addicted
   c. psychologically dependent
   d. physically dependent

   6. Avoid using terms in the correct response alternative that match or contrast sharply with words in the stem and thus give away the answer. Example A is better than Example B:

Example A
A dog has learned that a tone always precedes the delivery of shock in a shuttle box, so he now jumps over a barrier when the tone sounds. This process is called
   a. avoidance conditioning.
   b. escape conditioning.
   c. spontaneous recovery.
   d. extinction.

Example B
A dog learns to avoid getting a shock by jumping over a barrier at the sound of a tone that always precedes the shock. This process is called
  a. avoidance conditioning.
  b. escape conditioning.
  c. spontaneous recovery.
  d. extinction.

7. All response alternatives should be about the same length so as not to give away the correct choice. This can be trickier than it sounds because it is often necessary to include qualifying phrases in the correct answer to distinguish it from the incorrect alternatives. Write the correct answer first, then all the others. Example A is better than Example B:

Example A
Aggression is defined by psychologists as
  a. any social interaction in which people do not cooperate with each other.
  b. any social interaction in which one person threatens another.
  c. an act that involves the expression of anger or hostility.
  d. an act that is intended to cause harm or damage to another person.

Example B
Aggression is defined by psychologists as
  a. fighting.
  b. threats.
  c. anger.
  d. an act that is intended to cause harm or damage to another person.

8. The correct answer should be randomly placed in each of the alternative positions (e.g., a, b, c, or d), then adjusted if necessary to assure that it appears in each position an approximately equal number of times. Avoid the common tendency to place the correct answer in the third position, where test-wise students know it is likely to be.

9. Minimize the use of special alternatives such as "any of the above," "all of the above," or "B or C, but not A." These items can be challenging and useful for assessing particular learning goals, but overusing them can make an exam more difficult than you want it to be or—if the special alternatives are never the correct ones—easier than you want it to be.

10. Don't include in the question any information that is unnecessary or that is designed to teach new material.

Alternative Testing Formats

By tradition, most psychology faculty administer their tests in a classroom, where it is expected that each student will work alone and without reference material. Some, however, use open-book or take-home formats instead or in addition to this traditional format.

Open-Book and Take-Home Exams. Open-book exams are often given in classes, such as statistics courses, where the instructor's goal is for students to be able to solve problems or analyze data using formulas, information, and procedures that students cannot, need not, or should not be expected to memorize. In such courses, the textbook provides the formulas, tools, or other information students need to correctly deal with the problems or issues set forth in the exam.

Take-home exams—a subtype of open-book exams—are popular in psychology courses in which students are asked to respond to essay test items at a length and depth of analysis that could not occur given the time constraints of a classroom test session. Some psychology teachers prefer to give take-home essay exams in lieu of in-class essay exams because doing so affords students more time in which to research their facts, organize their thoughts, and create more considered—and more neatly presented—responses. Items on take-home final exams, for example, might ask students to integrate material learned throughout the academic term. This type of exam could be especially appropriate for a senior capstone course.

Some teachers don't give take-home exams because of concerns that students might get help from other people, not just from their textbook or other approved sources. This threat to test validity does exist, of course, even when students sign pledges to work alone, so you will have to decide whether the benefits of a take-home exam outweigh its potential disadvantages. If you do give a take-home exam, don't be surprised if not all of your students are pleased. With no time limits to guide them, some students worry that they have not spent enough time—or as much time as other students—answering the questions. As a result, some might allow a take-home exam—especially a take-home final exam—to consume so much of their time that they neglect their studying for exams in other courses. Setting a page limit on the students' responses can help with this problem. Another way of dealing with both the time-management and test-security problems is to use a "hybrid approach" (Jacobs & Chase, 1992) in which you give students a week or so to think about, study for, and even draft answers to all the essay questions that might appear on the upcoming exam. The students will thus be better prepared to give thoughtful answers to the questions you actually include on the in-class exam.

Collaborative Testing

Collaborative learning methods suggest yet another approach to testing (Lusk & Conklin, 2002; Mitchell & Melton, 2003). In this approach, students are allowed to take exams in groups and each member of each group earns the same grade. In a related option, students take part of an exam individually, then collaborate on another part. Some instructors offer students the option of taking an exam individually or as part of a group. If you decide to use any version of collaborative testing, be sure that you have thought through exactly what grading procedures you will use, and of course, announce them ahead of time. Used with care, collaborative testing provides an excellent way of encouraging student–student interactions in your course.

Tables of Specifications

Whether you decide to use essay, short-answer, multiple-choice, or other test items, and regardless of the format you choose, we suggest that you analyze each test and quiz by creating a *table of specifications* (Jacobs & Chase, 1992; Ory & Ryan, 1993). As you can see in Table 5.2, each row of this table should represent one concept, phenomenon, principle, theory, or other content element to be tested. Each column should represent a cognitive skill to be demonstrated, such as defining terms, comparing concepts, applying principles, analyzing information, and the like. Each of the table's cells thus represents the intersection of a particular bit of course content and the level of skill being tested. You can use this table to plan the content and level of the items you are about to write, or those you choose from a test-item bank. If you have already written or chosen a set of items, you can enter a digit representing each item into the cell that best represents its content and level. Looking at the resulting pattern of entries will tell you how well the test or quiz covers the lectures and assigned readings, and at what level.

TABLE 5.2
A Sample Table of Specifications

Content	Cognitive Skills		
	Knowledge	Comprehension	Application
Classical conditioning	1	1	2
Shaping			1
Reinforcement	1	1	
Observational learning		1	
Latent learning			1
Cognitive processes	1		

Note. This small table of specifications was created to plan a 10-item quiz on learning principles in an introductory psychology course. Tests and quizzes need not assess every possible concept at every possible cognitive level. Notice that, here, three items test basic knowledge (definitions), three more test deeper understanding, and four test students' ability to apply what they know about the concepts tested. Such tables can be created for any course using Bloom's taxonomy of cognitive skills: knowledge, comprehension, application, analysis, synthesis, and evaluation (Bloom et al., 1956; Jacobs & Chase, 1992).

 The test development and administration tips described here, along with a few others, are summarized in Checklist 5.1.

WRITTEN ASSIGNMENTS

Making writing assignments will help your students to improve their writing skills and will help you to better evaluate their knowledge of course material. In addition, as described later in this book, most writing assignments can be configured to serve as active learning and critical thinking exercises.

Term Papers or Term Projects

Writing assignments in small classes might involve term papers or a term project that runs to 15 or 20 pages, and even longer in graduate classes. In making such assignments, be sure to explain (in detail and in writing) what you expect from the paper or project, and when it is due (see Table 5.3). Students don't learn much by writing papers or finishing project summaries at the last minute, and these products are no fun to read, either, so be sure to set up a series of deadlines for

---

Checklist 5.1
Things to Remember When Writing
and Administering Tests

We hope the following checklist will be helpful to you in preparing your tests and avoiding many of the problems typically encountered when administering them (Clegg, 1994).

1. Don't wait until the last minute to start writing tests, especially multiple-choice tests. Write a question or two after each class session.
2. Use a table of specifications to match your test items to your testing goals and the level of skill to be assessed.
3. Spell-check your tests and ask others—including someone who can take a nonexpert student perspective—to read them for errors, inconsistencies, or confusing content.
4. Write tests using language that is respectful and inclusive of all your students. As described in Chapter 6, items should include ethnically diverse names and situations and should not perpetuate stereotypes.
5. Place similar types of items together—multiple-choice items should be in one part of the test, matching items in another part, and short-answer items in another part.
6. Provide explicit and clearly written directions for taking the test, including the maximum number of points possible on each item, and in the case of essay items, the recommended amount of time the student should allocate to each.
7. Allow a reasonable amount of time to answer all the items you have written. One minute per multiple-choice item, 2 minutes for each short-answer item, 10 to 15 minutes for each restricted response essay item, and about 30 minutes for an extended response essay item is about right (McKeachie, 2002).
8. Be sure that the test is printed clearly, and in a minimum of 12-point font, so that it is easy to read, and make sure that items are not interrupted by page breaks. If you have created alternative forms of the test for use in large classes or in crowded classrooms, use different-colored paper for each, but be sure the type is readable on both forms.
9. Create and double-check the accuracy of answer keys before administering multiple-choice tests. Do the same with rubrics for scoring essay and short-answer tests. Doing so will help you spot

(continued)

Checklist 5.1 *(continued)*

---

imbalances in the position—a, b, c, or d—of correct response alternatives and possible problems in how you will grade items.

10. To be sure you do not run short at the testing session, always duplicate more copies of the test than you think you will need.

11. Once tests have been copied for distribution, count the pages to be sure they are all there, and check to see that they have been collated in the correct order.

12. During the class session prior to each test, remind students about bringing pencils, erasers, calculators, or other materials they will need for the test. (Most experienced teachers bring a small supply of eraser-equipped pencils with them to avoid disruptions caused when students try to borrow them from other students.)

13. In large classes, develop a time-saving procedure for efficiently distributing test forms and answer sheets. We allow students to pick up answer sheets as they enter the room, and then have proctors distribute alternate test forms from collated piles along each row such that students seated next to each other always have different forms.

14. Administer each test yourself, even if you have proctors available to help, and stay active and engaged in the testing situation. Reading a newspaper during an exam tells your students that you don't care much about the test or the testing process.

15. Decide, and tell your students, whether or not you will answer questions during the test. If a student discovers a significant misspelling, a missing item, or other important problem with the test, announce the correction to the entire class immediately.

16. Minimize the stress of the testing situation by arriving early, being friendly, and staying calm. In addition to the pencils already mentioned, bring tissues for students whose sniffling colds are disturbing others.

17. Establish your plans for dealing with cheating on tests (see chapter 6).

---

completing various stages of the assignment (Angelo & Cross, 1993; Davis, 1993). If nothing else, give your students an early deadline to submit for your approval a short description of the topic they plan to write about or study. Taking this simple step will save you a lot of time and effort later, because many students initially choose a topic or re-

TABLE 5.3
A Sample Writing Assignment

PSYCHOLOGY 100/SECTION &JS
WRITING ASSIGNMENT #3
FALL 2003
Dr. Goss Lucas

DUE DATE: Thursday, November 20, 2003 by 5 p.m. (Two points deducted for every day late after that.)

ASSIGNMENT:

1. Watch a movie that deals with any psychological topic: It can be a movie about psychological disorders, therapies, mental abilities, obedience, conformity, gender roles, etc. Some suggestions for such movies are listed at the end of this assignment. If you want to watch a movie not on that list, please see me (and have a good idea of the psychological concept that the movie portrays). Also, if you would prefer to read a book, that's fine as long as you clear it with me.
2. Read about the psychological concept in your textbook. Note what information the textbook provides.
3. Find another source that discusses the same psychological topic or concept that you have picked. This can be a book, a journal article, talking to an expert in the area, etc. If you choose to read a journal article, it should come from a research journal such as *American Psychologist, Journal of Personality and Social Psychology, Developmental Psychology, Journal of Educational Psychology, Journal of Abnormal Psychology, Child Development, Journal of Counseling Psychology, Journal of Personality and Social Psychology, Journal of Experimental Psychology, Science, Neuroscience, Psychology of Women Quarterly,* etc. These journals can be found in the Education and Social Science Library (housed in the main library) or the Susan Stout Library (821 Psychology).
(**HINT:** Your textbook can often lead you to a journal article or book on the topic.)

WRITING THE PAPER:

4. Summarize the movie. (Approximately 2 pages)
5. Summarize the outside source. If you read a journal article what are the major conclusions that the authors reached? Who were the subjects in the study? How was the study conducted? (Approximately 1½ pages)
6. Summarize the textbook information. (½ to 1 page)
7. Critically analyze the movie. (**HINT**: Answer the five critical thinking questions in your text, Bernstein et al., 2003.)
   a. Does the movie portray this psychological concept accurately? Why or why not?

(continued)

TABLE 5.3 (*continued*)

   b. How does information from the outside source validate/dispute the information given in the movie?
   c. How does the information from your textbook validate/dispute the information given in the movie?
   d. How could the movie be changed to be a more accurate reflection of the psychological concept?
      (This is the bulk of your paper and should be 5–8 pages.)
8. Summary of the paper. Tie it together, give me your major conclusions.
   (1 page)

PUTTING THE PAPER TOGETHER:

1. Your paper should be about 10 to 12 pages long. (I'm not "hung up" on length—I'm just trying to give you some guidelines.) It should be typed, double-spaced.
2. Your paper should be assembled in the following order:
   a. The paper itself.
   b. A separate sheet of paper with your outside source referenced and the textbook pages cited.
   c. A copy of the important pages from the book, interview, or journal article.
   d. A separate sheet of paper with your name on it.

HOW THE PAPER WILL BE GRADED:

See the attached criteria sheet. Note that 30 points are available, but the maximum number of points that can be earned is 25.

IMPORTANT POINTS:

1. By Tuesday, October 21, 2003, you need to tell me what movie or book you are going to critique and what psychological concept will be your focus. Also, tell me if you have your outside source identified or not.
2. I would be more than happy to look over your outside source to help you decide if it is appropriate or not.
3. I will read rough drafts of this paper and return them to you with comments before November 14, 2003. I will not accept rough drafts after this date.
4. The due date is firm. Remember, 2 points are deducted from the paper for every day the paper is late.
5. Please ask me if you have any questions about this assignment.

---

search question that is too broad or vague to be addressed effectively within the page limits or by the deadline you have set. By helping students refine their original question at an early stage, you will not only ease some of their frustrations; you will also increase the chances of eventually reading a higher quality paper.

You can also set up a deadline for submitting an annotated bibliography. If you do this, be sure to specify exactly what are acceptable and unacceptable resources for the writing assignment. In the days before the Internet, applying this caveat mainly involved warning students against citing sources such as *Cosmopolitan* magazine or other less than scholarly sources, but today it requires teachers to warn students about Web sites that, although easily accessible, could be utterly unreliable.

Other interim deadlines might be set for submitting to you an outline, and then a rough draft, of the students' writing projects. The earlier these deadlines occur, and the more time you have available to critique the material submitted, the more students are likely to get out of the project and the more satisfying it will be for you to read and grade the final product. Some instructors ask their students to exchange their outlines and rough drafts, review each other's efforts, and then return them for further refinement. The peer review process can be useful to the students (and less work for you), but if you decide to adopt this approach, be explicit about what is expected of peer reviewers. Explain that, in addition to making general comments about the draft, reviewers should address a set of more specific questions—such as the strengths and weaknesses of the paper, are there sections that are unclear, and what additional problems need attention. Nilson (2003, p. 36) proposed a more extensive list of items to which peer reviewers should respond, including the following:

1. What one or two adjectives (aside from *short, long, good,* or *bad*) would you choose to describe the title of the paper?
2. In one or two sentences only, state in your own words what you think the writer's position is.
3. Use a highlight pen to mark any passages that you had to read more than once to understand what the writer was saying.
4. Bracket any sentences that you find particularly strong or effective.

You might even ask peer reviewers to "grade" rough drafts using the same set of criteria—the same grading rubric—that you yourself will use when reading the final drafts. This strategy will not only clarify the reviewers' task, but will give them a preview of how their own paper measures up to your expectations. In fact, even if you don't use a peer review system, it is a good idea to give students a grading rubric to guide them. Table 5.4 shows the rubric used with the term project outlined in Table 5.3; your own rubric would be designed to fit your own writing assignments.

Writing Assignments for Large Classes

It can be difficult or impossible to assign long writing assignments to large numbers of students, so you might consider using one-page papers that can be graded relatively quickly using the analytical approach or the grading rubric mentioned earlier.

Mini-Papers. You can assign several of these "mini-papers" to cover a broad spectrum of course material. For example, one of us

TABLE 5.4

A Grading Rubric

PSYCHOLOGY 100/SECTION &JS
FALL 2003
WRITING ASSIGNMENT #3
GRADING CRITERIA

SUMMARY OF THE MOVIE: 8 points

8   Adequately summarized the important aspects of the movie, put them into context, emphasized the psychological concept.

6   Summarized most of the important aspects, put them in context, emphasized the psychological content.

4   Summary lacking depth, context, or emphasis on psychological content.

2   Summary lacking in two of the above criteria.

SUMMARY OF THE OUTSIDE SOURCE: 10 points

10   Adequately summarized the outside source, including a discussion of subjects/population, research methods, and conclusions.

8   Summarized most of the important aspects of the outside source.

6   Summary lacking depth, discussion of population, research methods, or conclusions.

4   Summary lacking in two of the above criteria.

2   Summary lacking in three of the above criteria.

SUMMARY OF THE TEXTBOOK: 1 point

1   Provided an adequate summary of the textbook information on the psychological concept.

0   Did not provide an adequate summary of the textbook information on the psychological concept.

(continued)

TABLE 5.4 (*continued*)

CRITICAL ANALYSIS: 10 points

10   Excellent job of tying the outside source, textbook, and movie together; many examples of the psychological concept put into context and critical discussion.

8   Good job of tying the outside source, textbook, and movie together; many examples of the psychological concept put into context and critical discussion.

6   Fair job of tying the outside source, textbook, and movie together; lacking in examples of the psychological concept put into context or critical discussion.

4   Inadequate job of tying the outside source, textbook, and movie together; lacking in examples of the psychological concept put into context and critical discussion.

2   Lacking in combining all sources, providing examples of the psychological concept in context, and critical discussion.

PROPER FORMAT: 1 point

1   Paper presented in proper format
0   Paper lacked proper format

TOTAL POINTS: 25 points possible

---

assigns 12 mini-papers that require information from 12 of the 18 chapters in the course text in introductory psychology. These assignments include summarizing the culture-specific motivational messages contained in a children's book, describing subtle gender stereotypes in birth congratulation cards, writing a new item for an IQ test, and reporting on the results of an exercise in violating a social norm. Other short assignments can be used to assess students' content knowledge, such as by asking them to design an experiment on some topic, or to describe the sensory structures involved in blindness or deafness.

Journals. As an alternative to mini-papers, consider asking students to keep, and periodically submit, a course-related journal. Such journals can contain several types of entries (Bronstein & Quina, 1988), including responses to specific instructor questions (e.g., "If you had to give up one of your senses, which would it be, and why?"), reactions to a lecture or reading assignment, records of daily observations (e.g., dreams, moods, or stressors), questions about course material, and thoughts about how course topics are linked. In short, journals can provide a bridge between course content and student experiences and between instructor and student (Connor-Greene, 2000; Fisher, 1996). Writing brief comments about what students have written in their journals is yet another way to apply the first principle for good practice in teaching, namely encouraging student–faculty contact. This kind of contact can be especially important in large classes, where many students might not have the chance, or the inclination, to participate in class discussions. These students might welcome the opportunity to share their ideas with you in a written format, where they can better organize their thoughts, and can have greater control over what they say, and how much they choose to say (Fisher, 1996). Sensitive instructor responses to journal entries can also help build trust between the instructor and student, and reflect the seventh principle of good undergraduate education, namely respecting students' diverse talents and ways of learning.

Some instructors allow students to make their journal entries whenever they wish, but if you want journals to serve as a framework for learning particular course content or for integrating course content and student experiences, it is probably best to set up a series of deadlines for making entries and submitting journals for your review. Most instructors ask students to write in their journals outside of class, but there are also ways to make journal entries a part of class sessions (Steffens, 1987). For examples, students can be asked to make journal entries at the beginning of a class period, perhaps in the form of a question they have about the day's reading assignment, an example they have thought of, or a topic they would like to discuss. Students can also be asked to make journal entries that summarize part of a lecture or, just before the end of class, that draw conclusions about that day's session. Assigning, and later reading, these kinds of entries can help you maintain your connection with your students while increasing their involvement with course topics, keeping them up to date with assigned readings, and informing you about any misconceptions or unanswered questions they might have (Stevenson, 1989).

Many instructors report that journal writing increases student learning, and there is at least one study showing that grades in a class requiring journal entries were higher than in a comparable class that did not require journal entries (Connor-Greene, 2000). Further, in end-of-term evaluations students have reported that journal assignments deepened their understanding of course material (Connor-Greene, 2000; Fisher, 1996; Hettich, 1990; Stevenson, 1989). Students also say that they prefer journal assignments to term papers. This preference might relate to the perception that making journal entries is easier than writing term papers, but the students say it is because they are able to cover more topics, personally apply concepts, and write throughout the course rather than just at the end of the term. They also tend to think that making journal entries is more interesting and stimulating than writing a term paper (Hettich, 1990).

To maximize the effectiveness of journal writing assignments, be sure your students understand the purpose of the assignments, the structure of the entries, and how the entries will be graded. Be explicit about all these things. Are the journal assignments designed to increase students' understanding of their readings? To provide a dialogue with the instructor? To apply course material to life experiences? Are entries to be made on paper supplied by the instructor, in a looseleaf notebook, on disk, or perhaps in e-mail? How long should the entries be, and when are they due? Finally, how many points is each entry worth, and what criteria will be used for determining the grade?

Think about the answers to all of these questions before you make your journal assignments. Typically, instructors rate journal entries on criteria such as whether an entry is accurate, whether the examples are appropriate, the depth of thinking exhibited, the quality of writing, or the number of entries (Connor-Greene, 2000; Fisher, 1996; Hettich, 1990).

Other Kinds of Writing Assignments

There are many other types of writing assignments, as well. You can ask students to write letters addressed to friends or relatives in which they explain course material, or you can ask them to summarize what they find during a course-related search of the Internet (Davis, 1993; Erickson & Strommer, 1991). You can also ask them to write book reviews, letters to the editor, critiques of research studies, and even journal articles in APA style (Davis, 1993). In other words, in making writing assignments, consider options that go beyond the format of the standard term paper. Nontraditional assignments are likely to be especially interesting and challenging for your students to write, and especially interesting for you to read and grade (Davis, 1993).

Student Portfolios. One such assignment, the *student portfolio*, offers students a chance to reflect on their efforts, progress, and learning in your course (Jacobs & Chase, 1992; King, 2002b). Like the teaching portfolios discussed in Chapter 8, student portfolios contain a collection of a student's work over some period of time, including previous writing assignments, graded exams, course projects, and other materials. The portfolios are usually submitted at midsemester and at the end of the term and are evaluated by the instructor using a pass–fail criterion or a letter grade (as with all writing assignments, the criteria for evaluation of student portfolios should be outlined when the portfolio assignment is made). One instructor's portfolio assignment, which could be chosen as an option to writing a term paper, included the collection of "news and magazine clippings illustrating psychological concepts, articles and archival sources and data, photographic essays, animations, Internet sites and presentations, student produced videos and CDs, student constructed models, interviews and visits with specialists and experts, among other possibilities" (King, 2002b, p. 4). Each item in the portfolio was to be accompanied by a written reflection about what the student had learned about it, and how it was connected to the course's content. Portfolios might also contain critiques of journal articles, reflections on videos shown in class, summaries of presentations by guest speakers, and the like (Sanders, 2001).

Student portfolios do take a lot of time to read and grade, and unfortunately, some students spend too much time collecting items and not enough time reflecting on them (King, 2002b). However, many teachers feel that the disadvantages of assigning portfolios are outweighed by their advantages—including helping students to apply the theories and concepts they learn in psychology, encouraging students to engage course material more deeply, to display creativity, and to communicate their knowledge and understanding through a channel that goes beyond traditional exams and papers (King, 2002b).

Setting the Stage for Writing Assignments

Whatever writing tasks you set for your students, be sure to check with your library to be sure that they can provide the resources necessary for your students' efforts. This step is especially important if you assign all of your students to write on a relatively narrow topic. You might even consider asking a librarian to speak to your class about how to find the resources necessary to complete the assignment (Davis, 1993). To further assist our (primarily) first-year students in introductory psychology, we have sometimes arranged for a short class presentation outlining the services of the campus Writer's Workshop. Your campus might have a similar unit, perhaps in the English department, that offers students help with all types of writing assignments.

APPLYING THE PSYCHOLOGY OF LEARNING TO STUDENT EVALUATION

In the persona of Father Guido Sarducci, comedian Don Novello touted the advantages of the "Five Minute University," where students could spend 5 minutes learning all the information they would have remembered 5 years after completing a college degree. This hilarious notion is based on the not-so-funny fact that, no matter how you evaluate your students, the results all too often reflect their ability to store information until it is no longer needed for the purpose of earning a good grade. The fact that most students forget most of what they hear or read in a course within a few weeks or months (e.g., Rickard et al., 1988) is consistent with the results of laboratory research on human learning and memory in general (Anderson, 2000). Students' performance on course evaluations does not necessarily reflect long-term retention, which is what most teachers think of as learning. There is probably no way to prevent this forgetting process, but research in cognitive psychology suggests that certain study and evaluation procedures might help students to retain course information longer (e.g., Bjork, 1979, 1999).

Massed Versus Distributed Practice

Long-term retention is improved when students engage in numerous study sessions (distributed practice) rather than when they "cram" during a single session on the night before a quiz or exam (massed practice). With this in mind, consider giving enough exams and quizzes that students will be reading and studying more or less continuously. You can also promote distributed practice by including a few unannounced "pop" quizzes (Ruscio, 2001). Some instructors avoid giving pop quizzes for fear of creating a stressful classroom atmosphere, but there are ways to overcome this potential problem while allowing students to reap the benefits of the steady reading and studying and regular class attendance that pop quizzes encourage.

For example, you could use pop quizzes as extra credit events. In one case (Bayly & Spiker, 2003), the instructor gave six unannounced quizzes throughout the term, and allowed students to use the sum of their quiz scores to replace their lowest exam score. This arrangement motivated students to do well on pop quizzes, and to view them as opportunities to compensate for a poor exam performance. For 25% of the students, using pop quiz scores in this way resulted in an improved final grade.

Retrieval Practice

Students assume that if a term, concept, or phenomenon looks or sounds familiar as they study for a test, they will be able to retrieve information about it during the test. This is not necessarily the case. To help students correct this mistaken idea before it is too late, consider giving one or two noncredit quizzes to help them more realistically assess the state of their knowledge as they study. This is easy to do if your course has a Web site on which practice quizzes can be posted. You can accomplish the same goal by giving more quizzes than you plan to include in final grade calculations and allowing students to drop their lowest quiz scores.

Offering review sessions is another way to help students assess the state of their learning prior to taking a test. These can be conducted during class sessions, or as optional sessions scheduled outside of regular class hours (Jacobs & Chase, 1992). Specially scheduled review sessions can run for 60 to 90 minutes, and have the advantage of attracting students who are the most motivated to participate in the pre-exam review, but schedule conflicts might prevent some of those same students from attending. Some instructors conduct their review sessions on the day or evening before an exam (e.g., Sahadeo & Davis, 1988), but we prefer to schedule them several days sooner than that in the hope that students who use the session to find out what they still need to know will have enough time to focus their studying accordingly. Keep all these points in mind as you decide where and when to schedule your own review sessions.

The content of review sessions can vary widely (Jacobs & Chase, 1992; Sahadeo & Davis, 1988). Some instructors control the content by presenting an overview and summary of the concepts, phenomena, and other material that will be covered on the upcoming exam. Others simply show up and answer whatever questions students might raise, or respond to questions that students submit on 3 × 5 cards that serve as their admission ticket to the session. Still others read questions from previous exams covering the to-be-tested material, ask students to supply the answers, and then explain why correct answers are correct and why incorrect answers are not. Simply answering questions or discussing old exam items can create a disjointed experience for students, though, so you might want to consider a hybrid approach in which you begin by presenting an integrated overview of the material to be tested—concentrating especially on the most complex or difficult concepts—and then open the session up for questions. Whatever option you choose, you will probably help students to do better on their exam, you might improve their long-term retention of the material, and you will almost certainly reduce their anxiety about the upcoming test. In our experience, students feel more relaxed taking an exam if they feel that they have done all they can to prepare, and attending a review session can enhance that perception.

Desirable Difficulties

Long-term retention of course material can be improved by creating "desirable difficulties" (Bjork, 1999). For example, learning is aided not only by opportunities to repeatedly retrieve, restore, and again retrieve the same information, but especially when the student is asked to do so randomly, not in the same order in which material was originally presented (e.g., Bjork, 1999). In fact, it can be argued that random retrieval forces students to learn to access information without the help of cues provided by the order in which questions are asked. Consider giving "cumulative" exams and quizzes that require students to retrieve information about past as well as current course material, and present the items in random order.

Could randomly ordering exam items improve long-term retention at the expense of exam performance during the course itself? Teaching lore suggests that it might, because putting items in random order deprives students of cues that might remind them of the sequence in which information was presented during lectures and in the textbook (Balch, 1989). However, we have reason to believe that randomly ordered items do not impair test performance. Many years ago, because of a computer glitch, the 100 multiple-choice items on one form of our final exam in introductory psychology appeared in random order, but on the other form, the same items appeared in the order in which the material had been presented in class. We did not discover the error until it was too late, so we had no choice but to administer the exam to 2,500 students on the same day in 15 locations around campus. To our surprise, the difference between the mean scores on the random versus organized exams was less than one half a point. We have now conducted the same comparison, on purpose, for more than a decade with more than 40,000 students, and have consistently found the same results. In short, if you wish to use randomly ordered exams to help create desirable difficulties that can lead to greater long-term retention, you will probably not be placing your students at a disadvantage in the short run.

Rapid Feedback

Remember that learning is enhanced when students receive prompt and constructive feedback that helps them to identify and correct mistakes (Chickering & Gamson, 1987; Dinham, 1996; Ory, 2003). If many days, or even weeks, pass between taking a test and receiving feedback on it, an important learning opportunity will have been missed. See Chapter 6 for ideas about returning and reviewing student exams. For more information on applying the psychology of learning in your classroom, visit a Web site related to applying the science of learning (http://berger.claremontmckenna.edu/asl/tp.asp), and read documents linked to it (e.g., Halpern & Hakel, 2003; Huber & Morreale, 2002).

SOME FINAL COMMENTS

Like other aspects of your teaching, the perceived quality and fairness of the quizzes, exams, papers, and other graded assignments you give can have a significant impact on your students' reactions to you and your courses. Their reactions to being evaluated, and your reactions to their reactions, will either support or undermine the teacher–student relationship that we see as the touchstone for success in teaching psychology. We examine that relationship and its complexities in the next chapter.

Faculty–Student Relationships

Most students will enter your courses with positive expectations about you and with high hopes of enjoying themselves and doing well. These expectations provide the foundation for a good learning experience and a good teaching experience. The suggestions we have made in previous chapters should help you build on that foundation by offering a well-organized course in a fair and consistent manner that conveys your concern for teaching effectively. In this chapter, we offer additional suggestions that are focused specifically on forging productive and mutually respectful relationships with your students.

THE ETHICAL USE OF TEACHER POWER

Even if you have never taught before, your students will (correctly) perceive you as having power and authority, if for no other reason than you will be assigning their grades. For example, unless you tell them otherwise, students will probably address you as "Professor," or "Doctor," and they will look to you to establish the rules and the style of interaction that will prevail in the course. This power differential, which is inherent in all aspects of the faculty–student relationship, is an extremely valuable asset. It allows you to teach your class on your own terms, based on your plans and according to your preferences. Most students not only accept, but value this power differential. They have come to learn; they don't want the responsibility for deciding how their course will be organized and taught. Accordingly, even if a few students complain or offer alternative suggestions for, say, testing schedules, exam formats, reading assignments, or grading policies, don't abdicate your authority in an effort to make your students like you.

At the same time, don't let your authority go to your head. APA ethical standards, the basic principles of effective teaching, and common sense all dictate that you never abuse the power that is invested in you as a teacher (APA, 2002; Bayer & Braxton, 1998; Keith-Spiegel, Wittig, Perkins, Balogh, & Whitley, 1993). For example, it should go without saying that you should not date your students, although the APA's *Ethical Standards for Psychologists and Code of Conduct* confirms this point in Standard 7.07 (APA, 2002). Even when initiated with the best of intentions on both sides, such relationships contain inherently coercive elements that can be psychologically harmful to the student involved. Further, once the relationship becomes public (as it eventually will), it will also undermine your relationship with the rest of the class by raising doubts about your character and the fairness of your grading system.

It is also important to present lectures and assign readings that fairly represent the state of the science in the areas of psychology covered by your courses (APA, 2002, Standard 7.03). Although you might not be a great fan of certain theories, methods, or points of view in developmental, clinical, or cognitive psychology, for example, you owe it to your students to at least make them aware of that material, and of the research findings related to it. In the same vein, you should be careful not to purposely or inadvertently impose your political, moral, or religious beliefs on students. It is all too easy to err in this regard, because the views you express in a lecture or discussion about psychology, or anything else, will carry the weight of authority, and if you push those views too hard, students could feel coerced to accept them, or even adopt them—on papers and exams, at least. Remember, too, that casual remarks that appear to condone excessive drinking, illegal drug use, or the like, can legitimize these activities in students' minds, even though you might have meant them as a joke or to show that you are "hip."

MANAGING THE CLASSROOM CLIMATE

Upholding the highest ethical standards in your teaching is just one element of the social and psychological climate you create in the classroom. The nature of that climate will have a strong influence on your students' classroom attendance and their academic progress in your course (Erickson & Strommer, 1991; Leamnson, 1999). All else being equal, students tend to stick with and learn more from classes in which they feel comfortable and valued as individuals (Sleigh & Ritzer, 2001; Sleigh, Ritzer, & Casey, 2002). These perceptions are especially important among first-year students, who might enter the college classroom with the greatest trepidation and the strongest need for support.

Establishing Rapport

Students are more likely to feel comfortable and valued if you go out of your way to create rapport with them. In the context of teaching, *rapport* refers to the process of creating emotional connections between teacher and student (Buskist & Saville, 2001).

Establishing rapport is not a magical process. Student surveys suggests that rapport is built mainly by following the principles of good practice in teaching that we outlined in Chapter 1 and illustrated in other chapters. In one such survey, the teacher behaviors that contributed most to the development of rapport were, in order of importance: displaying a sense of humor; being available to students before, after, or outside of class; encouraging class discussion; showing interest in students; knowing students' names; sharing personal insights and experiences with the class; relating course material through everyday terms and examples; and understanding that students sometimes have problems that hinder their progress in the course (Buskist & Saville, 2001).

Rapport is also enhanced when teachers display a cluster of nonverbal behaviors that include eye contact, smiles, an expressive speaking style, establishing physical proximity during interactions, using appropriate movements and gestures, appearing relaxed, and spending time with students (Andersen, 1986). These behaviors are referred to as *immediacy* because they create the impression that the teacher is psychologically engaged with the students and the class, not an aloof figure who is merely going through the motions of teaching. Verbal behaviors that reinforce the sense of immediacy include asking students about their work, soliciting students' views on course-related matters, and offering praise for good work. As you might expect, students tend to like teachers who display immediacy, and to want to work hard in those teachers' courses (Anderson, 1999; Sanders & Wiseman, 1994). In short, you can go a long way toward establishing rapport with your students simply by being friendly.

Assuring Inclusiveness

Friendliness is not enough, however. To create a classroom climate in which all students feel comfortable and valued, you have to put yourself in the shoes of students who differ from you—or from the majority of their fellow students—in terms of ethnicity, religion, gender, age, sexual orientation, physical or sensory capacity, or the like. To take a silly example, imagine that you are one of only two left-handed students in a psychology class in which the teacher regularly asks you or the other southpaw to tell the class what left-handed people feel or think about, say, putting children in day care, the acceptability of drug use, the value of achievement motivation, or other course-related topics. Singling out students in this way can easily make them feel uncomfortable, not only because it's impossible for them to summarize the views of the group they represent, but also because asking them to do so suggests the existence of a stereotype that applies to everyone in that group. It is fine to ask students to speak for themselves, but asking them to speak for a whole category of people—at the same time highlighting their membership in that category—is not a good way to make them feel included. Doing so might actually have the opposite effect. Our point here is that, although most teachers would never deliberately make their students feel uncomfortable, it is easy to do so inadvertently. Here are some additional dos and don'ts that can help you create a climate of comfort and inclusiveness in your classroom.

Use Diverse References and Examples. In lectures and discussions, use references and examples that are diverse enough to let your students know that you don't presume they are all Americans, heterosexuals, Christians, males, Whites, Blacks, females, or representatives of any other particular group. Mixing male and female pronouns and using gender-neutral pronouns are the most obvious ways to convey awareness and acceptance of student diversity, but there are many others, too. If you are discussing research on religiosity and stress-coping, for example, be sure to mention churches, synagogues, and mosques, not just the institutions that you know best. In lecturing about interpersonal attraction, remember that attraction can be heterosexual, homosexual, or bisexual. Because in most places marriage is not an option for your homosexual students, they are more likely to feel included if you refer to "marriage or partnerships" and to "couples" rather than just "married couples."

Avoid repeated comments or references that presume everyone in the class is a sports fan, an avid hunter, a devotee of *Star Trek* or *Buffy the Vampire Slayer*, or has any other characteristics that give special access to the meaning of your lectures. Finally, don't make sarcastic or joking comments about any condition or any group of people. Comments meant to give everyone a laugh might do so, but perhaps not everyone will be amused. Consider how you would feel, for example, if your teacher made light of obesity or dementia or some other mental or physical disorder that was a problem for you or a loved one. It is easier to avoid making such mistakes if you keep in mind that every aspect of behavior and behavior disorder will be represented among your students or in someone they know.

Look at Everyone. In Chapter 4 we suggested that, as you lecture or lead discussions, you scan the entire classroom to make eye contact with everyone, not just your favorite students or the ones who are most responsive and interested. Doing so not only ensures that you can see all students who raise a hand or show a puzzled expression, but also lets all students know that they are part of the class. So be sure to include in your visual scanning the students who are in the last row or in the far corners, those who usually don't participate in discussions, and anyone else you might otherwise be tempted to pass over for some reason.

Create Mixed Work Groups. In setting up teams for class discussions or cooperative learning, assign students to their groups. If you let students form groups on their own, their choices might maintain pre-existing cliques or exclude certain individuals based on gender, ethnicity, or other demographic characteristics. Creating diversity in such groups benefits all students by assuring that they interact with peers who differ from themselves, peers with whom they might otherwise never have exchanged ideas or gotten to know (*Does Diversity Make a Difference?*, 2000).

Write Inclusive Questions. When writing quiz and exam questions, use ethnically diverse names for hypothetical people and make sure that the examples and terms used will be familiar to all your students. To take a blatant example, certain international students, and those who are not Jewish, might be clueless about an item that involves a Seder. Like fish unaware of the water they swim in, we can all be unaware of the cultural waters in which we are immersed, so whenever possible ask one or more colleagues (ideally someone representing the other gender and perhaps another culture) to review your exam items and give you feedback about exam items that might contain gender-specific or culture-bound content.

Dealing With Sensitive or Controversial Topics

Many psychology courses cover sensitive or controversial topics that students do not normally address and about which they hold strong, emotionally charged views. It can be challenging to maintain a comfortable classroom climate when lecturing about or leading discussions on such topics (Seward, 2002). We don't pretend to know how to handle these situations to perfection, but we can offer some general guidelines. These guidelines are based on the assumption that you will have established an atmosphere of openness and mutual respect early in the course (Anderson, 1999).

First, it is a good idea to remind students about sensitive or controversial topics that will be addressed at the next class. This reminder might motivate students to do the reading associated with that topic, and perhaps begin considering what they think about it and what they want to know about it.

Second, when lecturing on sensitive material, present that material in a mature and straightforward way. Model a serious academic approach that your students can emulate. If your lecture includes mention of masturbation or oral sex, for example, use the terms themselves, not vague references to "self-abuse" or "sodomy." Similarly, use these terms in a natural way. If you seem hesitant to use certain words or to address certain topics in your narrative, your students probably will be, too, when the time comes to ask questions or engage in a discussion. If you are not entirely comfortable describing or discussing certain topics in class, practice delivering the lecture material in private to help you get used to dealing with it.

If some students seem to be uncomfortable when the time comes to consider and discuss the first sensitive or controversial topic—perhaps it will be evolutionary theories of social behavior, the origins of sexual orientation, racial differences in behavior and mental processes, or the status of recovered memories—acknowledge that people might have strong feelings and differing views on the topic. If you encounter comments that are extreme or intemperate, point out that although everyone has the right to hold and express personal views, discussion in an academic classroom must occur in an atmosphere of mutual respect (Allen, 2000; Marin, 2000). This point might seem self-evident, but remember that you have long since learned to accept and follow the norms governing academic discussion and debate; some of your students might be less familiar with those norms (Condon, 1986). Make it clear to those students at the outset that although concerns for political correctness need not stifle the expression of opinions or the posing of questions, everyone must consider the rights and feelings of others and should expect others to do the same.

If inappropriate or harmful comments continue, don't ignore them, but handle them with care. As mentioned in relation to classroom discussions in Chapter 4, there is not much point in castigating students who make inappropriate comments because doing so is unlikely to alter—and might even solidify—those students' views. An overly harsh response will probably also lead these students to refrain from further discussions on any topic, and worst of all, will stop the current discussion in its tracks. Instead, as also described in Chapter 4, you can use such comments to create "teachable moments" that serve not only to enlighten the speaker and the class, but also to move the discussion forward (Anderson, 1999).

One way to minimize the likelihood of inappropriate classroom remarks about sensitive or controversial topics is to invite students to submit (possibly anonymously) written questions or comments about these topics on the day before each one is covered in class (Brooke, 1999). You can use these questions and comments to tailor your lectures and frame class discussions to characterize and address wide-ranging points of view in a nonprovocative manner. Another way to raise the level of discussions is to assign groups of students to study each of several different viewpoints on a sensitive or controversial topic, and then to summarize that viewpoint in a classroom presentation. This approach allows the class to consider differing perspectives on the topic that are based on each group's research, not on the casual and possibly ill-advised comments of one individual. The result might be a more moderate and balanced discussion from which everyone can learn (Allen, 2000; Heuberger, Gerber, & Anderson, 1999). This process has been described as disagreeing in an agreeable manner (Desrochers, 2000).

Yet another strategy for reducing the chances of triggering unproductive classroom comments, especially when addressing topics related to gender, culture, race, or ethnicity, is to refer in your lectures not only to groups such as women, African Americans, Hispanic Americans, and Asian Americans, for example, but also Jews, men, Native Americans, Italians, Irish, Arab Americans, and the like. Doing so makes it easier for everyone to remember that they, too, are probably part of a group that at one time or another has been the target of stereotyping, prejudice, and discrimination (Seward, 2002). That realization can help students see gender, race, and ethnicity as broad sociocultural variables that operate to alter their own behavior and mental processes, not just the behavior and mental processes of others.

This same goal can also be achieved by assigning students to read articles or essays that represent varying points of view on the topic to be discussed in class (Heuberger, Gerber, & Anderson, 1999). Before discussing the role of sociocultural variables on, say, achievement motivation or prejudice, you could make students aware of other perspectives by asking them to read a magazine or newsletter that was written for members of a particular ethnic group, gender, religious group, or sexual orientation (Seward, 2002). You might even ask students to write a page in which they speculate about how their behavior and thinking and motivation and outlook on life might have been different if they were of a different race, gender, or sexual orientation (Seward, 2002).

In short, and as always, some planning will help maximize the value of discussions of sensitive or controversial topics (Allen, 2000; Seward, 2002). Part of that planning involves recognizing your own strongly held views on these topics, and, in accordance with ethical standards, resolving not to let those views turn your teaching into persuasion or proselytizing.

So far, we have discussed strategies and tactics for fostering productive and supportive relationships with students in general, but psychology classes are made up of individuals whose varying needs, wishes, motivational levels, life situations, cultural backgrounds, and other characteristics might place special demands, and possibly some strains, on the faculty–student relationship. In the sections to follow, we offer some advice on dealing with students as individuals.

DEALING WITH STUDENTS' NEEDS, EXCUSES, AND COMPLAINTS

At some point in every academic term, some of your students will ask you for help or accommodation in relation to their special needs, requests, excuses, and problems. Your response to these students will significantly shape your relationship with them, and with the rest of your students, too. Remember, first, that you do not have to accommodate every request or accept every excuse to preserve good relationships with students. If your students perceive that you make your decisions carefully, fairly, and reasonably, even an unwelcome outcome need not permanently harm faculty–student rapport. In fact, dealing with students in a firm but fair fashion can go a long way toward reinforcing students' perceptions of you as a caring teacher.

Dealing With Special-Needs Requests

On most campuses, students who have special academic needs due to a physical or cognitive disability are responsible for letting you know about their situation and requesting special accommodations in your course, such as allowing a note-taker or American Sign Language signer to accompany visually impaired or hearing-impaired students in class. In our experience, the most common accommodation requests are for extra time to complete exams or for a distraction-free exam location. Less commonly, visually impaired students ask that exams and quizzes be made available in Braille or that the items be read to them under supervision in a special testing center.

Open the door for such requests on the first day of class by inviting special-needs students to contact you immediately. Put this invitation in your syllabus, too. We suggest that you take these steps even if your institution requires special-needs students to transmit their accommodation requests to faculty through some campus office. First-year students, especially, might not be aware of, or might not recall, this procedural requirement, so if they contact you directly, advise them about what they should do to meet official rules. Another reason to invite these special requests is that, on most campuses, special-needs accommodations cannot be made retroactively. For example, it might well be considered capricious—and certainly unfair to other students—if you allowed a student who did poorly on an exam to re-take it under different circumstances after suddenly claiming special-needs status (Curzan & Damour, 2000).

If you feel that the accommodation requested by a student is un-reasonable, explain to the student that you will take the request under advisement for a day or two. Then contact the campus office that can advise you about what options are available to you under campus policies, the Americans with Disabilities Act (ADA), and other relevant statutes. Our own policy has been to provide requested accommodations whenever possible, not only as required by the rules, but also in the context of fairness to all of our students. For example, because students with or without identified learning disabilities perform better on exams when time pressure is not intense, our exams are designed so that they can be completed in less than the allotted time. Further, although we routinely provide a quiet, supervised seminar room in which students with certain learning disabilities can take exams, these students must take the exam on the same day, and at the same time, as all other students.

In other words, deciding what is fair and reasonable accommodation will take you beyond the formal requirements of the ADA. Suppose that, on the basis of a cognitive disability, a student asks to be given essay exams instead of the multiple-choice exams you normally write. Would accommodating this request give you the same assessment information that you get from other students? If not, should you—and would you have time—to use essay exams for all students? Would it be fair to let international students use a dictionary during multiple-choice exams to look up the meaning of unfamiliar words? Such questions require you to ask yourself which accommodations you can and cannot offer in the context of preserving the academic integrity of your course. These questions are easier to answer after you have reflected on your course goals and on your views about what methods of instruction are necessary in reaching them, what outcomes are required of all students (and why), what methods of assessing student outcomes are necessary (and why), and what levels of student performance on these outcome measures are acceptable to you (Scott, 1997). (For additional resources on providing reasonable accommodations to special-needs students, visit http://www.disabilityresources.org/, a Web site that lists disability resources by topic and state.)

Dealing With Student Excuses

Your efforts to nurture good faculty–student relationships will be frequently challenged by the need to deal with students' excuses for missing (or delaying) a quiz or exam, or the deadline for a term paper or other assignment. As you probably know, these excuses can range from the tragic to the ludicrous, and everything in between (see Table 6.1). Any of them can be genuine and any of them can be phony (Caron, Whitbourne, & Halgin, 1992), so your tricky task is to discriminate one from the other without becoming too cynical or too gullible. Performing this trick is important not just because fictitious excuses should not be tolerated, but also because failing to detect phony excuses can give a few dishonest students an unfair advantage over the rest of the class, in terms of extra study or preparation time, and possibly information about exam content. Does this advantage translate into better grades? Not necessarily. One study of the relationship between frequency of excuse making and quality of course grades revealed a significant negative correlation (Schwartz, 1986).

The way you handle excuses conveys a message to your students about your teaching philosophy, and most particularly about whether you view students as partners or adversaries, the degree to which you trust them, and how much you care about them. Your excuse policies and procedures will also influence the number and nature of the excuses you will receive in the future. As those policies and procedures circulate on the campus grapevine, they will either encourage or discourage frivolous excuse making.

We recommend taking a firm, consistent, rational, and caring approach to excuses that incorporates a "trust, but verify" policy. Treat every excuse as genuine but, in fairness to the entire class, require that it be verified accompanied by supporting documentation (see Fig. 6.1). We have found that this authoritative approach is widely accepted by students, and gives us sufficient time to consider (and investigate, if necessary) the validity of each excuse instead of making snap decisions or ad hoc changes in course policy (Bernstein, 1993).

TABLE 6.1

A Taxonomy of Student Excuses

I. *Death of a loved one*

"My grandmother/grandfather died/is dying." (One student is said to have reported the deaths of 9 grandparents in 4 years.)

"Grandpa's heart exploded, but he's fine now."

II. *Personal illness*

"I caught dyslexia from another student last semester."

"I broke my nose on the alarm clock."

"I sprained my back lifting a corpse." (This student worked in a mortuary.)

(After failing an oral exam): "I have a split brain disorder, so the side that knew the answers could not communicate with the side that controls my speech."

III. *Accidents/illness of friends or relatives*

"My mother is having a vasectomy."

"My brother-in-law was struck by lightning."

"My father was overthrown." (from the son of a political leader)

IV. *Automobile problems*

"My tires are too bald to drive on."

"My windshield wipers won't work."

"I hit a toilet in the road."

"The police impounded my car with my term paper inside."

V. *Sleep disorders*

"My alarm clock didn't go off and I overslept."

"I will be oversleeping after getting drunk on my birthday."

VI. *Crime victimization*

"Someone stole all the tires off my car."

"A robber locked me in the basement of a convenience store."

"I have to take the exam early because my girlfriend's husband is threatening to kill me."

"My car was stolen—with my term paper inside."

(Message left on professor's answering machine): "I have been arrested for selling cocaine, so I won't make the midterm. This is my only phone call— can you please get me a lawyer?"

VII. *Poltergeist victimization*

"My diamond jewelry disappeared."

"I was consulting a ouija board and accidently called up a spirit who scared me so bad I couldn't leave the house."

"I couldn't finish my paper because my horoscope said that my jupiter was opposing my venus and that any writing I did would be used against me."

VIII. *Animal trauma*

"My rabbit swallowed a needle."

"My dog's eye popped out."

"My cat had kittens and I was her coach."

"I can't stay for class because someone just painted my dog pink."

"My paper is late because my parrot crapped in my computer."

(continued)

TABLE 6.1 (*continued*)

"The parakeet fell into the soup and I had to rush it to the vet."
"A flaming squirrel caught my yard on fire."
"My buffalo herd got loose."
"The dog ate my hearing aid."

IX. *Miscellaneous*

"I'm too happy to give my presentation tomorrow."
"I skipped class because I didn't want to get spots on my new leather jacket."
"I have multiple personality disorder and my good side wrote the paper but my bad side threw it away."
"It was either have sex for the first time or take your exam."
(From a student in prison): "I got shot while trying to go over the wall."

Note. These are some excuses students actually offered to their teachers. We have organized them according to categories suggested by Schwartz (1986).

Dealing With Complaints About Test Items and Grades

One of the greatest threats to the quality of the faculty–student relationship stems from students' perceptions that course grading is unfair, or that a teacher is callous and uncaring in the face of student requests to review and reconsider grading decisions. These perceptions might be inaccurate, but can be easily formed nonetheless if you fail to clarify the grading system in your syllabus, and especially if you don't offer a clear and accessible procedure through which students can respond to the grading of every quiz and exam item.

The first step in establishing a fair and open grading-review process is, as mentioned in Chapter 4, to develop an efficient plan for returning quizzes and exams in class. With such a plan in place, there will be enough time in class to review the scoring of some or all of the test items. It is just as important to have a plan for handling the complaints that will inevitably be made about some items by some students. Without such a plan, students who are unhappy with their scores might shout out questions about items they missed (e.g., "What was the right answer to number 11?"), after which others who missed the same item will chime in, too. Before you can answer, yet another student might ask, "How about number 22?" and this question will attract its own group of echoing voices. If you allow this process to continue, and simply try to cope with it, chaos and confusion will soon reign, leading to tension and hostility in your students, and probably in you, too.

To prevent the development of this unpleasant atmosphere, we recommend that you set up and explain an organized test-return system

APPLICATION FOR A PSYCHOLOGY 100
MAKE-UP EXAMINATION
FALL SEMESTER, 2003

Dr. Sandra Goss Lucas

After completing the information requested below and obtaining the necessary signature, please give, or fax (XXX-XXX-XXXX), this form to your instructor. Once we have verified the accuracy of the information you have provided, and confirmed that your reason for requesting a make-up exam is acceptable, an alternate exam date, time, and place will be arranged. All make-up exams will take place after the regular exam.

Important note: Unless you are requesting a make-up exam because of a last-minute illness or emergency, this form must be turned in at least 7 days before the date of the regularly scheduled exam. If you miss this deadline you will not be eligible for a make-up exam.

Please provide the following information:

I, _____ certify that I am unable to take the Psychology 100 exam scheduled for _____, 2004 because (please be clear and specific when describing your reason and be sure to obtain a confirming signature):

_____

_____

_____

_____

_____

Your name:_____ Your signature:_____

Your ID# _____ Your phone number:_____

Your e-mail address:_____

Confirmed by (please print name): _____

Signature:_____

Position or relationship to student:_____

Telephone number:_____

E-mail address, if available: _____

FIG. 6.1. An excuse-documentation form. We have used this form to help students establish the legitimacy of their excuse for missing an exam. You can create versions of this form for dealing with excuses relating to any academic situation.

well before you begin to return the first graded assignment. Then follow that system to the letter when returning your first quiz or exam, and in every instance thereafter. Your students will soon understand that your rules and procedures are designed to give them a fair forum for making comments and complaints, and that discussion of test items in class should focus on learning from mistakes, not fishing for points.

The system we use works well in classes large and small, and is especially useful in relation to multiple-choice tests, but it can also be adapted for use with short-answer items, essay tests, and even term papers (assuming that you have used a clear grading rubric—see chapter 5). Let's consider multiple-choice tests first. After grading a quiz or exam, we create a frequency distribution that ranks all the items from most missed to least missed. Next, before distributing the students' test results in class, we explain that our goal is to help everyone better understand the course material associated with the items they missed. We explain, too, that to satisfy the curiosity of the largest number of students as quickly as possible, we will review the test items in the order of difficulty, beginning with the one that was most often missed.

Like many other psychology faculty, we give students their test results, but not a copy of the test, so we have to refresh their memories about each item to be discussed. To make this task easier, we create a large-font copy of each test item on individual transparencies or PowerPoint displays. We then present the items, one by one, describe the correct answers, explain why they are correct, and explain why various frequently chosen options are incorrect. If you use this system to review short quizzes, you should have time to cover all the items. In the case of longer exams, reviewing the 10 to 20 most difficult items—or as many as time allows—should satisfy the questions and concerns of the vast majority of your students. If you don't get to all the items, be sure to invite students to discuss any remaining items with you during office hours or via e-mail.

As you review test items in class, invite students to ask questions, but don't get bogged down in long discussions. If students raise questions or suggest item interpretations that create uncertainty in your own mind about how items should be graded, don't feel compelled to make a decision on the spot. Later reflection might lead you to regret that decision. We suggest that, instead, you invite students to fill out a form on which they can present their argument in written form (see Fig. 6.2). On the days you are discussing graded assignments, place these forms on a chair or table where students can easily pick them up as they leave. Set a short deadline for submitting the forms, and explain that you will carefully review them before announcing your final decisions in class or via a group e-mail message. In our experience, only students with well-thought-out complaints take the time to complete these forms. If you decide that a complaint is valid, announce that you will give credit to everyone whose response deserves it. If you reject an appeal, announce that, too, and jot a brief response on all review request forms before returning them to the students.

A different version of the same system can be used to handle complaints about grades on essay exams or other written assignments. Here, too, it is important to give your students time to reflect on their

---

REQUEST TO REVIEW GRADING OF AN EXAM ITEM

Name _____ Student ID # _____

Instructor's Name _____ Section _____

Item # _____ Test Form _____

I believe that answer _____ should also be considered correct because:

_____

_____

_____

_____

_____

_____

_____

_____

_____

_____

_____

I found supporting evidence on page(s) _____ in the textbook.

FIG. 6.2.   Test item review form. Allowing students to submit forms like this one not only eases students' (and teachers') tension and emotional distress in class, but lets students know that you will seriously consider their questions, comments, and alternative interpretations about test item grading.

grade, and your reasons for assigning it, before they raise objections (Svinicki, 1998). Accordingly, we ask students to carefully reread their own work, and our comments about it, and then—if they still feel we have been unfair or misguided—to resubmit the work along with a detailed statement indicating why we should reconsider our grading decision. We do not allow students to submit a writing assignment for possible regrading on the day it was returned to them. Requiring students to carefully evaluate both their writing and our response tends to short-circuit many complaints as students become aware of the mistakes or misstatements that led to the grade they received. At the same time, reading the regrade justification statements of students who do submit them gives us the opportunity to thoughtfully reconsider our earlier judgment and to correct any mistakes we might have made.

When students take you up on your invitation to discuss test items or grades during your office hours, remember that your demeanor during these conferences can solidify or undermine the student–faculty relationship. The meetings might be only a minor part of your day, but your students will consider them important, even vital. The students might want to understand material that has eluded them, or they might be hoping you will find it possible to raise their grade enough that they can retain a scholarship or avoid academic probation. Whatever the case, they are probably not there simply to challenge your authority (Svinicki, 1998; Zlokovich, 2001). Keeping this in mind can help you avoid becoming defensive and turning the conference into an adversarial situation. It can also help you to listen more carefully to what students are actually saying, and what they are actually requesting. In many cases, for example, when students come to your office to complain about a grade, they don't really expect you to change it; they might simply want to tell you how they feel about your grading system, or about the course. If you are unapologetically firm about your course policies, but also sympathetic and ready to listen, these sessions could well become fruitful discussions of the demands of college life, of students' motivation and study habits, and of how they can best prepare for future quizzes and exams. Or not. Inevitably, a few students wish only to cajole you into giving them some kind of special consideration. They might not react well when you explain that it would be a violation of capricious grading rules to grant their request. Try to stay calm in such circumstances. It is far better for students to go away angry and feel apologetic later than for you—who occupies the power role in the relationship—to lose your cool and feel the need to apologize to your student.

DEALING WITH PROBLEM STUDENTS

Now that we have raised the specter of unpleasant interactions with students, we should consider them in more detail. Happily, the worst of these interactions are rare and will involve a tiny minority of your students. Nevertheless, it is important to understand what can happen and to be prepared to handle untoward teaching-related events, in the classroom and beyond. Here again, remember that the way you deal with one student can affect your relationship with the rest of your class.

Problem Students

Most students are nice people who are fun to teach and are in class to learn. Still, some of them do occasionally behave in ways that create problems for their teachers. The most common student behavior problems are known as *classroom incivilities*. These can include a wide variety of sins, such as coming to class unprepared, refusing to participate in classroom activities, and disrupting or distracting a class by arriving late, leaving early, talking during lectures, being hypercritical or overly argumentative, making inappropriate comments or disapproving sounds, and many other possibilities we cannot think of but you might encounter (Boice, 1998a).

As discussed later, the number and nature of the classroom incivilities you will encounter is influenced by your teaching style, but even the most organized, experienced, and caring teacher has to deal with problem students at one time or another. Try not to take their classroom incivilities or other problematic behavior as a personal affront. If you can remain calm and objective, it is easier to think rationally about why the behavior is occurring and what to do about it.

Handling Classroom Incivilities

By far, the most common form of classroom incivility takes the form of minor classroom disruptions, particularly when students talk to each other during your lectures. These disruptions require your attention because they can interfere with other students' ability to follow the lecture, and—if the students are talking loudly enough—can even derail your own train of thought. Again, try not to take this behavior personally. True, it is impolite, and it also sends a message that the talking students are not interested in your lecture. However, remember that, especially in larger classes, most students have the mistaken idea that you cannot see them, let alone hear them. In short, they might be in the process of trying to entertain themselves, not offend you.

We suggest that you deal with inappropriate talking as soon as you detect it, but that you start off slowly. Perhaps the simplest tactic is to stroll over to where the talkers are seated; this will usually put a stop to their talking. If the problem continues, you can pause, look at the offending students, and ask if they have a question about the lecture. This tactic has several advantages. First, it stops the talking. Second, by making the assumption that the students were talking about course material, you give them the opportunity to save face by actually asking a question. Third, this tactic lets the students know that you can see and hear them, and that their talking was disruptive (it sends the same message to other students who might otherwise have started their own conversations). Fourth, you have let everyone know that you care enough about your students to make sure they can hear you. Fifth, you have asserted your right to authority and control in the classroom without appearing to be too harsh.

We suggest that you also use this first talking incident to remind the class how important it is for everyone to be considerate of their fellow students. You might also invite students to let you know in private about students whose conversations habitually distract them but that are not loud enough to have attracted your attention. Students who are not assertive enough to ask their peers to be quiet truly appreciate this invitation.

If more than one student conversation is occurring at the same time, stop and ask for quiet, and if the same students are talking on a regular basis, ask to see them after class or in your office for a discussion of the problem (Tiberius & Flak, 1999). It is crucial that this discussion takes place in private. No matter how much you think the students deserve to be embarrassed in public, doing so is usually a no-win alternative. It engenders strong negative feelings in the embarrassed students, and can make you look petty, abusive, and out of control in front of your class. Instead, sit down with the offending students and remind them that their behavior is inappropriate, it is disrupting the concentration of other students, and it is interfering with your job as a teacher. Point out that, because you have already let them know that talking in class is a problem, their remaining options are to either agree not to sit near each other or drop your course. (On many campuses, interfering with a professor's teaching activities can lead to formal disciplinary proceedings and even dismissal. Check your campus's rules and regulations on student discipline to be sure of your ground before mentioning these possible consequences.)

We suggest that you follow the same general strategy of increasingly strong interventions in relation to other kinds of classroom incivilities, too. Remember that whether the inappropriate classroom behavior involves students kissing each other, sending or receiving text messages on a mobile phone, or using a wireless Internet connection to surf the Web (all of which we have personally seen in class), the way you deal with one person's incivility can have a ripple effect on the other students' perceptions of you (Kounin, 1970; Kuhlenschmidt & Layne, 1999). If your response style is reasonable and measured, it will solidify your standing as an authoritative, but fair, teacher. If it is excessive, capricious, or abusive, you run the risk of alienating the entire class. It might take some time, and some mistakes, before you learn to strike just the right note in such situations, but with experience and a caring attitude, you will do it.

Preventing Classroom Incivilities

Ultimately, the best way to deal with classroom incivilities is to prevent them. As described in Chapter 3, you can start the prevention process on the first day of class by summarizing whatever rules for classroom behavior you have outlined in your syllabus (Boice, 1998a; Carbone, 1999; Gonzalez & Lopez, 2001). Your students will probably come from diverse backgrounds and will have had diverse experiences with classroom etiquette, so don't assume that all students will already know what you consider to be acceptable and unacceptable classroom behavior (Astin, 1993; Appleby, 2001). Describe and discuss the reasons for your rules about arriving late, leaving early, talking during lectures, and the like. Some instructors even ask students to sign a statement affirming that they have read and understood the classroom rules (Carbone, 1999). In any case, don't keep your rules secret and then harshly punish the first example of classroom incivility.

Instead, use the first instance of problematic behavior to remind everyone of the rules and the need to abide by them. Above all, don't ignore early violations of classroom etiquette; if you do, those violations are likely to increase in number and severity (Gonzalez & Lopez, 2001). Indeed, failing to deal with uncivil student behavior often creates the impression that you are not in control of the classroom, an impression that makes students uncomfortable and threatens the quality of the learning environment.

In other words, whether classroom incivilities remain the small problem they normally are, or become a bigger problem depends largely on you—not only on how you handle problem students' uncivil behavior, but on whether your teaching style encourages or discourages such behavior. Teachers who habitually read their lecture notes in a monotone voice or who respond to students' questions with sarcasm or hostility can expect a higher incidence of student uncivility than those whose lectures are more interesting and who make it clear that they care about teaching and about their students. In one study, for example, instructors who, during their first few class sessions, displayed the behaviors described earlier as "immediacy" encountered far fewer and far milder instances of classroom incivility than other instructors. The most important elements of immediacy in this study were: (a) arriving in class early enough for informal chats with students; (b) a moderate amount of movement around the classroom during lectures; (c) maintaining eye contact with students; (d) use of active learning methods; (e) marking lecture notes with reminders to slow down, pause for questions, and check for student understanding; and (f) listening patiently to student questions (Boice, 1998a). As one observer put it, "the opportunity for disruption in the college classroom is directly related to students' perception of their treatment by the instructor and other students, their sense of security, their perception of the classroom as a comfort zone, and the quality of the interpersonal rapport that exists" (Anderson, 1999, p. 71). This assertion is especially accurate in relation to large classrooms, where a sense of anonymity and isolation from the instructor can foster the highest rates of uncivil behavior (Carbone, 1999). No wonder then that, in classes of any size, reducing students' perceived anonymity and isolation by learning students' names and employing lots of active learning techniques has been found to decrease classroom incivilities (Boice, 1998a; Carbone, 1999).

Addressing the Problems of Problem Students

The behavior that earns problem students their title might go well beyond the scope of classroom incivilities. Problem students' actions can run the gamut from pathetic to annoying to disruptive to unbalanced. Some of these people are very bright; some are less so. Some are highly motivated but scattered; others don't seem to care about much of anything. Some are a problem mainly in your class; others create problems for the entire campus. Problem students have been identified as falling into eight categories, including the compliant, the anxious-dependent, the discouraged, the independent, the hero, the sniper, the attention-seeker, and the silent (Mann et al., 1970). Most teachers recognize these descriptive categories and can even associate individual student names with each of them. When it comes to giving advice about how to actually deal with the problems of problem students, though, we prefer our own somewhat less extensive taxonomy. The tips contained in the following sections are based to some extent on classroom management research, and to a large extent on our own experiences (Goss, 1995).

The "Everything-Always-Happens-to Me" Student.
These students have the best of intentions, but some external force always seems to interfere with their plans to meet their academic responsibilities. They show up an hour late for the exam because they overslept because the alarm didn't go off (even if the exam was at 7 p.m.). They can't submit their term paper on time because the printer jammed just as they were trying to print it out 15 minutes before class. In other words, these are friendly students who seem utterly bewildered by all the "bad luck" that interferes with their best efforts to do the right things at the right times. Dealing with this type of problem student is relatively simple. Be sympathetic, but apply your rules, even if it means that the student gets a penalty—or even a zero—on an exam or a paper. In addition, advise the student to take advantage of any time-management or organizational skills workshops that might be offered on your campus. Many instructors are hesitant to take this "tough love" approach because they feel sorry for the student. However, in being lenient they fail to consider three things. First, the student's apparent misfortunes might be part of a long-standing pattern of irresponsibility, poor planning, and last-minute activity that has been excused and supported in the past by family, friends, and other teachers. Second, the basic principles of learning suggest that giving the student special consideration is likely to perpetuate this problematic pattern. Third, making ad hoc decisions to bend the rules for certain "unfortunate" students can be unfair to other students, and can even be construed as a violation of capricious grading regulations. In short, don't feel guilty about enforcing the course rules you set down in your syllabus at the beginning of the

term. You must be accountable for your behavior as a teacher, and you can do your students a service by helping them learn to be responsible for theirs.

The "I-Disagree-With-Everything-You-Say" Student.

Most teachers want to nurture students' critical thinking skills, including the tendency to question what they are told by authority figures. So we should be pleased and supportive when students challenge what we say in class, especially when they ask for more evidence, or present conflicting evidence of their own. Occasionally, however, you might encounter problem students who disagree with virtually everything you say as a way of challenging your credibility, attracting attention, or both. Research in classroom management suggests that these problem students fall into one of two subtypes: the low-achieving student whose challenges take the form of long, marginally relevant discourses or emotional arguments against your presentation, and the high-achieving student whose challenges are logical, but essentially mischievous attempts to disrupt and discredit your presentation.

The key to dealing with both subtypes of students is to first figure out what is going on, and not jump to conclusions. Are these students creating a problem because they enjoy causing trouble or because they are simply unskilled at the rules of academic controversy? You can find out by assuming the latter, especially in the first few class sessions when the classroom climate has not yet been established. Accept the student's critical comments at face value, and reply objectively. A harsh response to an early student comment—even if you suspect it was a bit hostile—can discourage other students from asking or answering questions later on. If the student's subsequent questions and comments appear to have little or no intellectual purpose or content, the pattern will become clear to you, and your diagnosis will be confirmed by the rest of the class. Irritated by the problem student's attempts to sabotage the lecture with disruptive comments and picky questions, your students will react strongly whenever the problem student raises a hand or begins to speak. If you see them roll their eyes, shift in their seats, tap their pens and pencils, and look away, and you hear sighs, giggles, or whispered comments, it is time to take action to solve the problem (Fritschner, 2000).

We suggest that your first intervention be a "soft reprimand," which consists of having a private talk. Tell the problem student that his or her classroom questions and comments are creating a problem for you and for the rest of the class. Explain what the problems are and ask if the student was aware of them. If, as sometimes happens, the student seems genuinely unaware that he or she has been creating problems, the solution is relatively easy. Let the student know that you are happy to discuss any aspect of course content and to listen to the student's views, but that in the interests of time it would be better to raise complex questions and challenging comments outside of class, in office hours, or in e-mail. A soft reprimand is usually enough to take care of the chronic disagreement problem. For one of us, a private chat with one such problem student ultimately led to a research project and a jointly authored journal article.

If a soft reprimand doesn't work, you will have to take further steps. The first of these is to refuse to call on the problem student in class, or to do so only rarely. Let the student know of your plans ahead of time, and provide a reminder during class, too, by saying something like, "I see your hand, Jack, but let's give someone else a chance to talk." Another method for dealing with the situation was suggested by a colleague who uses the system modeled after radio call-in contests. He tells the class that he will not always call on the first person to raise a hand, but will sometimes choose the third or fourth volunteer. This tactic not only allows him to call on a problem student only at his discretion, but it also encourages other students to participate more actively. Whatever method you choose, your students will love you for it!

If the problem student ignores such tactics by interrupting you without permission, have another conference in which you offer the options of behaving properly or dropping your course. In such cases, which you might never encounter, you should discuss the situation with your department executive officer to determine what campus security or student discipline proceedings might be necessary to remove the student from class.

The "Quick-to-Anger" Student. The label says it all. A quick-to-anger-student has a hot temper and might become highly irritated and even verbally abusive about a low exam or quiz score, about your refusal to adjust a grade, or about your negative response to his or her request for, say, a deadline extension. Fortunately, these students are relatively few in number, and their outbursts are even more rare—mainly because of the power differential that exists between teacher and student. Still, here are a few tips for defusing what can be a very disconcerting situation.

If the student's anger is expressed during a class session, explain that this is not the time or the place to deal with it. Offer the student the opportunity to discuss the situation after class, and in private, saying something like "OK, I can see you're unhappy about this, so let's meet in my office right after class and we can talk it over." No matter how disrespectful the student's behavior might be, try not to take it personally, and don't get into a shouting match or an exchange of criticism in front of your class. Your students will have more respect for you if your response is firm but calm in the face of inappropriate anger. In fact, your controlled and mature response might even serve as a model to them for handling such situations in their own lives.

If the angry outburst occurs in private, give the student a chance to speak without interruption. This can be exceedingly difficult, especially if the student is swearing, being disrespectful, or saying things that you believe are untrue. However, interrupting a tirade will accomplish nothing because the student will be unable to rationally process what you are trying to say; in fact, the interruption might make the student even angrier. At this stage, just listen, nod in understanding, and maintain steady eye contact and the most composed facial expression you can muster. As the student eventually runs out of steam, the emotional level of the situation will drop. You can usually be sure that the student has finished talking when the anger becomes tinged with sheepishness. The student might even apologize for having been so upset. At this point, you should acknowledge the student's anger, summarize your understanding of the problem or complaint, and offer whatever coherent, nonemotional, nonthreatening response you think is appropriate. For example, you might say something like, "Look, Jill, I realize how angry and disappointed you are in your midterm exam score, because it is obvious from what you have said that you studied long hours to get ready for it. And it is obvious from what you have said, too, that you blame me for giving an impossible exam. I wish I could just fix the problem for you, but I think you know that wouldn't be right, and it would certainly not be fair to the rest of the class. I think you know, too, that the exam was not really impossible because some people did pretty well on it. Let me make a suggestion. We still have eight weeks to go in this course; why don't we talk about exactly how you are preparing for exams in general, and how you should be getting ready for the next one in my course. If it turns out that you can use some help in learning how to use your study time more effectively, there is a workshop on campus you might want to join."

The "Unbalanced" Student. In some cases, a student's anger, hostility, criticism, disruptiveness, or other classroom behavior reflects a more general psychological problem that might be severe enough to qualify as a form of mental disorder. In these cases it is vital to remember that, even if you are a clinical or counseling psychologist, your responsibility as a teacher does not extend to providing psychological help. In fact, your responsibility is to treat troubled students just like other students. You can refer them to appropriate sources of help, or confirm that they are already getting such help, but trying to establish a therapeutic relationship with these students would be unethical (see the APA's *Ethical Standards of Psychologists and Code of Conduct*, Standard 3.05). The resulting dual role would create a conflict of interest that could easily lead to favoritism and capricious grading (Standard 7.06).

If you suspect—or your student tells you—that the problem you are trying to deal with privately involves a serious behavior disorder, be ready to make the appropriate referral if the student is not already getting help. This is not the time to be looking up phone numbers, so before you begin teaching on a new campus, prepare a list of contact details for the departmental or campus counseling service, local public and private mental health centers, inpatient psychiatric units and hospitals, domestic violence shelters, crisis services, and the like. It is also a good idea to become familiar with the services, clientele, and admissions criteria associated with each facility. Armed with this information, you will be better able to assist your student to seek help from the most appropriate source. Keep copies of your referral list in your office and at home, and bring it to class, too, because you might be asked for referral information when you least expect it.

In rare cases, a student's psychological problems might be so severe or potentially dangerous that you will have no choice but to discuss the situation with your department executive officer or with campus mental health professionals. They can advise you about how such cases should be handled, and can, if necessary, arrange to remove the student from your class, and perhaps from the campus.

The "I'm-Not-Here" Student. At the opposite end of the problem student spectrum is the person who avoids attracting your attention, never volunteers a question or an answer in class, never comes to your office hours, and accepts without complaint whatever grades you assign, no matter how poor those grades might be. Some teachers don't see these students as "problems," and in terms of actively causing trouble, perhaps these teachers are right. Students do have the right to structure their college experience in their own way. If they prefer to listen passively, do their reading, take their exams, and move on to the next course, so be it. In fact, many students consider "class participation" to involve nothing more than showing up regularly, remaining attentive during lectures, completing all assignments, and being prepared for class. This view probably accounts for why so relatively few students, especially in introductory psychology classes, participate in the active way that many instructors hope to see (Fritschner, 2000; Leamnson, 1999).

However, if quiet students are quiet because of shyness, fear, intimidation, or perhaps a culturally based reticence to attract attention, they might not be getting as much from your course as they could. We think that part of a psychology teacher's job is to reach out to these students and let them know that their active participation in class is not only desirable, but welcome (Bailey, 2003).

Perhaps the simplest way to do this is to greet quiet students by name when they come to class. Don't single them out at every class session, but if your initial greeting does not seem to make them uncomfortable, ask how they are doing, or if they had a nice weekend. If you require every student to come to an office hour early in the term (see chapter 2), you can use this opportunity to learn more about these students, and help them be more comfortable with you. This is also a good time to assess their expectations about the course, and how they prefer to learn.

You can also start a dialogue with reticent students simply by writing personal comments on the exams, quizzes, or other written assignments you return to them. For example, you might note that the student did a good job on the assignment, or seems to be doing better on quizzes now. These comments let the student know that you care, and this message can be reinforced by offering to discuss some aspect of the course content, or lending the student a book that might be of interest. Remind these students that they can contact you for a chat over e-mail as well as in person. Small-group discussions and other cooperative learning activities can also sometimes help reticent students become more active members of the class. Your efforts might not turn reticent students into feisty fireballs, but you might make it easier for these students to talk to you one-on-one and, as a result, get the help and advice they might need.

As already noted, students will inevitably present specific problems that we have not listed here. However, we hope that the advice we have offered (and summarized in Checklist 6.1) will provide a template that helps you to deal effectively with whatever problematic student behavior you might encounter.

Checklist 6.1
A checklist for dealing with problem students

Here, in summary, are some important things to remember when dealing with various kinds of problem students.

1. *Be prepared*. As far as possible, establish your plans, rules, and procedures for dealing with the most common types of problem students before you encounter them.
2. *Be proactive*. Try to prevent classroom incivilities and other problematic student behavior by developing your course and your teaching style to be as engaging and caring as possible. In addition, be sure your syllabus lists your rules relating to attendance, classroom conduct, missed deadlines, and other potential sources of misunderstanding and faculty–student conflict.
3. *Be firm and consistent*. Say what you mean, and mean what you say. Apply your rules and procedures in the same way with all students. Don't make rules that you can't (or won't) enforce and don't make ad hoc exceptions beyond those you previously stated.
4. *Remain calm and mature*. Display an adult, professional demeanor at all times. Listen to students' points of view, even when they are angry, and try not to take their problematic behavior as a personal affront.
5. *Ask for help when necessary*. Don't be afraid to involve your colleagues or department or campus administrators if you are not sure how to deal with a problem student. Experienced colleagues in psychology and in other departments are a particularly good source of advice about what strategies and tactics have and have not worked well in the past, and about the written and unwritten rules that might apply in dealing with problem students.

DEALING WITH ACADEMIC DISHONESTY

You might have noticed that we did not include "the dishonest student" in our taxonomy of problem students. This isn't because we don't see academic dishonesty as a problem. On the contrary, we think it is such an enduring, widespread, culturally supported, and harmful problem that it deserves more detailed attention. Estimates of the prevalence of academic dishonesty vary widely, depending on sampling techniques, the type of dishonesty studied, and whether data come from experiments or surveys.

Some studies suggest that about 9% of college students have been dishonest at least once in their academic careers; others have found the figure to be 95% (Maramark & Maline, 1993). The majority of studies report figures on the high side of this range. In one 1964 survey, for example, 75% of 5,000 students at 99 different colleges and universities admitted to cheating in their courses at least once (Bowers, 1964). Nearly 30 years later, a similar survey of 6,000 students on 31 campuses found the figure to be 67% (McCabe & Trevino, 1993). Other studies indicate that 40% to 76% of college students self-report dishonest behavior on at least one exam or other graded assignment (Davis, Grover, Becker, McGregor, 1992; Davis & Ludvigson, 1995). In short, even if the true prevalence of academic dishonesty falls halfway between the 9% and 95% extremes, you are going to have to deal with academic dishonesty in virtually all of your courses.

The problem is perpetuated, in part, by students' perceptions that "everyone does it," and that dishonest students are unlikely to be caught, let alone severely punished (Davis et al., 1992; Jendrek, 1992). This view seems to be popular even at smaller institutions where students are less anonymous; 89% of students at one small private college reported that they had been dishonest at least once (Graham, Monday, & O'Brien, 1994). The irony in the situation is that more than 90% of college students say that academic dishonesty is wrong, and that their teachers should not ignore the problem. Yet many faculty members do ignore it, and might thus serve to encourage academic dishonesty (Davis & Ludvigson, 1995). The literature on faculty responses to academic dishonesty suggests that as few as 20% of teachers report dishonest students to their department head or other academic official; some don't even talk to the offending student, perhaps because they prefer to avoid the interpersonal and administrative hassles that will ensue (Jendrek, 1989; McCabe, 1993). According to one report:

> Many faculty members have in fact disengaged from actively attempting to deter cheating, feeling that they will not be supported at the administrative level. Others just do not care. Institutions must demonstrate their commitment to the enforce-

ment of policies on academic dishonesty and must provide the resources necessary to deter cheating at the classroom level. (Diekhoff et al., 1996, p. 501)

When faculty do decide to confront dishonest students, many do so in an informal, one-on-one private meeting. This approach can be ill advised, for several reasons. First, it might violate the rules and policies set out by the psychology department or the campus for dealing with cases of suspected academic dishonesty. Second, it creates a situation in which the teacher assumes the roles of judge, jury, and executioner. Without an impartial hearing conducted in accordance with campus rules, the accused student is not only denied due process, but might be in a position to bring a complaint against the teacher—who was only trying to be "nice." Finally, if your suspicions about a student's academic dishonesty are upheld by a formal hearing, this fact will be noted in the student's file in the records office, where it can serve to inform those who might have to deal with repeat offenders. In other words, if you don't report dishonest students, they might be able to cheat their way to a degree (Jendrek, 1989). With all this in mind, we always follow campus procedures relating to incidents of suspected academic dishonesty, all of which begin with a letter to the student (see Fig. 6.3).

Academic dishonesty is less prevalent on campuses where there are strict honor codes and where faculty take academic integrity seriously enough to define it, announce consequences for violations, and then actively watch for and respond vigorously to infractions (Davis & Ludvigson, 1995; Genereux & McLeod, 1995; May & Loyd, 1993; McCabe, 1993; McCabe & Bowers, 1994). Dishonesty is also less common among students who believe that their peers disapprove of it (Davis et al., 1992; McCabe & Trevino, 1997). Indeed, the key to reducing academic dishonesty might lie in confronting our students early on with the moral and ethical issues involved, as well as with the possible consequences of infractions of academic standards (Jendrek, 1992). "In the final analysis, the most important question to ask concerning academic dishonesty may be how an institution can create an environment where academic dishonesty is socially unacceptable" (McCabe & Trevino, 1993, p. 534).

Categories of Academic Dishonesty

The code of student conduct published by the university where we have spent most of our teaching careers (University of Illinois, 2003-http://www2.uiuc.edu/admin_manual/code/rule_33.html) contains a

STUDENT NAME
ADDRESS
DATE

Dear Ms./Mr. _____ :

I am sorry to inform you that I believe you are guilty of an infraction of the code of academic integrity. Specifically, I believe that you and another student were sharing answers on the Psychology xxx examination, on the evening of October xx, 20xx. Under Rule 33, Section III, A of the Code of Policies and Regulations Applying to Students I am required to notify you of my belief; this letter is that notification. If you have any questions about the procedures, you may check with the Dean of Students in your college, or the Associate Head for Undergraduate Affairs in the Psychology Department.

You have a reasonable time in which to respond to the allegation. After receiving this notification, however, you may not drop my course. When I have received your response to this notification, or if I have not heard from you by [15 days after date of letter], I will continue following the procedures of Rule 33, Section III. Those procedures can include a hearing if you so desire. If after those procedures are complete, I conclude that you are guilty of academic dishonesty, I shall decide on the appropriate penalty and inform you of my decision, and of your right to appeal it.

You may contact me at [office address].

Yours truly,

INSTRUCTOR NAME

cc: _____ , Head, Department of Psychology

_____ , Associate Head for Undergraduate Affairs

_____ [Dean of the student's college]

FIG. 6.3.   Sample letters following suspicion of academic dishonesty. The first letter shown here establishes the allegation of academic dishonesty. The second letter reports the results of a hearing on the allegation. The content of these letters should be clear and specific and closely related to campus rules, regulations, and procedures regarding academic dishonesty.

(continued)

STUDENT NAME
ADDRESS
DATE

Dear Ms./Mr. _____:

As I recently informed you by letter, I believe you were guilty of academic dishonesty during the Psychology xxx examination on the evening of October xx, 20xx. As stated in that letter, I feel that you were sharing answers with another student on that examination.

I indicated in my letter that if you wished to respond to the allegation you should do so in a reasonable time as indicated in Rule 33, Section III, A, of the Code of Policies and Regulations Applying to Students at the Urbana-Champaign Campus. You have now had a chance to respond to this allegation. In a meeting attended by you, the Associate Head of the Psychology Department, and me, you indicated that you didn't think this infraction occurred. Nevertheless, on the basis of my observations, and that of an exam proctor who drew your behavior to my attention, I conclude that the cheating did in fact occur. As Section III, D, of Rule 33 indicates, I must decide on the penalty and inform you and the Department Head in writing of my decision.

I have decided to impose penalty 2 under Section II, A, of Rule 33: a reduced grade on the assignment. I am therefore, reducing your grade on the first examination in Psychology xxx from the "D" your score of 19 out of 30 would have earned to an "F."

As Section III, D, of Rule 33 indicates, you should be aware of the procedures in Rule 33 and that you have the right to appeal my decision. You may do so by writing to the Head of the Department of Psychology within 15 days of this notification. Her contact information is as follows: SUPPLY NAME AND ADDRESS OF DEPARTMENT HEAD.

If you have any questions about these procedures, you may check with the Dean of Students in your college, or the Psychology Department's Associate Head for Undergraduate Affairs.

Yours truly,
INSTRUCTOR NAME
TITLE

cc: _____Head, Department of Psychology

_____ Associate Head for Undergraduate Affairs

_____[Dean of the student's college]

section that, in our view, does a good job of defining various forms of academic dishonesty. Accordingly, we use the structure of this code as a framework for organizing our discussion of academic dishonesty and how to deal with it. We address academic dishonesty that takes the form of cheating; fabrication; facilitating infractions of academic integrity; plagiarism; bribes, favors, and threats; and academic interference. These categories, and their definitions, might or might not exactly match those prevailing at your institution, but we hope that the sections to follow will help you recognize (a) the scope of dishonest behaviors, and (b) the need to educate yourself, and your students, about what constitutes dishonest behavior and how it is dealt with in your department and on your campus. In the course of our discussion we suggest some ways in which you can help students avoid inadvertent acts of academic dishonesty, but the most important step you can take is to give each student a copy of your campus's academic integrity code, reproduce relevant sections of it in your syllabus, or assign it as required reading. Some of your students might not realize that they are bound by this code, so if you make a point of familiarizing them with its requirements, the code will be more likely to have a guiding, and deterrent, effect.

Cheating. *Cheating* is defined as "using or attempting to use in any academic exercise materials, information, study aids, or electronic data that the student knows or should know is unauthorized. During examinations, students should assume that external assistance (e.g., books, notes, calculators, conversations with others) is prohibited unless specifically authorized by the instructor."

If during an exam or quiz, you suspect that a student is looking at another student's answer sheet, or giving help to other students nearby, quietly move the suspected cheater(s), mark the student's answer form to identify the point at which you intervened, and allow the student to complete the test. The same goes for the discovery of a "cheat sheet" or other unauthorized material, which should be confiscated before allowing the student to continue. When the test is handed in, make an appointment to meet with the student as soon as possible, ideally later that day. We suggest allowing cheating suspects to finish their tests because, in the event that the student has a satisfactory explanation for the apparent cheating, you will not have to re-administer the test or create a new one.

It is also cheating if students allow others to conduct research or prepare any work for them without your prior authorization. This aspect of the cheating concept includes, but is not limited to, the services of commercial term paper companies. In addition, "substantial portions of the same academic work may not be submitted for credit more than once without authorization." This aspect of cheating is often misunderstood by college students, many of whom believe that once they create a piece of work, they can use it as they see fit. You can reduce the frequency of this form of cheating simply by referring to it when making a writing assignment. If you are assigning a book report or a paper, for example, be explicit that you want students to read a book they have never read before or address a topic they have not written about in the past.

Fabrication. *Fabrication* is defined as "unauthorized falsification or invention of any information or citation in an academic endeavor. 'Invented' information may not be used in any laboratory experiment or other academic endeavor without notice to and authorization from the instructor or examiner. Reliance upon the actual source from which cited information was obtained must be acknowledged. Fabrication also includes altering the answers given for an exam after the examination has been graded and submitting false documents for the purpose of being excused from a scheduled examination or other academic assignment."

This form of dishonesty is usually reasonably easy to detect by checking the source of suspect written material, but do take special care when allowing students to review their exam answer sheets, especially if they are multiple-choice forms. One of our students altered his answer sheet during the time we gave him to check it for scoring accuracy against our answer key. He then claimed that the optical scanner had erred in scoring his test and asked us to change his grade. Given that a scanner error is virtually impossible on a properly marked test form, we confronted the student with our suspicions and he admitted his deceit.

To prevent postgrading tampering with written work, we suggest that you not accept papers or other graded assignments unless they are typed. When grading essay exams or short-answer questions that were written in class, you might want to subtly mark areas where substantial erasures appear so that you can remember where these areas were later, if necessary.

You can also prevent fabrication by not allowing students to exchange and grade each other's quizzes or other assignments. In fact, as described later, this practice is actually prohibited in the United

States by the Family Educational Rights and Privacy Act of 1974 (FERPA), which makes it illegal to give students access to grade information about other students.

Facilitating Infractions of Academic Integrity.

Facilitating infractions of academic integrity is defined as "helping or attempting to help another to commit an infraction of academic integrity, where one knows or should know that through one's acts or omissions such an infraction may be facilitated." Both the person who facilitates the infraction and the one who benefits from it are guilty of academic dishonesty.

The most common example of this form of dishonesty occurs when students allow other students to see and copy from their work during an examination. To minimize this problem, we use two forms of every exam, and when space allows, we ask students to leave at least one empty seat between themselves and the person next to them. Before the exam begins, we announce that if we think anyone is looking at someone else's work, we will move them—or the person who was being watched—to a different seat. This warning not only puts students on notice to keep their eyes on their own work, but minimizes discomfort for any students we decide to move.

Another example of facilitating an infraction is impersonating another student for the purpose of taking an exam for that student. This scam is especially likely to occur in large classes in which the teacher and/or exam proctors do not know all students by sight. The best preventive measure in such cases is to require all students to show a photo identification card before entering the exam room.

Plagiarism.

Plagiarism is defined as "representing the words or ideas of another as one's own in any academic endeavor. This includes copying another student's paper or working with another person when both submit similar papers to satisfy an individual, not a group, assignment, without authorization. It also includes direct quotation without citation, and paraphrasing without prompt acknowledgment. Information obtained in one's reading or research that is not common knowledge should be acknowledged."

Aside from cheating, plagiarism is probably the most common type of academic dishonesty that you will encounter. Accordingly, find out what your institution's and department's plagiarism policies are before you have to deal with your first suspected case. Further, as with cheating and other forms of academic dishonesty, deterring the problem of plagiarism is easier than dealing with its aftermath. So design your writing assignments to be so specific that it will be difficult or impossible to find existing prototypes. A paper on "application of human factors technology to the design of hospital bed controls" will probably not be available on the Web, but there are probably several on "application of human factors technology in equipment design." If you allow students to choose their own topics, insist on reading and approving an outline of their proposed papers beforehand. Require students to turn in first drafts as they work on their papers; this not only helps assure that students are doing their own work, but it helps them get a better grade on the final draft.

Spotting plagiarism is often not too difficult. Look for papers that are only marginally related to the assignment; those with a tone or style that varies from the student's previous writing; that contains statistics and references not readily accessible to the student; that contain unexpectedly few grammatical errors; and, of course, papers that are extremely similar to one another (Curzan & Damour, 2000).

Bribes, Favors, Threats. Academic dishonesty can also include *bribes, favors,* or *threats.* As their names imply, these infractions are defined as "attempting to bribe, promising favors to, or making threats against any person with the intention of affecting a record of a grade or evaluation of academic performance." Although student behaviors in this category happen rarely, and might never happen to you, you should be aware that it is unacceptable for a student to offer you money, or anything else of value (including, say, free meals at a relative's restaurant, or discounts at a friend's store), or to propose washing your car or painting your house, or the like, in exchange for a better grade or other academic consideration. Threatening your health or safety, too, is a wholly unacceptable way to try to improve one's grade. In the only such case that either of us have experienced, a large, angry student threatened to "mess up" his instructor if the student did not get the extra points he felt he deserved. Remaining calm (outwardly at least), the instructor picked up his office phone and called the campus police to report the situation. The startled student realized he had made a serious mistake and was abjectly apologizing by the time officers arrived. You might decide to handle such a situation in a different way, but we recommend that you never ignore threatening behavior; the very few students who engage in it must immediately discover that it will get them nowhere.

Academic Interference.   *Academic interference* is defined as "tampering with, altering, circumventing, or destroying any educational material or resources in a manner which deprives any student fair access or reasonable use of that material or resource." These offenses tend to occur when a scarce resource, such as an article or book on reserve in the library, is stolen or damaged by one of the numerous students who are supposed to be sharing it. You can prevent this problem by placing multiple copies of required resources on library reserve, or better yet, by posting them on your course's Web site. As always, be sure that electronic posting does not violate any copyright laws. Indeed, a whole variety of computer-related academic infractions defined by applicable laws, contracts, or campus policies—such as unauthorized use of computer licenses, copyrighted materials, and intellectual property—apply to you to the same extent that they do to your students.

Responding to Proven Cases of Academic Dishonesty

As suggested by our earlier comments, the course syllabi for our introductory psychology courses incorporate a section on avoiding academic dishonesty. It defines each kind of academic dishonesty, and gives some illustrative examples. The section concludes with this statement:

> The psychology department and your instructor view all infractions of academic integrity as serious offenses. If it is determined that an infraction of academic integrity has occurred on examinations, papers, or other assignments, the policy in this class, and in the department, is that disciplinary action will be taken as follows: (1) a grade of "F" or "zero" will be recorded for the examination, paper, or assignment in question, and (2) a letter will be forwarded to the head of the psychology department recommending that procedures be implemented to drop the offending student(s) from the class with a grade of "F" and to recommend suspension or dismissal from the University.

ENHANCING STUDENTS' MOTIVATION TO LEARN

While we are dwelling on some students' less than ideal behavior, consider these assessments of college students in general:

> The general level of intellectual interest among undergraduates is low. Their collective life is not characterized by intellectual curiosity and intelligent discussion.

> With the general obscuring of college's original purpose and function, it has unfortunately become a kind of glorified playground. It has become the paradise of the young.

These sentiments might have been expressed last week at a psychology faculty meeting, but they were actually written more than 70 years ago (Angell, 1928, p. 2; Gauss, 1930, p. 18). Obviously, concern over students' apparent lack of motivation to learn what we want to teach them has a long and distinguished history. It is also a topic of lively discussion, and complaint, at every teaching conference we have ever attended. Some instructors feel responsible for motivating students to succeed in their courses and to invest the amount of time and work necessary to do so. The ideal student, these instructors claim, is the person who is driven by intrinsic motivation, especially by a love of learning and a desire to acquire knowledge for its own sake (McKinney, 1999). These instructors tend to be disappointed and scornful when they realize that the behavior of even their best students is motivated to a considerable extent by extrinsic factors, particularly grades, and the points that determine those grades.

The fact is that some students today seem to care only about getting high grades, and as research on academic dishonesty shows, will apparently do anything to accomplish this goal. Academic dishonesty is inexcusable, in our view, but the grade orientation that underlies it should come as no surprise. After all, achieving good grades is a main gateway to the occupational and financial success that students in Western cultures are taught to want. The irony, of course is that, in the 1960s, many professors were just as scornful of students who cared only about intellectual engagement, questioning what they were told, and rejecting the grades and other job-oriented goals that the "establishment" set for them. In any case, most teachers today find teaching more enjoyable when their students care about the material they are learning, as well as about the grades they will earn for learning it.

Making Your Course Intrinsically Interesting

We think there are several ways in which you can help students find a more balanced blend of extrinsic and intrinsic motivation in your courses (see Bergin, 1999). For one thing, as described in Chapter 3, be sure at the outset that your students understand the structure and goals of the course. If students see the course as an organized whole, they tend to be more motivated to succeed in it than if they perceive it as an obstacle course made up of seemingly pointless and unrelated tasks (Beard & Senior, 1980). Second, do all you can to make your course content and your presentations as varied and interesting as possible. Chapter 4 contains several suggestions for doing this, including the liberal use of demonstrations, active learning strategies, critical thinking exercises, and the like. Challenging your students to engage the material rather than just read about it can make it more likely that they will actually begin to want to learn more. Don't forget to describe and illustrate the importance of each new topic, and how it relates to aspects of everyday life that are important to your students (Forsyth & McMillan, 1991). For example, if you are lecturing on color vision, let students test themselves for color blindness; in covering memory, include demonstrations of how students can improve performance on a mock quiz by using mnemonics and other memory enhancement tools.

Students are also more motivated to learn when they are given a measure of control about what they are learning (Forsyth & McMillan, 1991). Rather than assigning all students to write about the same topic, offer them the choice of several topics, or several variations on a main topic.

Finally, let students experience your enthusiasm for the course content and for learning itself. Tell them about some of the psychology books you are reading, information you obtained at a conference, or recent news events that are related to the course (McKinney, 1999). One of us gives her students a list of "summer reading" suggestions about each topic covered in class; to increase students' motivation to actually read these items, she provides a preview of their most interesting aspects. In other words, assume that, once they begin to discover the course material, your students will become just as enthusiastic about it as you are; some of them actually will (Mester & Tauber, 2000)!

Teaching Style, Student Motivation, and Attendance

When psychology teachers fail to display the caring, enthusiasm, immediacy, and other elements of effective teaching that we have described in this book, students are likely to see class attendance as a necessary evil or a tedious chore (Sleigh et al., 2002). One survey found that over two thirds of students would miss class more often than they already do if they could get a copy of the professor's lecture notes (Sleigh & Ritzer, 2001). Another survey found that the most important factor influencing student attendance was the amount of lecture material they thought would appear on exams (Sleigh et al., 2002).

Yet students who attend classes on a regular basis tend to perform better on exams and papers than students who attend infrequently (Moore, 2003; Shimoff & Catania, 2001). If you believe that it is important for students to attend your classes, there are several ways you can motivate them to do so. For one thing, you can let students know that you will be testing them on material that will be presented only in class. Another alternative is to take attendance every day. This simple step can dramatically increase attendance, even if attendance does not affect final grades (Shimoff & Catania, 2001). Just knowing that their name will be called in class, or that it will not appear on a daily sign-in sheet, can be enough to bring some students to class. Giving unannounced quizzes or extra credit test items at the end of class on randomly selected days can also motivate students to attend more regularly. Finally, you can make attendance mandatory or penalize students for missing classes. One instructor, whose policy is to give a failing grade to students who miss more than three class sessions, included the following rationale in her syllabus:

> This course is based on the concept that working with other learners and creating a healthy exchange of conflicting ideas and differing viewpoints encourages rethinking of accepted perspectives. Because that kind of interaction involves taking some risks and making choices, it is important to have a supportive atmosphere and to use active listening. Everyone is expected to facilitate this with consistent attendance and input. (Heuberger, Gerber, & Anderson, 1999, p. 111)

Although many faculty disagree with us, we don't favor mandatory attendance policies. True, students who attend more classes tend to do better in the course, but this relationship only appears in situations where attendance is voluntary. It might reflect the impact of some students' generally high level of motivation (or stress tolerance), not necessarily the benefits of being in class. As one observer put it,

> Students who are motivated enough to attend class consistently are also probably motivated enough to study outside of class, read and study the course textbook, turn in assignments on time, and attend help sessions. Together, these activities greatly increase students' time-on-task and, as a result, increase learning and improve grades. (Moore, 2003, p. 370)

In other words, forcing students to come to class might expose them to more course material, but it might not improve their performance. Because most people don't like to be forced to do things, mandatory attendance policies can create resentment, hostility, and disengagement—even among students who would have come to class voluntarily.

Although we agree that attendance should not be mandatory, we long ago agreed to disagree on how much to emphasize attendance. One of us never mentions attendance. He sees himself offering a product and a service in which adult consumers have expressed at least a nominal interest, and he allows them to decide how much of that product and service they wish to use. At the same time, he sees it as his job to make the product (psychology) and the service (the teaching of psychology) as interesting and beneficial as possible. To him, patterns of voluntary attendance serve as a barometer of how interesting his classes are, at least in terms of motivating students to show up for them. If classroom attendance is relatively high regardless of the topic being covered (or when the next quiz or exam is scheduled), he can be fairly sure that his teaching style is sufficiently engaging to make students want to hear what he has to say (Friedman, Rodriguez, & McComb, 2001). If attendance is consistently lower than normal for certain scheduled topics, he tries to find ways to make those topics more interesting, while maintaining his standards for course quality. (He could probably fill every seat at every class by doing a comedy routine or showing provocative videos, but this is not what we have in mind.)

Your other author feels that many students, especially first-year students, do not recognize the potential value of coming to class. She feels that it is only when most students attend consistently that a good classroom environment can be established. Accordingly, she stresses the importance of attendance, offers regular reminders of the material to be covered at the next class session, and lets her students know that she hopes they will show up. Her syllabus states that "Attendance is very important in this class. You miss important information and the class misses your input every time you are not in class. I will take attendance every day, not to penalize you if you are absent, but to match names and faces. If you must miss class, be sure to talk to a classmate who was in attendance to get the day's notes and assignments." This information can be especially influential in large classes, where students often feel that they won't be missed and that they won't miss anything if they skip class (Moore, 2003).

Whatever attendance policy you choose for your own courses, stick to it. Make it explicit in your syllabus, and explain your rationale for it in person.

The Role of Students' Goals and Attributional Processes

As mentioned briefly in Chapter 1, research by Dweck and her colleagues suggests that students vary in their academic goals and attributional tendencies, both of which can strongly influence their response to you, your course requirements, your assignments, your grading system, and your efforts to motivate diligent study habits (Dweck, 1986; Molden & Dweck, 2000). According to Dweck, some students approach your course with a mastery orientation, whereas others tend to be performance-oriented. Those with a *mastery orientation* are more interested in acquiring skills and learning course content than in how their performance will be evaluated (Svinicki, 1998). These students, who are also referred to as learning-oriented, are motivated to increase their competence, to seek challenges that foster learning, and to persist in the face of difficulty (Mayer & Sutton, 1996). When they seek help, students with a learning orientation are likely to ask for explanations, hints, and other forms of task-related information, not for quick, easy answers that remove the challenge from the situation. They experience satisfaction in learning for its own sake. Further, mastery-oriented students tend to view intelligence as fluid, not fixed; thus they do not become too upset by obstacles or failures because they do not see these as indicating a general lack of ability (Dweck & Leggett, 1988; Svinicki, 1998).

In contrast, *performance-oriented* students tend to be more interested in appearing "smart" than in the process and benefits of learning itself. Dweck (1986) described performance-oriented students as being motivated to attain positive evaluations, and to avoid negative ones, which leads them to avoid challenges when possible, and to be less persistent at difficult tasks before asking for help. They usually just want the right answer, not tips on how to find the right answer themselves. Performance-oriented students tend to view their successes as personal achievements that make them "smart" relative to others (Svinicki, 1998). They also tend to view intelligence as a fixed characteristic; they are likely to be upset by failure at an academic task because it indicates a general lack of ability (Dweck & Leggett, 1988; Svinicki, 1998).

Notice that a key difference between these two motivational patterns lies in how students interpret failure:

> From the learning goals perspective, mistakes are a signal to try harder or to alter your strategy. From the performance goal perspective, mistakes are a signal that you lack ability and may as

well give up trying. When students encounter difficult material or when they receive a poor score on an early exam, there is a tendency to experience feelings of learned helplessness. Students may shy away from academic challenges because they believe that making mistakes or exerting too much effort both reflect low ability. (Eppler & Harju, 1997, p. 571)

These varying orientations tend to be consistent in particular individuals, but can shift somewhat in response to experience and situational factors. A student who is competent in, say, mathematics might display a mastery orientation in a new math course, but a lack of confidence in musical ability might lead the same student to adopt a performance orientation in a music class (Svinicki, 1998). Keep this in mind when you meet with students to discuss the problems they might be having in your course. It might be useful to help them identify the role that their goals and attributional tendencies play in creating these problems. This is particularly true when dealing with "grade-grubbers"—students whose utter focus on grades and tenacity in arguing over every point on every quiz or exam can drive teachers to distraction. You might be able to help these students see that their preoccupation with grades rather than with actually learning course content makes it all too easy to become discouraged about a low quiz score, especially if they see failure as indictment of their mental ability. Point out, too, that if they let a failure experience make them feel stupid, they might start devoting less time to your course and more time to courses that make them feel "smart." The end result could be an unnecessarily poor grade in your course. Encourage these students to view low scores as a wake-up call, not a threat to their sense of self-worth, and work with them to develop a specific plan for spending more, not less, time studying material for your next quiz.

PROVIDING ACADEMIC HELP

Our discussion of students' goals and attributional patterns should serve as a reminder that students arrive in your classroom with widely varying amounts of ability, motivation, and academic preparation. Some researchers also suggest that students have differing learning styles that respond best to certain channels of information input. It would be nice to have the time and energy to work with students individually to improve their study habits and organize their academic efforts, but most psychology teachers don't have enough of either. Fortunately, there are other, more general things you can do to help all your students do their best in your courses.

For example, you can include in your syllabus a section on "How to Do Well in This Course," which offers a detailed list of what it takes to succeed in the course (Pastorino, 1999). In our own syllabi, we stress the importance of keeping up with the readings, we encourage students to study for the quizzes and exams by using the practice quizzes and exams that appear in their student study guide, and we have even provided statistical summaries from previous classes to show given grade breakdowns based on the percentage of assignments completed, showing how students' efforts in completing various assignments are related to final grades.

Let's now consider some additional suggestions for helping your students more effectively organize and think about the material to be learned, develop their study skills, and keep up with their reading assignments.

Providing Advance Organizers

Advance organizers serve to help students fit new course information into the framework of previously learned material (Ausubel, 1968, 2000; Ausubel, Novak, & Hanesian, 1978). This idea stems from research in cognitive psychology showing that it is easier to learn and remember new information if it can be related to information already in memory (Hilton, 1986; Palmisano & Herrmann, 1991).

For example, we typically jot down an outline of each day's lecture in a corner of the blackboard. If it is a continuation of a previous lecture, we include the earlier topics, too. This way, students can not only see how today's session will be organized, and how the topics are related to one another, but how new topics are related to what we covered earlier. You can also build advance organizers into your lectures. If you have already presented information about attachment theories in the developmental section of your introductory psychology course, you can refer back to that information (perhaps spending 5 minutes on it as a refresher) when covering object relations theories of personality and psychopathology later in the course. By reintroducing the concept of attachment, you are providing an advance organizer that can make it easier for your students to learn and remember information about object relations theory. We think that advance organizers are especially important in an introductory course, where the pace of presentation tends to be rapid and where it is easy for students to lose focus on how seemingly unrelated topics are in fact linked to one another.

Draw your students' attention, too, to the advance organizers that might appear in their textbook. These organizers usually take the form of chapter outlines, preview questions, or features that highlight linkages between new material and material covered in previous chapters.

Promoting Effective Study Skills

Students who come to college with marginal study skills will face an uphill battle in many of their psychology courses. Some of them might be aware that they are at a disadvantage, but even some students who did well in high school might suddenly discover that they lack the study skills required for success in psychology. To help our students, especially those in their first year of college, we distribute and discuss a list of basic "Studying Dos and Don'ts" (see Table 6.2). One of our colleagues distributes a similar, but much longer handout to just those students who fail his first exam (Hendersen, 2002b). Entitled "Responding to Failure: A Survival Guide," the handout encourages these students to meet with the instructor, but also provides detailed information about developing effective study strategies, including questions to ask oneself while reading the textbook, how to best use lecture notes, how to use the textbook, the value of study groups, the pitfalls of rote memorization, the importance of a proper study environment, and the need to devote adequate time to studying.

Note-Taking.   A clear and organized set of lecture notes is an important resource for effective studying, but many students are not as skilled at note-taking as they should be. If you want proof of this assertion, try this: At the end of a lecture, ask a few of your students to show you the notes they took for that class session. The results of this exercise can be disconcerting, because although you might have presented a first-rate lecture, full of well-organized content, vivid examples, and clever mechanisms for showing how all the topics are related to each other, some of the information might have been distorted in translation into students' notes, and the essential elements of the lecture might never have reached the students' notebooks at all. One study of student note-taking found that, at the end of a lecture, about half of the students had written no more than half a page of notes.

One way to help students to improve their note-taking skills is to expose them to information on the importance of good note-taking,

TABLE 6.2

A Handout on Study Dos and Don'ts

GENERAL STUDY SUGGESTIONS

There are two important keys to doing well in psychology and most other academic areas. First, you must be an *active* learner, not a passive sponge. Second, you must organize course information and understand how it all fits together.

In order to remember information you must actively process that information at more than a surface level. Listed below are three study "Don'ts," some study methods that rob you of the chance to process the information you are learning beyond a surface level.

1. *Don't underline your textbook.* It is too easy to underline material without thinking very deeply about it.
2. *Don't study by simply repeating material to yourself.* It is easy to fool yourself into believing that you understand material when you actually don't.
3. *Don't "cram" for exams.* Cramming is not an effective way to learn the material. Consolidating your memories and finding "hooks" that help you to hold new information in long-term memory take some time, but work better. Many relatively short practice sessions distributed over a period of time have been proven to aid memory better than one long practice session immediately before a memory test.

Instead, we suggest you follow these study "Dos" because they are more likely to help you learn and remember course material.

1. *Do take notes during lectures and while reading the textbook.* After completing each chapter, take time to integrate your notes from the text and from the related lectures into a comprehensive outline of the material. Review this outline periodically throughout the term, and use it as a study aid when a quiz or exam approaches. Studying a familiar outline will make it much easier to do well on a test.
2. *Do study with other people, if possible.* Ask each other questions about the material, and even give each other mini-lectures on the material to be sure you understand it. You benefit in two ways when you study with other people. First, hearing material presented again by a peer might make it easier to understand. Second, in getting ready to teach material to someone else, you will process the material more deeply yourself, and you will discover what information you do and do not yet understand. If you can't study with another person, try posing questions to yourself, then answering them aloud without using notes or the textbook.

OTHER SUGGESTIONS FOR SUCCEEDING IN YOUR CLASSES

1. *Keep up with the reading.* Many courses, especially survey courses, require extensive reading. You need to read the assigned material when it is assigned, so that you will be able to ask questions and know what you don't understand during the lecture.

(continued)

TABLE 6.2 *(continued)*

2. *Attend class regularly.* Being in class on a regular basis allows you to make the best use of the lecture material and administrative announcements concerning the course. When you do not attend class, you may be missing crucial material.

3. *Apply what you learn.* Many exam and quiz questions will require you to apply the concepts that you have learned. If you have only memorized definitions without understanding how the concepts fit together and how they are applied, you may have a difficult time. To help you think more deeply about course content and how it can be applied, we offer the following suggestions.

   a. If there is a study guide for your course, use it to review what you have read and as a double-check on your understanding of the course material.

   b. Take a practice exam if one was provided to you by your instructor. To get the most out of a practice exam, take it under realistic conditions. This means finding a quiet place to work (such as the library), limiting yourself to the amount of time you will actually have during the exam, and not looking up answers until you have finished. After you score the practice exam you should have a good idea of which concepts you understand and which require further study.

4. *Be responsible in completing all course requirements.* Use a calendar to keep track of all quizzes, exams, paper assignments, and other course requirements, and mark their deadlines so you can get ready for each of them in plenty of time.

5. *Seek out your instructor if you have questions about the material or need help with study skills.* All instructors have posted office hours, and most offer the opportunity to ask for help via e-mail.

Following our suggestions requires a time investment, but it is time well spent, and it will pay off when you take your exams. GOOD LUCK!!

and how to do it more effectively. We recommend to our students that they read *How to Study in College* (Pauk, 2001), and those who have done so tell us that the section on note-taking was extremely valuable.

A second way to improve students' note-taking is to make it clear during lectures that certain kinds of information are of special importance. Accordingly, as suggested in Chapter 4, be sure that key terms and main concepts appear on your blackboard, overhead projector, or computer screen as you talk about them. Students are more likely to take notes on information that arrives through more than one sensory channel. One study found that almost all students took notes on all the information a lecturer had presented both orally and in writing, but that only about 27% did so when important information was only presented orally. Further, it was the academically marginal students who benefitted most from the instructor's use of visual displays (Baker & Lombardi, 1985).

A third way to encourage students to take good notes is to plan activities that require them to use their notes for purposes other than studying for a quiz or exam. If students have to rely on their notes to do well at the next class, they will be more likely to review, clarify, and reorganize those notes soon after they take them. This process, in itself, helps students to process the information more deeply and remember it longer (Ashcroft & Foreman-Peck, 1994). For example, the day after a lecture on the brain, we describe the symptoms of various neurological disorders, one patient at a time, and then ask our introductory psychology students to work in groups to determine which brain areas are impaired in each case. To guide them in this activity, the students are allowed to use only the notes they took during the previous lecture (and while reading the biological psychology chapter). The experience helps them realize how valuable note-taking can be—especially if the notes are complete and well-organized. Groups with the best notes tend to come up with good answers quickly. Students who come to class without notes are placed in "no-notes" groups and have to come up with answers using only the textbook. These students tend not to do as well on the activity, and soon recognize that there is no substitute for good notes.

To further emphasize this point, you might consider giving quizzes, or even exams, during which students can refer to the notes they have taken in class and while reading the textbook. A variant on this idea is to allow students to bring one page of notes into a quiz or exam (specify a minimum font size). This option virtually guarantees that students will not only study for the exam, but will more actively process course material, if only to decide what information is important enough to include on their one precious page of notes.

Some psychology teachers believe that the ultimate way to assure that students have good lecture notes is to give them copies of the notes the teachers use to deliver their lectures. It is not uncommon nowadays for faculty to post their lecture notes on a course Web site and to ask their students to download them before coming to class. This option assures that the students will have the lecture information in written form, but it runs the risk that these printed notes will become just another batch of written material that many students will ignore until it is time to cram for the next quiz or exam. We prefer a version of this plan whereby the instructor provides students with a handout containing a bare-bones outline of each lecture, with lots of space between sections in which students can jot down the important details of each topic (Ashcroft & Foreman-Peck, 1994). Our preference is based on the notion that putting lecture content into a student's own words will help the student to better process and remember the information.

Encouraging Students to Read

One of the most frustrating experiences we know of in teaching psychology is to give a lecture to students who have not read the material that provides the basis and the background for the presentation. Unfortunately, it is also a common experience. Without taking special steps to encourage students to complete their reading assignments, you can safely assume that many, and perhaps most, of them will not have done so. This realization can undermine the faculty–student relationship because it is easy to take offense, and to attribute the students' behavior to lack of motivation, irresponsibility, or other negative characteristics. These attributions, in turn, lead some teachers to become less caring and responsible themselves (e.g., "If they can't bother to do their reading assignments, I can't be bothered to show up for my office hours.")

The truth is, of course, that some students don't care about you or your course, and you might not be able to do anything about that. Try not to take this personally, and don't let those few students poison the classroom atmosphere or your relationship with the rest of the class. Remember that when it comes to reading assignments, most students have every intention of being responsible. When they fail to keep up with their reading, the problem could be poor time management; the demands of work, family, and other courses; or even some form of reading disability. In talking to students who experience these problems, suggest that they seek help through whatever time-management, study skill, or rehabilitative programs your campus has to offer. In many other cases, though, students who initially kept up with the readings stop doing so simply because they see no obvious connection between what is going on in class and what they are being asked to read (Satterlee & Lau, 2003). If students see your reading list as irrelevant to understanding your lectures, some of them will devote their study time to reading assignments in other courses until your exam or quiz is imminent.

To prevent this situation, make sure that your students are rewarded during lectures for completing their reading assignments. During lectures, refer to the readings whenever it is appropriate, and stop occasionally to point out, or to ask students, how something you have said is dealt with in that day's reading assignment. Another way to reward students for reading is to assign short take-home exams that require students to read the text and critically analyze the material (Boyd, 2003). Yet another is to give points in class for correctly answering one or two questions from the material that everyone should have read. Finally, to help reinforce the idea that you expect students to be reading their assignments, you might use a classroom assessment technique related to those assignments. For example, you could hand out 3 × 5 cards on random days and ask students to tell you, anonymously, what parts of that day's reading assignment they found clearest or most interesting, and what parts they found most confusing (Angelo & Cross, 1993; Satterlee & Lau, 2003).

At the very least, as described in Chapter 3, spend some time on the first day of class talking about the texts and other materials you have chosen and how they will relate to your course outline (Eble, 1988). Then, as the course proceeds, remind students of each week's reading assignment, why it is important, and how it will help them to understand the lectures (Boyd, 2003). This information is especially important when teaching first-year students. If, as is usually the case, time constraints prevent you from lecturing about everything that the students will be reading, let them know this at the outset. Let them know, too, however, if they will be tested on all that they read. If they will, point out that it will be easier to learn and remember the material if they read it as the course progresses rather than in a rush at the end. If the readings really do have nothing to do with the lectures, tell your students that, too. As we pointed out in Chapter 3, we know of a rather extreme case in which a student felt stupid because he couldn't see the relevance of the assigned readings, and went to his instructor for help with this "problem." The student was stunned when the professor revealed that though college rules required that a textbook be assigned, it played no part in the course and that students didn't actually have to read it (Satterlee & Lau, 2003). It would have been a much better idea to convey this information to the entire class on the first day!

In addition to explaining the relevance of the reading assignments, help your students to understand and use the book's pedagogical features (Boyd, 2003). Talking about the importance of boldface terms, highlighted text, critical thinking exercises, and chapter summaries and questions will help students get the maximum benefit out of their assigned readings. We have found that students often skip pedagogical features such as an introduction, or information that is set apart from the regular text, unless they are helped to see how important and valuable this information can be.

If your students require additional assistance with reading, consider offering them an advance organizer in the form of a list of major points to look for in each week's reading assignment. Some instructors even give students a list of lecture-related questions that they should try to answer as they do the reading. You might also offer your students some guidance in how to best organize their reading. For example, suggest that, before beginning to read, they scan each chapter's outline and headings, and perhaps read the chapter summary to get an idea of what the chapter covers and how its topics are organized and related. Tell them, too, about any methods that you have found helpful in reading books and journal articles. Showing students what works for you might encourage them to try the same strategies as they approach their own reading (Satterlee & Lau, 2003).

If your students persist in ignoring their assigned readings, there is not much point in punishing them. Doing so will only create hostility in the class, and besides, students who fail to read will be punished enough on exams and quizzes. Instead, delve a bit into the cause of the problem. For example, you might hand out 3 × 5 cards on which students can anonymously tell you whether or not they are keeping up with the reading, and if not, why not (Satterlee & Lau, 2003). Reading these cards can give you a starting point for deciding what to do next, whether it be to consult with colleagues, set up (or alter) a reading-reinforcement system, or perhaps change textbooks.

Remember, though, that there is a limit on what you can and should do to help your students. Trying endlessly to save them from themselves could be counterproductive, especially in the case of individuals who choose not to put in the time or effort necessary to succeed (Coffman, 2003). In such cases, the consequences of students' past choices might ultimately be more influential in shaping future choices than anything that you can do. In other words, we urge you to do all you can to provide help and resources for students who are motivated to succeed but who lack certain skills and information. However, we don't think you are obligated to assume total responsibility for your students' learning.

PROTECTING STUDENTS' PRIVACY

Among the obligations that you do assume as a psychology teacher is the legal and ethical obligation to protect students' rights to privacy. This obligation is outlined in the APA's *Ethical Standards for Psycholo-*

gists and Code of Conduct (APA, 2002; Standard 7.04), as well as in FERPA, mentioned earlier. As outlined in FERPA, students' privacy rights extend to all educational records, including grades, and affect, but are not limited to, procedures for posting grades and returning graded assignments.

Many instructors are surprised to find, for example, that it is illegal to post quiz, exam, or final grades on an office door, or on a physical or electronic bulletin board using the last five digits of Social Security numbers to identify students. The only legally appropriate method of posting grades in a public place is to use a unique identifying number other than a Social Security number. To ease this process, many institutions have created random student ID numbers or established computerized grade books through which students can have access to their own score or grade, and can view statistics such as the mean, standard deviation, and frequency distribution of the class's scores, but cannot see anyone else's score or grade.

FERPA also bars teachers from returning papers, quizzes, exams, or other graded assignments in a manner that might allow students to see any score or grade other than their own. Accordingly, it is not acceptable to pass out stacks of graded material for students to pass through the classroom after finding their own result. Nor is it legal to place piles of graded material in the classroom and allow students to sort through them.

For further information about FERPA, visit the Web site of the University of Illinois, Urbana-Champaign, Office of Admissions and Records, where you will find a helpful tutorial at www.oar.uiuc.edu/staff/systems/ferpa_trng .

WRITING LETTERS OF RECOMMENDATION

One of the most common, but least anticipated, aspects of the faculty–student relationship appears in the form of requests from students to write letters of recommendation in support of their efforts to obtain employment, financial aid, study abroad, admission to graduate or professional school programs, or other opportunities. Many teachers find these requests to be a burden, not only because they can require considerable time and effort—especially when the student is an unknown quantity or when the student's characteristics are well known but not particularly commendable.

Our advice is to be honest with every student who requests a letter of recommendation. If you know the student well and feel comfortable writing a strong letter, say so, and perhaps ask for further information, such as the student's vita, a grade transcript, and a summary of the job or scholarship or program for which the student is applying. Having this information will allow you to write a personalized and appropriately targeted letter. Be sure to include in that letter as many details as truthfully possible about the student's excellent performance in your class. Employers, graduate schools, and scholarship committees are often looking for evidence of a well-rounded personality, so mention the student's extracurricular activities, communication skills, class participation and presentations, written work, and ability to interact with you and with fellow students. Go into as much detail as possible, describing, for example, the nature of the course requirements, the group work done in your class, and the student's role in it. End your letter by comparing the student with the other students you have taught and provide a short reprise of the student's strengths (Curzan & Damour, 2000).

If you don't feel that you can truthfully write a strong letter, tell the student. If the problem is simply that you do not know the student well enough (a common situation in larger classes), advise the person to seek a letter from another instructor who does. If these unfamiliar students tell you that none of their other instructors know them well, either, or that they have two good letter-writers lined up, but need a third letter to meet the requirements of an application package, you can offer to write what is essentially a form letter. Be sure to explain that this letter will contain only a statement that the student was a member of your class and earned a particular grade. Mention that you might also add a note about the grade distribution, and your general impression (if any) about the student's motivation and demeanor in the class. If you can't write a strong letter because you have little or nothing good to say about the student, and in fact, have some rather negative things to say, we suggest that you lay your cards on the table. In such cases, we say something like this: "Look, because of _____ , _____ , and _____ , I am really not the best person to write a letter for you. In fact, my letter might hurt rather than help your chances." Most students who hear this will immediately go elsewhere, but there have been a few cases in which such students urged us to write a letter anyway. Under these circumstances, your letter can be a fair-minded but candid assessment of the student's characteristics, abilities, and potential.

The first few letters of recommendation you write will probably be the most difficult and will take the most time, simply because you will not yet have a template to follow. To make the task easier, ask colleagues for examples of letters they have written (they will first have to remove identifying information), look at sample letters in other sources (e.g., Curzan & Damour, 2000), then ask one or more colleagues to read and comment on your first draft (again, identifying information should be removed). We offer some sample letters in Fig. 6.4.

Some students will give you printed recommendation forms on which you can write your letter, or which are to accompany your letter. Many of these forms have a place where the student can waive the right to see the letter you write. Some students fail to waive this right, but we recommend that they do so because the letter will have greater impact on the recipient if it is clear that the letter writer's comments were not influenced by concern over the student's reaction to them. This advice is especially appropriate, in our view, when you have been honest with the student about the kind of letter you can write.

ETHICS IN THE FACULTY–STUDENT RELATIONSHIPS

The APA's *Ethical Standards of Psychologists and Code of Conduct* (APA, 2002) does not focus much attention on ethical issues associated with teaching, but it does include some guidelines, some of which we have already mentioned. For example, Standard 7.03, Accuracy in Teaching, states that "psychologists take reasonable steps to ensure that course syllabi are accurate regarding subject matter to be covered, bases for evaluating progress, and the nature of course experiences. This standard does not preclude an instructor from modifying course content or requirements when the instructor considers it pedagogically necessary or desirable, so long as students are made aware of these modifications in a manner that enables them to fulfill course requirements." In other words, as described in Chapter 2, you should give thoughtful consideration to the construction of your syllabus and you should not arbitrarily deviate from it.

The same standard requires psychology teachers to "present psychological information accurately." Earlier, we applied this standard in recommending that you provide fair and balanced coverage in your courses, but we think it also refers to the obligation to keep your course material as current as possible. It is not only misleading to present out-of-date information in a psychology course, it is also unethical.

Dear _____:

Mr. Tyrone _____ has asked me to write in support of his application for _____. I am happy to do so. Tyrone was a student in my introductory psychology course at the University of Illinois, Urbana-Champaign during the fall semester of 2000. In a class of 110, Tyrone still stood out as an excellent student. He earned one of the highest grades in the course and demonstrated a wide variety of academic skills. For one thing, he was very responsible and involved in his education. My class met at 8:30 in the morning and he had a perfect attendance record. He was also an active participant in the class, and all of his assigned work was turned in on time and complete.

I require extensive writing, and different types of writing in my course. In addition to short-answer and essay questions on quizzes and exams, I make 12 "mini-assignments" (1–2 pages each) that require students to either apply a concept that they have recently learned or to be creative in developing new material. I also assign a major paper (10–15 pages) that requires students to watch a film with psychological content and then critically analyze how that film presented the psychological concept. The students are also required to read a journal article related to the film's psychological content and tie that article, the information presented in class, and their textbook information to a critical analysis of the film's portrayal of the psychological issue. I also require students to select a popular cartoon that relates to some topic in psychology and to tie the cartoon back to the textbook and classroom presentations. Tyrone received full credit on all of these writing assignments—an outstanding accomplishment.

Tyrone is not one to just follow the crowd. In class discussions he was articulate and thoughtful. And he was not afraid to present a viewpoint that was opposite to that of most students in the class. He was very attentive during class, making appropriate comments, asking and answering questions, and helping other students solve problems in some small-group exercises I assign in class.

Finally, Tyrone is a genuinely nice person. He is enthusiastic about learning, open to new experiences, optimistic, and gets along well with others. I very much enjoyed having him in my class. He is definitely in the top 10% of all undergraduate students that I have worked with in my 25 years of teaching.

If I can answer any further questions or provide any additional information, please do not hesitate to contact me. My office phone number is _____ and my e-mail address is _____.

Sincerely,

(continued)

(continued)

Dear _____ :

Ms. Tasha _____ has asked that I write in support of her application for admission to _____. Tasha was a student
in my introductory psychology class at the University of South
Florida during the fall semester 2000.

She earned only a C in the course, but I found Tasha to be a very
enthusiastic student, one who is more interested in learning course
material than in what grade she will receive at the end. She not
only displayed this interest in class discussions, but went beyond
normal course requirements in pursuit of current psychological information. Tasha was also faithful in attending class and turned in
all her assignments on time. She was also one of the few students in
the class who took advantage of the opportunity to have me read a
first draft of her term paper.

In summary, I believe that Tasha is a fine person and an eager student. While not outstanding academically in my course, she was a
pleasure to have in class. I hope you will give her your most serious
consideration. If I can be of further help, please do not hesitate to
contact me.

Sincerely,

___

Dear _____ :

Mr. Tom _____ has asked me to write in support of his application for _____. Tom was one of 350 students in my introductory psychology class at the University of Illinois, Urbana-
Champaign, during the spring semester of 2004 In such a large
class, it was difficult if not impossible to get to know all of my students, so my comments on Tom must be brief and limited. I do recall that he came to class regularly, and my records show that he
completed all course requirements on time and with distinction. He
earned an A in the course, and in my recent discussions with him,
he struck me as a student who is seriously interested in pursuing a
career in psychology.

I hope these few remarks are of use to you in your decision-making
process.

Sincerely,

FIG. 6.4. Sample letters of recommendation. Here are examples from our files of
a strong letter of recommendation for "Tyrone," a student we knew well; a weaker
letter for "Tasha," a student who did not impress us as much; and a "form" letter
for "Tom," a student whom we did not know at all well, but still wanted to support.

Much of the advice we give in this chapter about returning and reviewing quizzes, tests, and other graded assignments as soon as possible is consistent not only with effective teaching principles, but with APA Standard 7.06, which requires psychology faculty to provide timely and specific feedback to students. Similarly, our advice in Chapters 2 and 3 about clearly announcing your grading system, and sticking strictly to it, is in accord with another aspect of Standard 7.06, namely that students should know how they are going to be evaluated in the course and that evaluation be based solely on the announced criteria.

Of course, as already mentioned, Standard 7.07 warns psychology teachers not to engage in sexual relationships with students or anyone else over whom they have, or are likely to have, evaluative authority. In our view, there are no exceptions to this rule, and those who violate it are likely to be guilty of sexual harassment.

A much more extensive and specific treatment of the many ethical issues that arise in teaching is available in *The Ethics of Teaching: A Casebook*. Written by Patricia Keith-Spiegel and her colleagues, and sponsored by STP, the book discusses the ethics of teaching in relation to cases that have arisen in several different "venues" (Keith-Spiegel et al., 1993).

The first set of cases focus on the classroom, including issues related to classroom policies and decorum, student deportment in the classroom, and teachers' lecturing style. Another set of cases raises issues surrounding lessons and evaluations—including activities and assignments, assessment of students' progress, letters of recommendation, bias toward or against particular students, and academic dishonesty. The third set of cases centers on ethical issues relating to teachers' availability outside of the classroom, including their interactions with students when off campus.

The next section, called "Relationships in Academia," deals with cases involving dual roles, conflicts of interest, relationships with colleagues, sexual issues, exploitation of students, and supervising and collaborating with students. Cases in the section "Responsibilities to Students and Colleagues" pertain to instructor competence, confidentiality, political and public statements by teachers, and faculty use of campus resources. The casebook concludes with a consideration of ethical issues that are unique to teachers in psychology departments, including issues relating to supervising research, therapy, and psychological assessment.

We recommend that you read *The Ethics of Teaching*, and keep it handy so that you can easily refer to it whenever an ethically ambiguous situation arises in your own teaching.

SOME FINAL COMMENTS

We think that the best part of teaching psychology is the opportunity to work with and build productive relationships with students. We think that the worst part of teaching psychology is dealing with students whose characteristics and behavior make it hard to remember the best part. We hope that the guidelines and suggestions that we have provided will help you minimize the number of negative interactions you have with your students and maximize the positive ones

 (see Checklist 6.2).

Checklist 6.2
A checklist of items related to establishing
and maintaining productive
faculty–student relationships

1. Use your authority and power as a teacher in an ethical manner.
2. Establish rapport with your students by being positive, keeping a sense of humor, being available to students, and showing interest in them.
3. Display immediacy behaviors such as appearing relaxed, smiling, making eye contact with students, using an expressive speech style, and using appropriate movement and gestures.
4. Be inclusive of all students—use diverse references and examples, create mixed student groups, make eye contact with all students, and write inclusive questions for your quizzes and exams.
5. Invite students with special needs to contact you early in the semester. Evaluate these students' requests for accommodations in light of the integrity of your course and its goals.
6. Establish policies at the beginning of the term for dealing with late papers, missed exams, complaints about test items, grades, and other academic work issues, then adhere to those policies in relation to all students.
7. Minimize the likelihood of classroom incivilities by developing rules for classroom conduct, letting students know those rules, and then enforcing them.

8. If you have to deal with an angry student, maintain a composed and professional demeanor while allowing the student to vent views and feelings without interruption. Then discuss the problem in a rational manner to help the student learn what helpful steps or resources might be available.

9. Before teaching on a new campus, create a list of campus resources for helping students who are upset, troubled, or otherwise in need of assistance that are beyond the scope of your role as a teacher.

10. Become familiar with campus and departmental policies and procedures regarding academic dishonesty. Follow these guidelines carefully when you act on suspected cases of academic dishonesty in your classes.

11. Try to make your course intrinsically interesting by relating its content to students' lives, incorporating relevant new material, and presenting it in the most compelling manner possible.

12. Develop your attendance policy in light of your course goals; be sure your students know and understand your policy.

13. Become familiar with FERPA and your institution's guidelines concerning students' privacy rights. Always adhere to these guidelines in planning and teaching your courses.

14. Be aware of and follow the APA's ethical guidelines related to teaching.

Using Teaching Technology

The teaching tools that psychology faculty relied on in past decades—such as chalk and blackboards, marking pens and "whiteboards," overhead projectors and write-on transparencies, and audio- or videotape players—are now considered low-technology, or old technology. These labels make us feel old, because we can easily recall the days when VCRs were hailed as the high-tech replacement for the venerable 16mm film projector that most of us actually knew how to use. Today, of course, DVDs, PowerPoint slides, CD-ROMs, the Internet, and other computer-based digital devices offer a whole new range of high-technology teaching aids that, to the computer-literate, digitally immersed students enrolled on most campuses, are just another part of the educational landscape. They are not surprised—or even impressed—to find that their classroom is wired for live Internet access and allows all sorts of computer-driven displays to be dramatically and colorfully presented on giant screens. In fact, we suspect it won't be long before students will find it quaint, if not jarring, to encounter faculty who persist in using blackboards and overheads to get their classroom message across.

HIGH-TECH TEACHING TOOLS

There is no doubt that modern teaching technology provides exciting new ways for you to present information, as well as endless opportunities for creativity in communicating with your students and linking them to the rest of the world. When used appropriately, each of the technologies discussed in this chapter is capable of advancing the basic principles of effective teaching described in Chapter 1, especially encouraging student–faculty contact, active learning, and cooperation among students; providing students with prompt feedback; respecting diverse talents and ways of learning; being organized and prepared; and communicating enthusiasm about teaching and about psychology. However, if ill-chosen or misused, each of these technologies also has the potential to detract from the quality of your courses. So although we encourage you to use some or all of the high-tech teaching technology that is available, don't feel obligated to use it simply because it is available. First consider the pros and cons of each technology as it relates to your teaching style and teaching goals, then decide which, if any, will maximize the effectiveness of your teaching and promote students' learning. More specifically, ask yourself these questions: Is there evidence that the technology I am considering will make it easier for me to teach effectively? Is there evidence that this technology will help my students to learn more and remember it longer? Will the technology be more trouble than it is worth? Will the technology complement my teaching style and help accomplish my teaching goals?

It is not always easy to answer such questions in advance, largely because there might not be enough empirical data on the short- and long-term effects of every new kind of teaching technology, and because you might have to try some of it yourself before drawing conclusions. At the very least, read all you can about the technology in question, and be sure to ask the advice of colleagues in your department, on campus, and around the world who have experience in using it. In short, make sure that the technology you choose for your courses will advance your goals in the course without taking over the course.

Let's now consider some of the teaching technology tools that are increasingly available to psychology teachers today, including PowerPoint slides, classroom Internet access, CD-ROM ancillaries, textbook Web sites, Web links and resources, asynchronous Web components, instructor Web sites, student–instructor e-mail, and Web-based courses.

POWERPOINT SLIDES

Just as *Kleenex* has come to refer to any brand of facial tissue, *PowerPoint* has come to refer to any presentation software that enables teachers to project slides from a computer onto a screen. However, Microsoft PowerPoint is only the most popular of several similar programs, such as Corel Presentation, Apple's Keynote, and a growing number of other presentation software titles. Many psychology teachers use PowerPoint slides simply as digital versions of the overhead transparencies or printed handouts they once used to present topic outlines, lists of concepts and theories, photos, figures, tables, and the like. This makes sense, but you can get the most out of PowerPoint by using its impressive capabilities to engage your students' interest and attention in ways that overhead transparencies and handouts cannot match. In addition to displaying text and figures, PowerPoint can present audio and video clips, animations, and simulations, and it can contain links to an endless variety of Internet resources. It has even been used to create a version of the *Jeopardy!* game for reviewing material in introductory psychology (Stevens, 2003).

Pacing Lectures with PowerPoint

Even when simply presenting text material, you can use PowerPoint to time the appearance of main lecture points, definitions, and the like to create maximum impact and minimum distraction. For example, if you were to present a slide that lists several neurotransmitters or theories of prejudice, or whatever, your students will stop listening to your lecture until they have finished copying all the slide's information into their notes. By the time they start listening again, you will have moved on, leaving many students lost. To prevent this problem, use PowerPoint's animation capabilities to make each item appear when you begin to talk about it. This strategy gives you more control over the flow of visual information during your lecture and increases the chances that your students are paying attention to the information you are presenting at any given moment.

In the interest of promoting active learning, try to provide at least some opportunities for students to interact with, rather than just watch, your PowerPoint slides. For example, you could hand out incomplete versions of some or all of your slides in advance of each lecture, or post them on the course Web site for downloading. This allows students to fill in the blanks and jot other notes on the slides as you lecture on the slide material. You can also distribute your slides in finished form, but some psychology faculty argue that doing so invites students to skip class or, at best, to passively follow along as each predictable image appears in a predictable order. We tend to agree with this view. We recognize that having slides in hand can ease students' note-taking task, but you might want to distribute just those slides—such as a summary of a case study or a set of MRI photos—that will be the focus of your presentation on a particular day, and present the rest of the slides as you go along. This strategy will provide students with the basic material they need to follow your presentation, but still requires them to listen and take notes as your lecture unfolds in interesting and unpredictable ways. To generate interest in attending future classes, even when students have some of your slides in advance, provide a list of coming attractions—such as a brief description of the PowerPoint audios, videos, and simulations that can only be appreciated in person.

PowerPoint Internet Links

If your classroom allows live access to the Internet, you can create links in your PowerPoint slides that will take your class to Web sites that present sights, sounds, and other information that can bring your lecture material to life and stimulate students to explore it on their own later. In one developmental psychology course, for example, the instructor used a link in a PowerPoint slide to take her students to the Human Genome Project Web site, where she used her computer's cursor as a pointer to highlight images of DNA, chromosomes, and the like. She then clicked on several articles about genetic testing that were part of her students' assigned readings. Many Web sites provide animated demonstrations that illustrate brain anatomy, neurotransmitter activity, learning principles, and many other psychological phenomena. Spend a little time exploring such resources—many are listed in the instructor's manuals of psychology textbooks and on publishers' Web sites—and you will soon have more options than you can use in a lifetime of teaching. When accessed during your class sessions, these resources can have great instructional value.

Multimedia PowerPoint Slides

Many psychology publishers, as well as some Web sites, offer slides of textbook graphics, lifelike simulations of complex processes, and audio or video clips that can be easily integrated into your lectures without the need for a live Internet connection. You can find a wide variety of interesting pictures and animations related to virtually any aspect of your psychology course simply by conducting an Internet search through Google.com or other search engines. Once you have found what you want, download the material to your computer, and then move it into PowerPoint (as always, be sure to check for copyright restrictions before doing this).

If a picture is worth a thousand words, these multimedia materials can be worth even more. When discussing neurotransmitters, for example, you can use PowerPoint to enhance your lecture with vivid simulations of neural communication activity at the synapse that demonstrate the processes you are describing. Video clips of children engaged in Piaget's cognitive development tasks, or of dogs in Pavlov's original experiments are just two more examples of the types of video material currently available for a PowerPoint presentation.

Multimedia slides can be powerful teaching tools, but they cannot teach for you. Stay involved in the teaching process by, first, putting the slide material in context. Always let your students know what to watch for before you present an audio or video clip, or provide your own narration as the clip runs. Second, choose clips that last no more than a few minutes; edit them if they are too long to hold students' interest.

Mastering PowerPoint

Remember, too, that although PowerPoint in all its forms can highlight, guide, animate, and provide structure to a psychology lecture, it can also take over the lecture if you let it. We have all had to sit through PowerPoint presentations that were too text-heavy, that involved the mere recitation of each slide's content, or that employed so many distracting gimmicks that the point of the presentation was lost (Tufte, 2003). When this happens in the classroom, PowerPoint technology can become an impediment to learning. Keep these experiences in mind, but don't let them keep you from exploring the potential of PowerPoint in your classes. Remember, PowerPoint doesn't kill lectures; PowerPoint presenters kill lectures! We encourage you to experiment with the PowerPoint options we have described and look for ways in which they can best be adapted to your course goals and teaching style. When you use it for good, not evil, you will be amazed at the positive effect PowerPoint can have on your lectures.

CLASSROOM INTERNET ACCESS

As just described in relation to PowerPoint, classroom access to the Internet can open up a universe of possibilities for teaching and learning, especially when it comes to animation, illustration, and simulation. Via the Internet, your students can sit in on interviews with mental patients, take personality tests, explore the brain, participate in a social psychology experiment, experience perceptual illusions, and watch crimes caught on videotape, just to cite a few examples. After finding a Web site (www.soundportraits.org) featuring audio documentaries about the lives of young people, one psychology teacher visited the site in her developmental psychology class and, as her students listened, she clicked through the online links to slides that illustrated the content of a documentary. This exercise led to a lively classroom discussion and students were later assigned to write a short essay based on the documentary. To help them do so, the students were able to review the material by revisiting the Web site on their own outside of class.

Finding such Web sites and bringing them to your students is a great way to convey your enthusiasm for psychology and your preparedness and organization in teaching it. Indeed, you do have to be highly organized to use the Internet effectively in class. For example, you must check the computer system before each class to make sure that it and the Internet connection are working. You must also recheck to assure that the site(s) you plan to visit are still live and accessible. It is no fun to integrate a Web site into a classroom presentation only to find that the Web link has changed or that the material loads so slowly that you are left with lots of awkward "dead time" to fill while you wait for something to happen. As discussed in Chapter 3, be sure you know how to use all the computer equipment, Internet connection devices, projection screens, and remote controls in your classroom before you ever try to employ them in a lecture. As you probably know from watching certain conference presentations, there is no better way for a speaker to lose an audience's interest than to spend long minutes fumbling with unfamiliar or malfunctioning computer equipment.

Of course, sometimes you might encounter lecture-destroying events that are beyond your control. It is not unheard of for a local network administrator to temporarily shut off Internet access without informing the faculty, for a hard drive to crash, or for the power to fail, so it pays to hope for the best, but be prepared for the worst. For every class session that includes an Internet connection, plan what you will do as an alternative if the connection or a Web site is down at the time you need it. If the Internet material you plan to use lends itself to offline display, and if it can be downloaded to your own computer without violating copyright laws, consider loading each page into a separate browser window and minimizing it until you are ready to show it. This alternative can save a lot of time and trouble.

CD-ROM ANCILLARIES

Many psychology textbooks are accompanied by CD-ROMs that contain digital versions of student study guides, instructor's resource manuals, and other useful material. These can be excellent resources, especially if they contain useful Internet links. The quality and value of the disks can vary greatly, but as digital teaching technology becomes more commonplace, the resources supplied on text-related CD-ROMS are becoming increasingly sophisticated. Only a few years ago, many instructional CD-ROMs were poorly drawn, awkward to use, and of limited value. Some of today's CD-ROMs are amazingly elegant in design and well-integrated with the textbooks they accompany.

However, the devil is in the CD-ROM architecture. The fact that a faculty- or student-oriented CD-ROM contains flashy resources does not automatically qualify it as useful for your course. Embedding simulations and media in an interactive medium like a CD-ROM required the CD developer to make important decisions for you— decisions about what to present and how to present it. You might agree with some of these decisions, but some of them might not reflect the goals you have for your students, let alone capture your students' interest. Accordingly, before you decide to incorporate any CD-ROM in your course, review it carefully. Are there portions of the CD-ROM that might not be relevant to your class, or that might be incompatible with the way you teach it? Are there portions that will be especially valuable for you to build on or to integrate into your own presentations? Keep the good stuff, and ignore the rest. Remember, there is no law that says you have to use, assign, or recommend everything that is on an instructional CD-ROM.

Instructor Resource CD-ROMs

Make a point to ask your textbook's publisher for full details about any Instructor Resource CD-ROMs (IRCDs) that are available to you. These days, publishers are supplying more and more material on IRCDs, including instructor's manuals, digital copies of textbook art and graphics, prepackaged PowerPoint presentations and media clips, and the like. As described earlier in relation to PowerPoint itself, these resources provide endless opportunities to enliven your lectures and draw your students into the course material. Even if you don't wish to use PowerPoint, remember that the graphics, PowerPoint slides, and other material on an IRCD can be printed out onto transparencies and projected as overheads. Don't let functional fixedness prevent you from using high-tech material in low-tech ways if that is your preference! If you are a PowerPoint user, remember that many of the simulations and media clips on CD-ROMs can be copied onto your own computer and integrated directly into your lectures. Explore your instructor CD-ROM (and the student-oriented CD-ROM, too) to determine how best to use these materials. Ideally, you should review all your CD-ROM resources before you finalize your course planning so that you can smoothly integrate material from the instructor's CD-ROM into your lectures.

Student CD-ROMs

If your textbook comes with a study guide on CD-ROM, or if you can order a version that does, take time to preview the disk before deciding whether to recommend (or require) your students to use it. Is the CD-ROM just a duplicate of the printed study guide, or does it offer links to the textbook's Web site where students can take practice quizzes, engage in interactive learning activities, and the like? We think that unless the CD-ROM provides students with opportunities for active learning and a chance to engage in some self-directed exploration of psychology, the high-tech version of the study guide might not be worth the cost. Of course, if the CD-ROM is free, you can let your students decide which version of the study guide they prefer. Whether you assign, recommend, or simply offer the option of a digital study guide, check to see whether it tells students to submit to their teacher (you) the results of their study guide work. If it does, you will have to decide whether you want students to follow those instructions (will you have time to read or grade this work?) or to retain completed study guide assignments for their own reference and review.

TEXTBOOK WEB SITES

As with CD-ROMs, the pedagogical value of a textbook's Web site depends on the features the publisher has created. The most desirable textbook-related Web sites are those that give students opportunities to actively interact with course material rather than just clicking through a computerized version of the book or the study guide.

Typically, these Web sites are organized around the topics of particular chapters in the textbook. Most sites include a summary of each chapter, but the better ones go well beyond the text-based material. They provide interactive learning modules that include a brief tutorial on the chapter's subject matter, a chance to work with or manipulate examples of concepts, an online demonstration of various phenomena, a challenge to think critically about a concept or a piece of research, and links to online articles and other Web sites where further self-directed exploration can take place. The better textbook Web sites also offer review and self-testing facilities that allow students to assess their progress in learning chapter material. Some, for example, include "flash cards" that students can click on to review and test their knowledge of key terms. Many also offer practice tests that students can take, and have scored online to give them immediate feedback on their progress. Ideally, these tests should not only provide information about the correct answer to each item, but in the case of multiple-choice items, information about why each of the incorrect choices is wrong. When students miss an item, the online program should refer them to the textbook pages where they can review the material in question. Some Web sites even allow for students' practice test performance to be submitted to the instructor. Instructors can then use this information to monitor students' progress in learning course material and to help assess their effectiveness in teaching it.

WEB LINKS AND RESOURCES

We have seen that the Web site links contained in study guide CD-ROMs, on publishers' textbook-related sites, and in other resources can be extremely valuable, but their usefulness depends on the relevance of their content, the quality of the material they contain, the currency of their Web addresses, and the degree to which students take advantage of their availability. Even the most stable Internet sites might change their web addresses (URLs) with amazing frequency, often when they update their pages or add new features. If students try to reach a site using an out-of-date URL that does not automatically take them to the new one, the value of the link will be lost, and you will be in for lots of e-mailed queries about what to do next. Even links that appear on publishers' Web sites can be out of date if the site administrator does not perform frequent updates.

Dealing with the problem of outdated Web addresses can involve a lot of work, but it is a necessary evil. Before each term begins, try to reach each Web site to confirm its current URL. If the address has changed, you will have to change the URL accordingly. If no forwarding address is offered, you can search for it by typing the name of the site at www.google.com or at some other search engine to see if it is still available. If you have reconfirmed the accuracy of all the Web sites to be used during the first few weeks of class, at least, your students are unlikely to face early frustrations and are more likely to enjoy their course-related use of the Internet. Once the course has begun, remind students that URLs often change and ask them to help you update them by following the procedure just outlined and reporting to you via e-mail the correct URLs they find. You can then pass on this information to the rest of the class. This procedure not only makes the updating process easier for you, but also hones your students' abilities in using the Internet.

Visiting the Web sites your students will visit is important not only to confirm the URLs, but to be sure that the content they will find there is reputable and relevant to your course. This is particularly true in the case of links appearing in study guides and even on publishers' Web sites. Some of these links take students to sites that are so generic as to be useless. If you see links to Yahoo associated pages or to huge portals, they are often too broad to be of much value. Finally, be sure that the links that you recommend to your students will take them to information that is accurate, up-to-date, reputable, and scientifically credible. These should form the foundation of your Web-based teaching, but it is also possible to make good use of the many scientifically marginal, even bizarre, Web sites out there in cyberspace that are related to topics in psychology. Sites relating to facilitated communication, therapeutic touch, phrenology, or astrology, for example, can provide useful material in research methods or other courses in which the goal is to promote critical thinking about unsubstantiated claims.

ASYNCHRONOUS WEB COMPONENTS FOR TRADITIONAL CLASSES

Many campuses now have available Web-based teaching and learning platforms such as Blackboard, WebCT, or E-College; others maintain their own proprietary platforms. Unlike public Web sites, such platforms allow instructors and students to exchange information in a secure and confidential manner. You can make good use of these platforms to enhance active learning, provide immediate feedback to students, and encourage student–teacher contact because the platforms provide (a) a place to post syllabi and assignments; (b) course-specific e-mail; (c) a discussion area open to students and the instructor; (d) a chat area open only to students; (e) an area for posting instructor learning aids, including PowerPoint demonstrations and samples of completed assignments; (f) an area where students can post completed assignments for grading; (g) test administration and grading facilities; and (h) individual student grade books.

Posting Course Information

Using teaching and learning platforms to post your syllabus and course assignments saves you the trouble of duplicating and distributing printed versions of these documents. In fact, some teachers who use Blackboard or other platforms no longer hand out any written material, either because of personal preferences or because of campus cost-saving policies that require students to absorb the costs of printing. At the very least, having access to asynchronous Web components should allow you to distribute written material only once; if students lose this material, you can send them to the Web site to print fresh copies.

Posting Learning Materials

The opportunity to post various kinds of learning materials is one of the best features of learning platforms. You can post PowerPoint slides (with or without Internet links), samples of high- or low-quality assignments submitted by past students, PDF documents, text files, and even streaming audio or video clips. These can be made available to an entire class or to selected students, at your discretion. (Again, if you plan to post copyrighted material, check with knowledgeable people in your department or on campus to assure that you will not be violating any intellectual property rights by doing so.)

Receiving Student Work

Once students have completed a course assignment, whether it be a paper, a research project, or even a multimedia PowerPoint presentation, they can use the online learning platform to post it where their instructor can read and respond to it with comments, suggestions, or a grade, and then repost it where students can see the results. This work-submission capability of learning platforms can make the student–teacher relationship more dynamic and immediate, but it can create a lot of extra work for you—especially if you invite students to submit first drafts of papers or other assignments. Unless you are teaching a very small class, if even a third of your students take you up on your offer, you will spend many hours at the computer reading and responding to works in progress, in addition to grading completed assignments. Keep this possibility in mind as you decide how to use the assignment-posting feature of your teaching and learning platform.

Test Administration, Scoring, and Grade-Keeping

A useful feature of most learning platforms is the option to create quizzes or tests that students can take at the Web site and, unless they involve short answers or essays, get immediate feedback about their performance. (They can submit short answers or essays using the posting feature described earlier.) The feedback can range from a simple total-correct score to a full summary of the results, including their response to each item, the correct response to each item, information about why incorrect responses were incorrect, and even suggestions for further reading on the topic of the missed item. The results of online quizzes and tests can count toward students' grades, or can be offered as nongraded warm-up exercises to help students prepare for—and perhaps improve their performance on—upcoming in-class exams (e.g., Brothen & Wambach, 2001; Daniel & Broida, in press). Whatever the case, the tests or quizzes can be made inaccessible until the day and time you want students to open them, and they can be made available for a limited or unlimited testing period. Some learning platforms require that you open the test result for each student, check the grading, and then enter the student's grade in a computerized grade book. Others are capable of automatically placing the student's score in a grade book for that individual.

The automatic entry of grades into a student grade book is a useful function for recording the results of tests or other assignments that are submitted and read online. You can use this same grade book to enter the results of papers, projects, and other graded assignments that are submitted to you offline. Although it takes some time to set up the grade book properly, you will save time in the long run because the grade book feature will tally each student's total points for the term, make any adjustments you programmed (e.g., dropping the lowest quiz score), calculate final grades, and generate grade distributions and other statistical summaries. In addition, students tend to love the grade book feature. They can see their records in the same format that you do—as a "big-picture" summary that shows them how they are doing, and what work they might have failed to submit. They can easily confirm that they have received proper credit for work that they did submit.

E-mail

The advantage of using a learning platform for e-mail is that all messages associated with each class, or even each section of each class, will appear in a course-related location on the platform server, not in your departmental or personal e-mail inbox. This advantage is partially offset by the fact that it usually takes a bit longer to access and download e-mail from the learning platform because before you can read your course e-mail, you must first log on to the platform. Further, e-mail messages containing attachments might take longer to download from a learning platform than via your normal e-mail program.

For this reason, some instructors prefer not to use the e-mail function offered by the learning platform and create instead, for each course they teach, a new e-mail identity within their personal or departmental e-mail account. This speeds the downloading process, but if you choose this option, you will have to remember which identities belong to which class and check for e-mail messages in all identities every day (see our more detailed discussion of student–faculty e-mail later).

Student–Faculty Discussion Areas

The student–faculty discussion area feature of your learning platform allows you to raise discussion topics and invite students to enter comments and reply to the comments of their peers. The result, known as a *threaded discussion*, can be extremely useful as an interactive community-building tool. Whether or not you decide to make use of this feature is a matter of personal taste and personal commitment. If you are to help guide and inform the discussion, you will have to read all the comments, respond to all or most of them, and perhaps even grade them. This can be a tedious process, to say the least.

Student Chat Rooms

Learning platforms also make it possible to create chat rooms that are open only to students. The discussions that develop in these chat rooms might arise spontaneously or in response to questions or topics that you assign. They can be ungraded opportunities to address course-related material, although some teachers offer points merely for "showing up" and participating in the discussion. Although these chat rooms are for students only, you will obviously be able to monitor the proceedings and intervene on the off chance that an unpleasant or inappropriate situation develops, especially in relation to potentially emotionally charged topics. If you don't like the idea of eavesdropping on your students' discussions, you might prefer not to make use of this feature of learning platforms.

Course Cartridges for Online Learning Platforms

Many textbook publishers offer content "cartridges" containing quizzes, demonstrations, activities, and other material that is linked to their psychology books and ready for use in your course. This material is also available on the publishers' free Web sites, but when your students interact with it on the learning platform cartridge, you can monitor their activity and even receive summaries of their performance.

As with CD-ROMs, it is up to you to decide whether and how to use course cartridges. For example, you might find it necessary to alter the content or format of a cartridge's chapter quizzes to conform to your preferences and to increase their effectiveness as a learning tool. In other words, as with CD-ROMs, you might have to spend some time reviewing cartridge content and features to develop the precise menu of material and functions that will work best for you and your students. The first time you use a course cartridge, you might want to include only its most basic features, and then gradually add some of the fancier ones as you become more comfortable with this aspect of the learning platform. We think that these cartridges have enormous potential to enhance your teaching, and your students' learning, but like all teaching and learning tools, they take some getting used to.

INSTRUCTOR WEB SITES

If your institution maintains a learning platform, it will support a Web site for each of your courses, and for you as an individual. Even if no such platform is available, you can still create your own instructional Web site where you can post information about yourself; your research and publications; and the syllabi, sample tests, and other course-related information you wish to distribute to students. Creating a useful personal Web site will take some thought and planning, and it also requires frequent attention to make sure it is up to date and operating properly. It can be disconcerting for your students to find dead links on your site, or to receive a "file not found" error message when they try to reach your home page. Is a personal instructional Web site worth the time and effort it takes? Only you can answer this question, and you might not know the answer until you try creating and maintaining one. As with other high-tech teaching tools, you will have to consider whether having your own Web site adds value to your course and serves your students. If not, don't hesitate to drop it from your instructional kit bag.

STUDENT–INSTRUCTOR E-MAIL

There is good news and bad news about the explosion of student–instructor e-mail. The good news is that it advances an important principle of effective teaching, namely encouraging student–faculty interaction. The bad news is that all this e-mail communication can create so much student–faculty interaction as to be overwhelming for the teacher. Although staying in touch with your students is an admirable goal, remember that the road to that goal can be strewn with potholes, including the possibility of (a) too much e-mail, (b) too much trivial content, (c) communication errors, (d) ill-advised or overly emotional messages (e.g., "flaming"), and (e) creating student overdependency. We think that, to maximize the benefits of e-mail while avoiding most of its pitfalls, you must set firm guidelines for its use, carefully manage the flow of messages, and demand proper e-mail etiquette of yourself and your students.

Establishing E-Mail Guidelines

It is just as important to set firm guidelines for students' use of e-mail as it is to set up all your other course-related rules and policies. And it is just as important to enforce those guidelines. The specifics of the guidelines you establish will reflect your own preferences, of course, but they should address, at minimum, the nature and content of student e-mail, the use of identifying information, and whether or not you will accept attachments to e-mail messages.

For example, if you have a large class and you wish to limit the volume of student e-mail you will receive, you might only accept messages containing questions about course assignments, or messages containing completed assignments submitted as attachments. Perhaps you prefer that students use e-mail to transmit their formative teaching evaluations, grading complaints, excuses for missed exams or deadlines, and the like, but that they address personal problems in person. Whatever your preferences about the nature and content of acceptable and unacceptable e-mail, clearly state those preferences in your syllabus, and on the course Web site if there is one. Your e-mail policy should also appear as a reminder on the Web page that students use to compose their e-mail messages to you.

Your e-mail rules should also specify how students should identify themselves. Some teachers are willing to accept virtually anonymous e-mail from students, but others—especially those who have been inconvenienced by harassing, incomplete, or otherwise inappropriate messages—will only open messages in which the sender and subject boxes of messages contain the sender's full name, ID number, course number, and message topic. You will have to decide, too, whether to accept graded assignments or other materials that come as attachments to e-mail messages. Opening attachments can expose your computer to a virus or worm, so make sure you understand how much virus and worm protection software your computer or computer network has in place, then set your attachment policy accordingly. If in doubt, err on the side of caution. Even the best virus detection programs do not catch all threats, and the cost in time, lost productivity, and aggravation caused by a computer infection might not be worth the risk of accepting attachments en masse. Unless those file attachments are very large, it might be better to ask students to paste their completed assignments into the body of their e-mail messages.

E-Mail Management

If you allow students to contact you via e-mail, take some time to set up an effective e-mail management system. As noted earlier, it might be best to establish multiple e-mail identities, each of which has a unique address that is associated with a particular course or section of a course. This multiple identity strategy avoids cluttering your main inbox with dozens or even hundreds of student messages while creating a filing system that sorts messages according to the sender's course and section. Although this arrangement requires that you check all of your e-mail identities on a regular basis, it does provide an orderly way of dealing with student messages. If you decide not to create multiple identities, consider creating separate e-mail folders into which you can file messages from students in each course or course section.

Your e-mail management system should also allow for long-term storage of students' e-mail messages and your replies. We treat e-mail like all other information about our courses, which means that we retain it for a minimum of 2 years, first on a computer hard drive, and later on floppy disks or rewritable CDs (we retain records of students' graded performance permanently). If you do not plan to keep e-mail messages and online assignments for that long, let your students know about your storage policy and encourage them to retain printed or electronic copies of all their course-related e-mail and assignments, just in case.

E-Mail Etiquette

If you have ever regretted sending an e-mail message to a friend or colleague, or have received one that caused you distress, you are well aware of e-mail's potential for poisoning social relationships. The dangers of impulsiveness, inflammatory language, and miscommunication are just as real in student–faculty e-mail. Your casual remark that might have been perceived as lighthearted in the classroom can come through as sarcastic or demeaning in an e-mail message. Worse, because you cannot see students' reactions to your e-mail messages, you might never know that you have caused significant discomfort. Students, too, might send messages that are inadvertently or purposely inconsiderate, rude, or insulting, because they—like the rest of us—feel empowered to speak more freely on e-mail than they would in person.

To minimize such problems, be sure to include some rules of etiquette in the e-mail policies you establish at the beginning of each term (Shapiro & Anderson, 1985). First, remind your students that e-mail messages create a permanent record of student–teacher interaction, and can thus have unintended long-term consequences. Accordingly, offer your students (and remind yourself about) the following suggestions:

1. Never send an e-mail message that you have written while angry, resentful, or otherwise emotionally aroused, unless it is to ask for a personal meeting to discuss a problem or concern.
2. Never respond to an e-mail message while you are having an emotional reaction to it. Wait a day or so, reread the message, and then write a thoughtful, emotionally neutral response that does not raise the emotional stakes. If possible, arrange a personal meeting or phone call to discuss the topic at issue.
3. Give the other person the benefit of the doubt when you receive an e-mail that seems sarcastic, flippant, troubling, puzzling, or hurtful. Unless the message contains a blatant attack, assume that the sender did not mean to offend and that the message's attempt at humor or harmless teasing was lost in cyberspace. Try to clarify the sender's meaning, perhaps by asking if the previous message was meant as a joke. If it wasn't, it is time to arrange a meeting or phone call.
4. Treat your e-mail recipient as you would like to be treated, and don't say anything on e-mail that you would not say in person. Read and reread your messages before you send them. If you have any doubts about their appropriateness or their potential for miscommunication, ask the advice of someone who is not involved in the situation.

WEB-BASED COURSES

Teaching and taking courses on the Internet is not right for every teacher or every student, but it can be of great benefit in many cases. These courses support diverse learning styles (and schedules), but students who choose Web-based courses over traditional classes must be highly motivated, well-organized, self-disciplined, persistent, open to new experiences, and technologically savvy enough to navigate the Internet and contend with the frustration it sometimes creates. Teachers of Web-based courses must have these same traits, and must also be willing to work harder, especially at the beginning of each term, than they would in teaching a traditional course.

Synchronous Web Courses

Synchronous Web courses are conducted much like traditional classes, but are delivered in a distance format on the Internet. The class sessions are presented live on a fixed schedule, as students around the county, around the country, or around the world watch, listen, and participate. Using an audio streaming program such as Real Producer, students can hear their teacher speak, but the teacher usually cannot hear the students, and the students cannot hear each other. However, everyone can see on their computer screens the questions, comments, or other classroom contributions offered by all the others in the virtual classroom. The instructor can lecture while displaying a variety of material on screen, including PowerPoint slides, live Web sites, and virtual "handouts." Each class session is usually recorded, not only for accreditation purposes, but also so that absent students can listen to the teacher's presentation and view the associated slides and handouts that are saved on the course Web site. Even students who were present for the class might want to see and hear it all again for review purposes.

Synchronous Web-based courses work best when the instructor's personality fits the distance learning format. Perhaps because of the headphones she wears during her Web course, one experienced instructor we know describes herself as feeling like a radio disc jockey. Like a DJ, she cannot hear or see her audience, but she knows they are out there (most synchronous Web course platforms generate a running attendance sheet as students "enter" and "exit" the class session). The trick is to present course material in a way that involves and engages this disembodied audience such that most or all of the students actively participate in the course. Instructors who can perform this difficult trick make a synchronous Web class almost as active and interactive as a traditional class.

Asynchronous Web Courses

In contrast to synchronous Web classes, which simulate the traditional classroom setting, asynchronous Web classes allow students to interact with a wide variety of course materials at times of their choosing. Although there is obviously no fixed time for lectures or discussions, lectures and other presentations can still be a part of asynchronous Web courses in the form of online videos and their accompanying PowerPoint slides. Asynchronous courses can also offer classroom-style lectures, recorded by the instructor using a program such as Real Producer and uploaded to the course platform. Audio lectures require far less bandwidth than videos, and even students who do not have a high-speed Internet connection can access them with relative ease.

Asynchronous course platforms typically include the following components (all of which were described earlier in relation to their use as supplements to traditional classroom courses): e-mail, an online student discussion area, a chat area open to students and instructors, an area where the instructor can post learning aids such as PowerPoint demonstrations and samples of completed assignments, an area where students can post assignments to be graded, capabilities for online test administration and grading, online grade books, and a place for posting syllabi and other course materials.

Interactions between students and the teacher of an asynchronous psychology course are not the norm, but immediate communication via e-mail or audio link can occur by arranging for the instructor to "appear" in an online chat area at a specified day and time. More commonly, student–teacher and student–student interactions are asynchronous and take place via chat area bulletin boards. Some teachers of asynchronous Web-based psychology courses require all students to participate in these chat area "discussions." The discussions are usually begun by the instructor, who poses a question, challenge, or issue and invites students to respond. For instance, a teacher might ask the students to report examples of how positive reinforcement has influenced their behavior in the past week, or to post examples of social norms appearing in television commercials.

Teaching an asynchronous Web-based course is probably the most time-consuming of all high-tech teaching formats, but it can also be one of the most satisfying.

SOME FINAL COMMENTS

When used as an adjunct to excellent teaching and solid pedagogy, the technology tools we have described can make teaching and learning more fun, promote active learning, and enrich students' contacts with course material, and with the broader community of learners. Still, as noted earlier, choose your technology with care, and with your teaching style and learning goals in mind. Don't use a fancy technology package just because it is available or because your colleagues are doing so. There are many good teachers out there who are still doing a fine job with blackboards and overhead transparencies. Indeed, your knowledge of and excitement about psychology, your clear and organized delivery, your enthusiasm about teaching, and your concern for students form the core of effective teaching. Use technology to amplify these core qualities, and it will further enhance your impact as a teacher and make the learning experience even more fulfilling for your students. Use technology as a substitute for that vital core of qualities, and it will be little more than an entertaining distraction.

To gauge how students are reacting to your use of teaching technology, be sure to ask about it on the surveys, questionnaires, or other early feedback instruments you use to help assess and improve your teaching—an enterprise that we discuss in detail in the next chapter.

RESOURCES

Here are just a few of the many online resources that are available to assist you in using teaching technology in your psychology courses.

1. University of Maryland—Teaching with Electronic Technology:
   http://www.wam.umd.edu/%7Emlhall/teaching.html
2. Web Learning Principles:
   http://eduserv.edu.yorku.ca:8080/~ron_owston/article.html
3. Online Teaching:
   http://www.oucs.ox.ac.uk/ltg/projects/jtap/reports/teaching/
   http://www.firstmonday.dk/issues/issue6_6/brabazon/

4. Links on Teaching and Learning on the Internet:
   http://carbon.cudenver.edu/~mryder/itc_data/net_teach.html
5. University of Illinois Report on Teaching at a Distance:
   http://www.vpaa.uillinois.edu/reports_retreats/
   tid_report.asp#Traditional%20Classroom%20Teaching
6. Integrating Technology Into the Traditional Classroom:
   http://www.gsu.edu/~wwwdls/its/internet_teaching/
7. E-Mail in Learning and Teaching:
   http://www.lgu.ac.uk/deliberations/eff-interact/index.html

Chapter 8

Assessing and Improving Your Teaching

Sources of Evaluative Feedback on Teaching
Student Evaluations
Evaluations by Colleagues
Self-Evaluation
Faculty Development Activities
Some Final Comments

The previous chapters have focused on helping you to carefully plan, thoroughly prepare, and effectively teach your courses. Now it is time to consider how you can evaluate the outcome of your teaching efforts, identify areas of weakness, and develop a plan for making improvements in those areas. These considerations are important not only because they can affect your prospects for salary increases, retention, promotion, and tenure, but also because teaching is more satisfying and enjoyable—for you and your students—when you have found ways to do it to the best of your ability.

Let's first identify several sources and varieties of evaluative information about your teaching, and then look at some of the ways in which you can most profitably use that information to help you become a better teacher. As you read, remember that the process of regularly gathering, carefully considering, and constantly adjusting to teaching evaluations is not just for new teachers. No matter how experienced they are, all teachers can always find ways to do better in one area or another. In our view, only those who have stopped caring about the quality of their teaching have stopped seeking or attending to feedback about their performance.

SOURCES OF EVALUATIVE FEEDBACK ON TEACHING

You can get evaluative feedback on your performance as a teacher from four main sources: students, colleagues in your department and in other psychology departments, faculty development activities, and yourself. The timing of the feedback can make it either formative or summative. *Summative* feedback comes at the end of the course, or perhaps the end of the academic year, and serves to "grade" your teaching and suggest improvements. *Formative* feedback, in contrast, is gathered during a course and serves to tell you about what you are doing well, and not so well, while there is still time to make adjustments to the way you are handling that course. Although policies and traditions vary at different institutions, most teaching evaluations tend to be summative, and tend to come in the form of end-of-course evaluations provided by students.

Collecting summative feedback might be voluntary on your campus, but don't be surprised if you find that it is mandatory, especially for faculty who are not tenured or at the highest academic rank. Although most of your attention (and concern) might be focused on the summative evaluations that affect administrators' decisions about you, don't forget to gather formative evaluations, too. Formative evaluations can alert you to problems, or the need for changes in your teaching style or methods that will ultimately affect summative evaluations.

STUDENT EVALUATIONS

Given what we have said in other chapters about the basic principles of good teaching, the value of creating an inclusive classroom atmosphere, and the importance of establishing productive relationships with students, it should come as no surprise that teachers who try their best to teach well, and who care about their teaching, tend to get the best evaluative feedback from their students (Cashin, 1995; Junn, 1994; Lowman, 1995, 1998; Marsh & Roche, 1997; McKeachie, 1997a, 1997b; Murray, 1997; Seldin, 1999a).

When students in one study were asked to describe the best college courses they had taken, they reported a comfortable classroom atmosphere and interesting course content as the most important components (Levy & Peters, 2002). They also said that instructors in those courses "had a sense of humor and were entertaining; were excited about the material, ... (had) a caring attitude toward students, and ... were approachable" (Levy & Peters, 2002, p. 47). These teachers were lauded for blending lecturing with a variety of other more active teaching techniques.

By contrast, in two retrospective surveys, former students portrayed their worst teachers as having shown no enthusiasm for their subject matter, having been detached and aloof, and having provided students little encouragement, support, or help (Carson, 1999; McKinney, 2001). These teachers were described as arbitrary, unfair, contradictory, and autocratic, not only in their grading systems, but in relation to individual students. They were said to have belittled and embarrassed some students, sometimes by making sexist or racist comments, while showing favoritism toward others. They were remembered, too, as showing scant concern for how they presented material, and especially for disorganized, confusing lectures that were delivered in a monotone voice and came straight from the textbook. Also included among the "worst" teachers were those who were entertaining and lenient, but who were perceived as holding their students, and themselves, to a low standard. These teachers were described as giving "Mickey Mouse" assignments, and offering "light and painless" classes in which lectures were aimed at the least able students and from which little was learned (Carson, 1999). Respondents in both surveys said that their worst teachers made them feel some combination of fear, anger, and frustration; caused them to lose interest in the course content; and taught them little or nothing (Carson, 1999; McKinney, 2001; see Table 8.1).

Formative Student Evaluations

As mentioned in earlier chapters, you can prevent these negative reactions simply by letting students know you care about them, and by staying in close touch with them throughout the course. This communication process includes giving students plenty of opportunities to let you know what they think of you, your teaching style, the course organization, and the like. You might not be able to address some of their criticisms (e.g., "This class meets too early in the morning"), but

TABLE 8.1
Seven Deadly Sins of Teaching

1. *Arrogance*: Presenting yourself as superior in status and knowledge, always presuming oneself to be right, and failing to consider other viewpoints.
2. *Dullness*: Boring your students with tedious, unrelenting lectures or other unchanging routines of teaching; offering no opportunities for active learning.
3. *Rigidity*: Teaching so as to convey the authoritarian idea that you know what is best for those over whom you have power.
4. *Insensitivity*: Saying things that show you do not empathize with your students and/or failing to respond to students' signals of interest, confusion, or concern.
5. *Vanity*: Engaging in self-promotion or self-congratulation in class, including by overemphasizing one's own work or point of view.
6. *Self-indulgence*: Allowing oneself to meet only minimum standards as a teacher; exhibiting laziness, lack of effort, and disinterest in the course and the students.
7. *Hypocrisy*: This one appears in many forms, but one of the most common is seen in teachers who decry their students' lack of motivation to learn, while themselves displaying a lack of motivation to teach.

Note. These were described by Eble (1983). Teachers who commit these sins tend to receive unfavorable summative evaluations from their students.

others might be easy to fix (e.g., "We could hear you better if you shut the hallway door."). Whatever the case, you can be sure that your students will appreciate the chance to provide you with formative evaluations, and to hear more about why you have chosen to teach the course as you have. In fact, asking for formative evaluations can impress students enough to elevate your summative evaluations, even if it was impossible or inappropriate to make all the changes they requested! Collecting formative evaluations can even affect students' impressions of faculty in general by countering the prevailing view that teachers ignore the evaluations they are forced to collect at the end of the term (Sojka, Gupta, & Deiter-Schmelz, 2002).

What's the best way to gather formative evaluations from students? In the Middle Ages, university faculty in Europe counted the cash that served to evaluate lectures back then. At the end of each class session, they would remove their trademark mortarboard cap and stand, literally "hat in hand," at the back of the lecture hall. As the students filed out, they would place money on the mortarboard. The more they gave, the more they thought the lecture was worth (Weimer, 1988). Trust us: Your students will not do this, even if you wear a mortarboard, so you will have to find other ways of collecting their formative evaluations.

One-Minute Papers.   We suggest that you start this process early, but that you start small. For example, to get feedback about the clarity of your lecturing, you can pause after completing a section on, say, Kohlberg's model of moral development, and ask students to write a "one-minute paper" (Angelo & Cross, 1993) in which they list anything that confused them about the material. Reading these papers later that day can tell you what to clarify at the next class session, and can also provide more general guidance about the pace of your lectures, the number of examples you give, and the like.

Another option is to begin a class session by asking students to write a one-minute paper about their reactions to the lecture, demonstration, or activity that took place at the previous session. This method allows students more time for reflection, and also provides you with an indication of how much they recall about the earlier class. We recommend that you ask for this kind of feedback whenever you feel that a particular classroom presentation or activity did not go as well as you had hoped. Your students might or might not feel the same, but your next effort will undoubtedly benefit from their comments, and they will feel good about having the chance to help you improve. Our advice to focus on less-than-stellar class sessions might run counter to some teachers' tendency to avoid dwelling on "failure," but remember that one (or even several) bad class session does not make a bad course (Curzan & Damour, 2000). It is only when you miss the opportunity to correct mistakes that you harm your chances to teach more effectively.

Interim Evaluation Forms.   You can collect more general evaluations of your teaching style and your course by asking students to complete a structured evaluation form as the course proceeds. We think that the best time to gather this interim evaluation is after the first 3 or 4 weeks, when students have become familiar enough with you, your course, and your quizzes or exams to comment knowledgeably, but when it is still early enough for you to make any changes that you think might be appropriate. To assess the impact of those changes, you might want to repeat the interim evaluation a few weeks later.

An interim evaluation need not be elaborate or time consuming (see Table 8.2 for some samples). You can simply ask students to take

TABLE 8.2

Sample Forms for Use in Gathering Formative Student Evaluations

PSYCH 100
EARLY FEEDBACK EVALUATION
(Instructor's Name Here)

Circle your response to each question below.

How would you rate the instructor's overall teaching effectiveness?

1	2	3	4	5
poor				excellent

How would you rate the overall quality of this course?

1	2	3	4	5
poor				excellent

Most of the time, I find this class interesting.

1	2	3	4	5
disagree strongly	disagree somewhat	neutral	agree somewhat	agree strongly

How would you rate the pace at which material is covered in class?

1	2	3	4	5
much too slow	a little too slow	just right	a little too fast	much too fast

It is easy to remain attentive during lectures.

1	2	3	4	5
disagree strongly	disagree somewhat	neutral	agree somewhat	agree strongly

The instructor is friendly toward students.

1	2	3	4	5
disagree strongly	disagree somewhat	neutral	agree somewhat	agree strongly

The instructor is well-prepared for class.

1	2	3	4	5
disagree strongly	disagree somewhat	neutral	agree somewhat	agree strongly

I find the lecture notes useful.

1	2	3	4	5
disagree strongly	disagree somewhat	neutral	agree somewhat	agree strongly

(continued)

TABLE 8.2 *(continued)*

I find the Web page useful.

1	2	3	4	5	6
disagree strongly	disagree somewhat	neutral	agree somewhat	agree strongly	never used it

Use the following scale to indicate how much you have enjoyed each of the topics below.

1	2	3	4	5
strongly disliked	somewhat disliked	neutral	somewhat liked	strongly liked

_____ Research Methods
_____ Development
_____ Biological Aspects
_____ Sensation & Perception

Open-ended comment section

What aspects of this course do you like? What do you think the instructor is doing well?

What aspects don't you like? What would you like to see the instructor do differently?

EARLY SEMESTER FEEDBACK
(Instructor's Name Here)

Early semester feedback will help me improve my instruction. I need feedback on how well I'm presenting the material, how well you are learning the material, and how you feel about my evaluation of your work. This feedback is not meant to be an evaluation. This feedback is a way for you to help me adapt my teaching style to your learning style so that my teaching can be more effective. Your evaluation of my teaching will occur at the end of the semester. Please answer in ways that will help me understand how I can change my methods for the better. The examples cited in the questions are not meant to limit your responses.

1. What things do you like about this course; how can these things be made even better?

2. What things don't you like about this course; how can these things be changed?

3. What problems are you having learning the material? (For example, your and my preparedness, my teaching style, your study skills.)

TABLE 8.2   (*continued*)

4. If you were I, what would you change? (for example, my style, grading procedures, my accessibility to you, course format, workload)
5. What can I do to structure the course so you will feel like participating?

The lecture material is

Too simple	1	2	3	4	5	Too complex

The course is paced

Too slowly	1	2	3	4	5	Too fast

The instructor speaks

Too slowly	1	2	3	4	5	Too fast

The grading procedures are

Obscure	1	2	3	4	5	Well known

The main points are understandable

Almost never	1	2	3	4	5	Almost always

The level of student participation is

Not enough	1	2	3	4	5	Just right

The instructor's use of the blackboard is

Confusing	1	2	3	4	5	Very helpful

The instructor's use of the overhead is

Confusing	1	2	3	4	5	Very helpful

MIDSEMESTER EVALUATION
PSYCHOLOGY 100
(Instructor's Name Here)

What do you like best about the course so far?

What do you like least about the course so far?

Have you found the lectures to be helpful/and or enjoyable? Why or why not?

Have you found the extra materials (handouts, online notes, etc.) to be helpful? Why or why not?

Do you have any concerns or comments about the quizzes or mini-assignments? Is there anything your instructor can do to make the class better or improve the classroom environment?

Is there anything you feel should NOT be changed in this class?

(*continued*)

TABLE 8.2   *(continued)*

INFORMAL EARLY FEEDBACK
(Instructor's Name Here)

1. Rate my overall teaching effectiveness.

   Excellent   5   4   3   2   1   Poor

2. I appear to be enthusiastic about teaching the course.

   Enthused   5   4   3   2   1   Not enthused

3. I make good use of examples and illustrations.

   Usually   5   4   3   2   1   Seldom

4. How would you characterize my ability to explain?

   Excellent   5   4   3   2   1   Poor

5. I am well-prepared for each class.

   Usually   5   4   3   2   1   Seldom

6. I provide adequate instructions for proceeding with course work
   (e.g., mini-assignments, class discussions, etc.).

   Usually   5   4   3   2   1   Seldom

7. I communicate the objectives of course work.

   Usually   5   4   3   2   1   Seldom

8. I am easily approachable when students have course-related questions.

   Usually   5   4   3   2   1   Seldom

9. I raise challenging questions in class.

   Usually   5   4   3   2   1   Seldom

10. Mini-assignments, quizzes, and thought papers are returned with
    explanations of errors and suggestions for improvement.

    Usually   5   4   3   2   1   Seldom

11. Are my supplementary handouts valuable as learning aids?

    Usually   5   4   3   2   1   Seldom

12. I promote an atmosphere conducive to work and learning.

    Strongly agree   5   4   3   2   1   Strongly disagree

13. I make you afraid to make mistakes.

    Strongly agree   5   4   3   2   1   Strongly disagree

14. I listen attentively to what class members have to say.

    Always   5   4   3   2   1   Seldom

15. I give advice on how to study for the course.

    Strongly agree   5   4   3   2   1   Strongly disagree

TABLE 8.2 (continued)

16. I use humor effectively.

    Usually   5   4   3   2   1   Seldom

17. I encourage you to take an active approach to learning.

    Strongly agree   5   4   3   2   1   Strongly disagree

A. What do you like best about this class?

B. What are the major strengths of the instructor?

C. What are the major weaknesses of the instructor?

D. What changes can you suggest to make the course a better learning experience for you?

STEPHEN BROOKFIELD'S CRITICAL INCIDENT QUESTIONNAIRE

1. At what moment in the class this week did you feel most engaged with what was happening?
2. At what moment in the class this week did you feel most distanced from what was happening?
3. What action that anyone (teacher or student) took in class this week did you find most affirming and helpful?
4. What action that anyone (teacher or student) took in class this week did you find most puzzling and confusing?
5. What about the class this week surprised you the most? (This could be something about your own reactions to what went on, or something that someone did, or anything else that occurs to you.)

Note. From Brookfield, S. (1996). Brookfield's Questions. *The National Teaching and Learning Forum, 5,* 8. Reprinted with permission.

out a sheet of paper and list three things they like about the class so far, three things they don't like, and three suggestions for change. This format can be especially useful to new teachers because it virtually guarantees getting positive feedback as well as constructive criticism (McKeachie, 1997b). Another option is to create a short survey about aspects of the course that are of greatest interest to you. You might ask students to complete sentences such as: "The textbook _____ ," "The teacher's ability to explain concepts is _____ ," or "The organization of the course _____ ." You might also ask students to "describe something that the instructor did not do that you personally would have found helpful" (Cashin, 1999).

To increase the chances that you will get candid and thoughtful responses, let students know that their comments should be made anonymously, and reinforce that message, if you wish, by appointing a student to collect the forms and place them in a large envelope that he or she seals and delivers to you. (Some psychology faculty we know distribute their interim evaluation forms near the end of a class session so that they can leave the room while the students complete them.) In addition, emphasize the fact that you are asking for interim evaluations because you want to use the feedback to improve this course as well as your teaching skills in general.

Analyzing Formative Feedback. Reading student evaluations can be a bit depressing because even the best teachers of psychology leave some students dissatisfied, and because new teachers, especially, tend to take positive comments for granted and brood about the negative ones. To help yourself view formative comments in an objective and rational way, create a two-by-two table, and label its four cells as follows: Positive Comments, Negative Comments, Suggestions for Improvement, and Factors Beyond My Control. A student's comment that "lectures are interesting" would go in the Positive Comments cell. "The quizzes are difficult" could go in either the Negative Comments or Positive Comments column, depending on your goals. If you deliberately give difficult quizzes to better prepare students for your tests, this would be a positive comment, but it should prompt you to tell the class why the quiz questions are difficult. "I hate early morning classes" goes into Factors Beyond My Control, but let the students know that you are aware of how they feel, and perhaps plan to include a few more active learning events to keep everyone involved. "Put an outline on the board" would go in the Suggestions for Improvement cell.

As already mentioned, you won't want to, or might be unable to, follow every student recommendation and correct every perceived fault, but after you have read and analyzed your formative evaluations, take a few minutes in class to thank your students for their comments, discuss their feedback, and explain any changes you will (or won't) be making. Before deciding what to change, tally the number of students who made various comments and suggestions. If only one person claims the lecture pace is too slow, the problem probably lies with that student, so during your classroom discussion of feedback, you might offer to discuss the problem with the person who made that comment. Similarly, if a few students find your pace too fast, and a few others think it is too slow, you are probably teaching at about the right pace. Again, however, mention that you realize that not everyone is satisfied with your teaching tempo and offer individual help to those who are struggling. Of greater concern are comments suggesting that students are nearly unanimous in perceiving your lectures as confusing, boring, or overwhelmingly detailed. Such feedback should be a signal for you to consider how to address the problem. When in doubt about how to respond to student feedback, discuss it with an experienced colleague or someone at your campus instructional development office. These consultations can be extremely helpful in guiding changes that significantly improve teaching effectiveness (Marsh, 1987; Marsh & Dunkin, 1997).

Summative Student Evaluations

As you might expect, the same set of teacher behaviors that shape students' evaluations during a course tend to affect their ratings when the course is over. Accordingly, if you have gathered formative student evaluations throughout your course, you will probably not be surprised by the summative evaluations you receive at the end of it. Nevertheless, some psychology teachers misinterpret the meaning of summative student evaluations. In particular, and regardless of their academic rank or tenure status, many believe that students give higher ratings to instructors who teach less demanding courses or grade more leniently (Sojka et al., 2002). Some of these faculty members appear to employ a self-serving cognitive bias, in that they treat the poor ratings they might receive as the misguided comments of the disgruntled or the ungrateful while dismissing their colleagues' more favorable ratings as the inevitable result of offering an easy course in an entertaining manner. We even know instructors whose view of student ratings as a popularity contest causes them to worry that their academic standards are slipping if student evaluations get "too high."

In short, whereas most students would like to see their summative evaluations given more weight in the salary, promotion, and tenure decisions that administrators make about their teachers, many of those teachers see student ratings as having little or no value. In fact, there are psychology faculty—including some renowned for scientific research on other topics—who argue that it is impossible to accurately measure the quality of teaching because no criteria for "good teaching" have ever been, or ever will be, established.

We would not argue that student ratings alone define teaching effectiveness, but a considerable body of research does show that summative student evaluations can have value, not only in guiding administrative decisions but in helping teachers to teach better. For one thing, the interrater reliability of students' evaluations of their teachers has been found to range from .74 in classes of 10 to 25 students to .95 in classes of 50 students or more (Marsh & Roche, 1997). Further, high summative student evaluations are strongly associated with desirable teacher characteristics such as enthusiasm, energy, and interest in teaching the course, but not with teachers' gender, age, ethnicity, teaching experience, or research productivity (Cashin, 1995). These evaluations are also not significantly related to potentially confounding factors such as the level or type of course taught, the time of day classes meet, class size, or students' age, gender, year in school, grade-point average, personality traits, and prior interest in the subject matter (Cashin, 1995; Marsh & Roche, 1997).

Summative evaluations are related to the amount of work assigned and to the leniency of the grading system, but the direction of the correlation is opposite to what critics of student ratings might predict. As suggested by the student survey data mentioned earlier, teachers who employ more stringent grading standards and assign heavier student workloads (up to a reasonable limit) tend to receive higher summative student evaluations than those who are more lenient and less demanding (Cashin, 1988; Centra, 1993; Marsh & Roche, 1997, 2000; Watkins, 1994). One series of studies did find negative correlations between workload and student ratings (Gillmore & Greenwald, 1994; Greenwald, 1997; Greenwald & Gillmore, 1997a, 1997b), but those studies appear to suffer from methodological flaws that severely compromise the conclusions that can be drawn from them (Marsh & Roche, 2000). Even the famous "Dr. Fox" studies have limited applicability. These studies have been used by critics of student ratings to support the conclusion that entertaining lecturers who present no course content receive higher student ratings than those who present substantial course content, but in a boring manner. In reality, though, this "Dr. Fox effect" appears only on the "instructor enthusiasm" dimension. On other dimensions, such as knowledge of material, "Dr. Fox's" ratings were not higher than the boring instructor. In other words, although students enjoy an entertaining instructor, they can easily discriminate between style and content, and they recognize that style alone is not enough to justify high overall ratings. In fact, students appear to value a course more, and to be more satisfied with it, when teachers require them to work hard to learn challenging material (McKeachie, 1997a; Marsh & Roche, 2000).

Finally, student evaluations are positively correlated with a variety of commonly agreed-on indicators of good teaching, including the amount of material students learn in the course (Lowman, 1998; Marsh & Roche, 1997). The validity of student ratings is also suggested by the fact that these ratings tend to improve after teachers engage in structured efforts to improve their teaching (Marsh & Roche, 1997).

Even if your institution or department doesn't require that you collect summative student ratings, we suggest that you do so. Like students who never see the teacher comments that earned them a particular grade on a paper, it is hard to know what you are doing right and what you are doing wrong as a teacher if you get no end-of-term feedback about your teaching and your course. Remember, too, that even if you are required to collect summative evaluations, the standard feedback form might not have been created by a measurement expert. It might not give you the summative information you need to evaluate your teaching in enough detail to guide good decisions about what changes to make. For example, many summative feedback forms ask students to provide only global ratings of the instructor (from, say, "good" to "poor") on just a few dimensions, such as "quality of teaching" or "personality" (see Fig. 8.1). These forms are quick and easy to complete, but are not particularly informative because they do not provide much detailed feedback, and they do not address enough of the many dimensions on which a teacher's performance can and should be evaluated (Marsh & Dunkin, 1997; Marsh & Bailey, 1993; Marsh & Roche, 1997, 2000; Seldin, 1999a). We prefer to use more elaborate forms that allow students to rate us on a wide variety of dimensions and that allow us to insert dimensions in which we have a particular interest (e.g., "value

---

1. Rate the instructor's overall teaching effectiveness.

    Exceptionally high   5   4   3   2   1   Exceptionally low

2. Rate the overall quality of this course.

    Excellent   5   4   3   2   1   Poor

FIG. 8.1. Example of a global summative student evaluation form. This form is easy for students to complete, but actually conveys relatively little information to teachers, or to those who must evaluate their performance. Global forms that focus on too few dimensions can also create frustration in students who, at the end of a course, might like to offer more substantial and detailed feedback.

of classroom demonstrations"). There are many of these more elaborate forms available. Some of them provide space for students to summarize in their own words what they think of the teacher and the course (see Fig. 8.2).

Reading statistical summaries of students' ratings, combined with the (often humbling) experience of reading students' written comments, gives you two useful categories of evaluative information. The first is an aggregated profile of your strengths and weaknesses, a profile that can be plotted as a graph, and compared from one term to the next, or from one course to the next, to evaluate the effectiveness of your efforts to improve various aspects of your teaching. The second is a more immediate and personal portrait of students' reactions to you and your course, a portrait that often contains telling and useful elements. As we suggested in relation to formative feedback, you can get the most out of written summative remarks by creating a two-by-two grid to analyze them. Then consult with experienced colleagues about what changes you can or should make in your teaching style and methods in response to the quantitative and qualitative summative feedback you have received.

EVALUATIONS BY COLLEAGUES

Like summative evaluations from students, summative feedback from an experienced colleague or two can be of enormous value in improving your teaching, especially in areas such as your selection and mastery of course content, course organization, the appropriateness of course objectives and instructional materials, appropriateness of student evaluation instruments, and application of appropriate methodology for teaching specific content areas (Cohen & McKeachie, 1980). As just noted, colleagues can help you to objectively interpret and respond to end-of-term student evaluation forms.

In many psychology departments, administrators or members of a teaching evaluation committee review summative student evaluations, along with copies of your syllabi, exams, paper assignments, and other course materials to determine ratings that affect decisions about your salary, retention, tenure, and promotion. If these summative ratings by colleagues are not as high as you had hoped for, we urge you to seek further information about the factors that shaped them. Ask what specific aspects of your teaching need improvement, and consider getting outside help in making those improvements. However, don't let low ratings or less than complimentary comments in one area blind

1. Did this course improve your understanding of concepts and principles in this field?

Yes, Significantly   5   4   3   2   1   No, Not Much

2. The instructor's knowledge of the subject was

Excellent   5   4   3   2   1   Very Poor

3. How would you characterize the instructor's ability to explain?

Excellent   5   4   3   2   1   Very Poor

4. Did the instructor make good use of examples and illustrations?

Yes, Very Often   5   4   3   2   1   No, Seldom

5. The instructor was able to answer questions clearly and concisely.

Almost Always   5   4   3   2   1   Almost Never

6. Was the instructor enthusiastic about teaching?

Very Enthusiastic   5   4   3   2   1   Very Unenthusiastic

7. The instructor listened attentively to what class members had to say.

Always   5   4   3   2   1   Seldom

8. The instructor synthesized, integrated, and summarized effectively.

Strongly Agree   5   4   3   2   1   Strongly Disagree

9. The instructor encouraged development of new viewpoints and appreciations.

Strongly Agree   5   4   3   2   1   Strongly Disagree

10. Did the instructor treat you with respect?

Yes, Always   5   4   3   2   1   No, Seldom

11. There was a positive interaction between students and instructor.

Almost Always   5   4   3   2   1   Almost Never

12. How accessible was the instructor for student conferences about the course?

Available Regularly   5   4   3   2   1   Never Available

13. How would you rate the instructor's quiz and exam questions?

Excellent   5   4   3   2   1   Poor

14. The instructor respected my individual characteristics (race, gender, etc.).

Almost Always   5   4   3   2   1   Almost Never

15. The course material was interesting.

Strongly Agree   5   4   3   2   1   Strongly Disagree

PLEASE TURN THIS FORM OVER AND, IN YOUR OWN WORDS, ANSWER THE FOLLOWING QUESTIONS:

(continued)

(continued)

A. What are the major strengths and weaknesses of the instructor?

B. What aspects of this course were most beneficial to you?

C. What do you suggest to improve this course?

D. Comment on the grading procedures and exams.

E. What was the best day of class and why?

F. What was the worst day of class and why?

FIG. 8.2. Example of a multidimensional summative student evaluation form. Forms like these result in detailed profiles of a teacher's strengths and weaknesses, as perceived by students, and as conveyed through quantitative ratings and qualitative statements. Completing such forms can also help students to "think about their own educational experiences—to develop clearer conceptions of the kinds of teaching and educational experiences that contribute most to their learning" (McKeachie, 1997a, p. 405). Adapted from the University of Illinois, Urbana-Champaign, Instructor and Course Evaluation System (ICES); www.oir.uiuc.edu/dme/ices.

you to the fact that you are doing well in others. Those areas of strength are the foundation on which you will eventually build and extend your teaching skills.

Summative evaluations from colleagues can be stressful, partly because the feedback you get can be so surprising. Accordingly, as with formative student evaluations, we urge you to seek formative collegial evaluations, too. There are probably sympathetic colleagues in your department who have repeatedly taught the course you are teaching, or are about to teach, and who will be happy to give you the benefit of their experience if you ask for it. Don't be afraid to ask. As described in Chapter 2, new teachers and even experienced teachers tackling a course for the first time can avoid a multitude of mistakes simply by getting sage advice on everything from writing a syllabus and choosing a grading system, to planning lectures and attendance policies (DeZure, 1999). We are not suggesting that you ask colleagues to plan your course for you; just ask them to review what you have planned (Weimer, 1996).

In addition, don't be afraid to ask for formative evaluations of your lecturing style, your classroom demonstrations and group activities, and other aspects of your teaching behavior. The simplest way to get these evaluations is to ask a colleague to visit a couple of your classes each term. The ideal visitor is someone who can be both candid and supportive. These visits can provide many insights, especially if you schedule them on days when you are giving a particularly difficult lecture, administering or returning a quiz, performing a dramatic demonstration, or engaging in some other aspect of teaching about which you feel less than confident or would like to improve. If this prospect sounds too intimidating, arrange for the first visit on an "easy" teaching day, just to help you get used to being observed.

More and more colleges and universities are actually requiring such classroom visits as part of a peer evaluation program (DeZure, 1999). Some of them arrange for pairs of faculty—usually from different departments—to sit in on each other's classes. At others, the department executive officer, a member of a teaching evaluation committee, or someone from the campus instructional development office makes the visits. A peer-review-of-teaching program at one large university, for example, included not only classroom visits, but written exchanges of information on course content and goals, reviews of exams, paper assignments and other student evaluation instruments, and a 2-week summer seminar on improving teaching (Bernstein, Jonson, & Smith, 2000).

Whether colleagues' visits to your classroom are required or you request them on your own, try to focus on what they can tell you about your teaching. To get the most from each visit, meet with the visitor beforehand to describe your goals for the class to be observed, outline and explain the methods you will be using, and identify the aspects of your teaching that you are most interested in improving. After the visit, meet to discuss the visitor's observations. Be open and willing to accept criticism as well as praise, and thank the visitor for helping you to strengthen your teaching skills. You might also want to ask the person to visit again later in the term to assess the results of your efforts to improve in areas of weakness. In fact, the true value of colleague visits lies in the formative feedback that comes during the detailed discussion that follows them. Unfortunately, some campuses require colleague visits, but not this vital follow-up meeting. Feedback might thus come only in the form of quantitative peer ratings that are revealed much later as part of a summative evaluation. These peer ratings tend not to be terribly reliable, and not well-correlated with either student ratings or other indicators of effective teaching (Marsh, 1987; Weimer, 1996).

In summary, keep in mind that colleagues can provide information that is unavailable from other sources, including helping you to decide on the content of your course, correcting flaws in exams and quizzes, and discussing many other course-related issues. Remember, too, that advice and feedback are available via e-mail from willing colleagues who teach in your subfield of psychology or who share your interest in teaching particular courses. We list some especially valuable mailgroups for psychology teachers in Chapter 2.

SELF-EVALUATION

There is no doubt that the process of collecting, reviewing, and analyzing feedback from others can be of enormous benefit in improving your teaching skills, but self-evaluation can be valuable, too. Let's consider two approaches to self-evaluation: teaching portfolios and structured reflection.

Teaching Portfolios

You can conduct a long-term self-evaluation of your teaching by creating a *teaching portfolio*, which is a dossier containing syllabi, exams, quizzes, student evaluations, and the like from all the courses you have taught. Detailed suggestions about how to create a teaching portfolio are available in several sources (Centra & Gaubatz, 2000; Davis, 1993; Edgerton, Hutchings, & Quinlan, 1991; Knapper & Wright, 2001; Seldin, 1991; Shore et al., 1986), but we suggest that you start by collecting and saving portfolio-type materials as soon as possible, ideally during the first course that you teach—even if you are still a psychology graduate student. Starting early allows your teaching portfolio to grow more quickly as you acquire packets of material related to each course. The *course portfolios* that go into your overall teaching portfolio allow you to focus not only on what you did in each course and how you evaluated your students, but also on "what, how and why students learned or did not learn what they were taught (or what the instructor intended them to learn)" (Cerbin, 2001, p. 16). Studying and analyzing discrepancies between your goals for the course and what you actually achieved, and between what you hoped the students would learn and what they did learn, provides some clues about where teaching problems lie, and what you might want to do to solve them.

As your teaching portfolio expands in tandem with your teaching experience, it should include material that goes beyond syllabi, exams, and the like. It should also contain your written reflections about each course, about specific teaching experiences, and about teaching in general (Rodriguez-Farrar, 2003). A statement of your philosophy of teaching is an important component of these reflections (Korn, 2003). In fact, most teaching portfolios begin with a teaching statement that describes how teachers see themselves as teachers, and especially what they do and do not value in the teaching domain. Each teaching philosophy statement is unique, of course, but they often begin by posing and answering questions such as, "Why do I teach? How do I teach? Why do I teach the way I do? What are my teaching goals, methods and strategies?" (Rodriguez-Farrar, 2003). As noted in Chapter 2, having your teaching philosophy clearly in mind can ease decisions about course organization, planning, policies, and rules. For example, reviewing your teaching philosophy from time to time can remind you of why you decided on requiring (or not requiring) class attendance or why you use so few (or so many) definitional items on exams, and therefore whether it now makes sense to change those elements of your courses.

Your teaching portfolio should ultimately encompass all material related to your teaching, including (a) descriptions of the courses you teach and the way you teach them; (b) explanations and reflections about each course syllabus; (c) a summary evaluation of your teaching and the steps you have taken to improve; (d) a description of new courses you have developed and other curricular revisions in which you have participated; (e) copies of your writings or publications on teaching and learning (including research articles, talks and workshops, and poster presentations at conferences); (f) statements from colleagues or consultants who have observed your teaching; (g) student and course evaluations; (h) any departmental statements about your teaching; (i) a list of the teaching honors, awards, or other recognition you have achieved; (j) statements from former students; (k) a videotaped sample of your teaching style; (l) summaries of your students' scores on standardized tests; (m) examples of graded student assignments and samples of especially creative work produced by students in your courses; and (n) any other documentation that reflects your teaching (Perlman & McCann, 1996; Rodriguez-Farrar, 2003; Zubizarreta, 1999).

Organize these materials in a logical way, and be sure that each section is clearly labeled to make it easy to read and understand. You might also want to include a cover letter summarizing what is to be found in the portfolio. This letter can be useful to those who are about to review and evaluate your teaching. Before submitting the portfolio to anyone else, though, you should probably show it to one or more friendly colleagues, and perhaps even some students, and then make whatever revisions their feedback suggests might be appropriate (Rodriguez-Farrar, 2003).

Structured Reflection

Your teaching portfolio constitutes a formal body of material, but the quality of what you put into it at the end of each term will depend partly on your willingness to engage in some informal end-of-term reflection about what went right and what went wrong (Korn, 2003). Think, too, about which students, or types of students, you enjoyed teaching, which ones made you uncomfortable or seemed beyond your ability to influence, whether you are satisfied with class attendance, the distribution of final grades, and the nature and quality of your out-of-class contact with students (Chesler, 2003). Ask yourself whether these reflections reveal consistencies or inconsistencies between your teaching philosophy and teaching practice, and summarize your conclusions as you add to your teaching portfolio (Korn, 2003). Ask yourself these questions, too: If my next course were the last one I would ever teach, would I do anything differently, and if so, what? What is the one criticism that am I most fearful of receiving from a student? From a colleague? What has been my greatest accomplishment as a teacher in the last 3 years, and what has been my greatest failure? (Seldin, 1999b).

You will probably be surprised and pleased about the extent to which this kind of structured self-reflection can lead to beneficial changes in your teaching philosophy, improvements in your teaching methods, and a more informative teaching portfolio.

FACULTY DEVELOPMENT ACTIVITIES

A lot of valuable feedback about your teaching, and about how to improve it, will inevitably come from your students, from colleagues in your department, and from your own self-evaluative efforts. However, the broader community of psychology teachers and faculty development experts can also offer a wealth of ideas about how to increase the effectiveness of your teaching.

Local Workshops and Seminars

Consider participating in local workshops and seminars for new teachers (and even for graduate teaching assistants) that might be offered by your campus's instructional development office, or by faculty development services on nearby campuses. Attending such events can help make you a better teacher, especially if they continue for several weeks and offer opportunities to practice and refine your skills and receive continuing feedback on your efforts (Weimer & Lenze, 1997). If these faculty development activities are not readily available, we recommend that you seek out, or even create, a teaching support group. The group might be made up of new teachers, or perhaps a mixture of new and experienced instructors from around campus or in the local area who are interested in improving, and helping others improve, their teaching.

One such group was formed more than a decade ago at the University of Illinois, Urbana-Champaign, by a group of graduate students from various departments who had just completed a course on college teaching. They decided that there should be a campuswide forum at which teaching problems and issues could be discussed. The result was the College Teaching Effectiveness Network (CTEN), an organization that continues to offer two or three evening programs, seminars, or workshops each semester. The graduate students who serve on the CTEN steering committee choose program topics and invite speakers from around the state. Over the years, these speakers have presented sessions on balancing time commitments, helping students read more effectively, teaching in a diverse classroom, the role of gender in the classroom, developing teaching portfolios, and the like. The audience is typically made up of graduate students from across the campus, but quite a number of young faculty members from many different departments also attend these sessions, which always include time for discussion and the opportunity to raise and discuss topics that might not have been on the formal program.

Consultants

The faculty development offices on most campuses offer individual consulting for teachers who wish to improve their teaching skills, and if this is true on your campus, take advantage of it. Faculty development consultants can offer a variety of services. For one thing, they will discuss with you the meaning and implications of your student and peer evaluations. As suggested earlier, those evaluations are more informative when they are systematically analyzed with the help of a consultant (Marincovich, 1999; Marsh, 1987; Weimer & Lenze, 1997).

To help you address your weaknesses and solidify your strengths, your faculty development consultant might invite you to participate in *microteaching exercises* in which you give a 5- or 10-minute lecturette to a small audience of colleagues who are also seeking consultation. These lecturettes will be videotaped so that you and your consultant can review and discuss them in detail. Depending on your preferences, these discussions can occur in private, or in a group session in which all members offer each other support and constructive criticism.

Your consultant might also arrange to videotape one or more of your regular classes to provide an even more representative sample of your teaching behavior for analysis. On the day of these tapings, be sure to tell your class what is going on, explain why the tape is being made (i.e., to help you improve your teaching), and ask the students to try to behave as if the camera were not there. Most experienced faculty development staff members will have the camera set up before your students arrive and will be as unobtrusive as possible during your lecture.

Discussion of these tapes usually takes place in private, and although watching the tapes can be a bit stressful at first, it can also be very valuable—at least as valuable as reviewing evaluative comments from students, colleagues, administrators, or faculty development experts (Centra, 1993). For one thing, seeing yourself as your students see you provides a new perspective on your appearance, demeanor, teaching style, and teaching behaviors. After viewing your tape, you will be better able to put yourself in your students' shoes and perhaps gain a better understanding of the basis for some of their evaluative comments. While watching the very first minute of his first teaching tape, one of our teaching assistants exclaimed, "I will never wear those pants again!" You too might be less than happy with your classroom fashion statement, but more important, you might notice speech habits—such as repeatedly saying "uhm," or "well," or "OK?," or "you know?"—that detract from your presentation (Lowman, 1995). The tape will also tell you if you are speaking loudly enough and slowly enough to be easily understood. It will be easy, too, to spot habits or rituals that might be annoying or distracting to your students. For example, it was only after watching herself on a video that one of us discovered that she held a piece of chalk as she lectured, constantly rolling it in her hand and creating an irritating sound as it clicked repeatedly over her rings. No student had ever complained about this habit, but they were happy when she stopped it! To help you focus more carefully on both visual and auditory aspects of your teaching, your consultant might suggest that you first play the tape as you normally would, then listen to the soundtrack alone, then watch the video without the sound. If you are speaking too quietly or too quickly, you will recognize this immediately while listening to the sound of the video without being distracted by its images (Lowman, 1995).

Your consultant will help you to address and alter these and other even more substantive teaching behaviors, and will remind you that the things you might wish to change are problems for other teachers, too. If you find yourself exclaiming that "I never realized I was so boring," your consultant will probably tell you that this is one of the most common self-criticisms that faculty express (Braskamp & Ory, 1994). Realizing that you are not the only teacher who struggles with the problems you see in yourself can be comforting, and knowing that others have overcome those problems can also provide additional motivation for change. Faculty are most likely to show improvement in areas of teaching weakness when their consultants offer concrete and specific suggestions for behavioral changes (e.g., "Stop and ask for questions at the end of every main heading in your lecture outline"), not vague suggestions, such as to "be more organized" (Weimer & Lenze, 1997). Don't be surprised to receive highly specific prescriptions for change, and if you are in doubt about what a consultant is suggesting, ask for examples and even behavior samples until you are sure about what you should be doing.

Consultants in one institution's "Program for the Enhancement of Teaching" (PET) not only give faculty ideas for effective teaching, but help them make better use of student evaluations, and develop departmental mentoring efforts (Kemp & O'Keefe, 2003). They also created "Bright Ideas Lunches" at which faculty members from across campus can talk about teaching techniques that have (and have not) worked in their classrooms.

Teaching Conferences and Events

Excellent advice, helpful ideas, and invigorating support for your efforts to evaluate and improve your teaching are all available at conferences on the teaching of psychology. For example, the National Institute on the Teaching of Psychology (NITOP), which convenes in Florida in early January of each year, offers dozens of speakers, more than a hundred poster presentations, and a wide variety of roundtable discussion sessions, all aimed at helping psychology faculty do a better job of teaching, and evaluating their teaching. You can find out more about this Institute by visiting its Web site at www.nitop.org; information about many other outstanding psychology teaching conferences is listed in Table 8.3.

Remember, too, that the conventions of many regional, national, and international psychology organizations offer preconvention institutes, workshops, or other programming dedicated to the teaching of psychology. For example, the American Psychological Society (APS) offers a Preconvention Institute on the Teaching of Psychology at its annual convention, and the annual convention of the APA always includes workshops and entire program tracks devoted to teaching psychology. The teaching events at both conventions are organized under the auspices of the STP. To find out more about what is being offered this year, visit the STP Web site listed in Table 8.3, or the Web sites of the APS and the APA (http://www.psychologicalscience.org/ and http://www.apa.org/). If you are teaching psychology at the high school level, you should be aware of the psychology teaching pro-

TABLE 8.3

An Incomplete List of Conferences on the Teaching of Psychology

Conference Name	Location/Timing	Web Site
Annual National Institute on the Teaching of Psychology	St. Petersburg, FL; January	www.nitop.org
Southeastern Conference on the Teaching of Psychology	Kennesaw, GA; February	http://ksumail.kennesaw.edu/ ~bhill/setop/16a.html
Southwest Conference for Teachers of Psychology	Rotates among various locations in Texas	Contact Scott Bailey at sbailey@tlu.edu
Mid-Atlantic Teaching of Psychology Conference	Prince George's Community College; October	http://academic.pg.cc.md.us/ ~dfinley/matop.htm
Annual Conference on Undergraduate Teaching of Psychology: Ideas and Innovations	Upstate New York; March	http://www.farmingdale.edu/ CampusPages/ArtsSciences/ AcademicDepartments/ Psychology/call4pap.html
Annual Midwest Institute for Students and Teachers of Psychology	Glen Ellyn, Illinois (near Chicago); March	http://www.cod.edu/people/ faculty/puccio/MISTOP.htm
Northeast Conference for Teachers of Psychology (held in conjunction with the New England Psychological Association convention)	Various locations in New England; November	Contact Ted Bosack at tbosack@providence.edu
Terman Teaching Conference (held in conjunction with the Western Psychological Association convention)	Various locations in the West; April	http://www.westernpsych.org
Rhode Island Teachers of Psychology Annual Teacher/Student Conference	Various locations in Rhode Island; April	Contact Ted Bosack at tbosack@providence.edu
Iowa Teachers of Psychology Annual Conference	Pella, Iowa; November	http://www.central.edu/itop/

Note. These conferences on the teaching of psychology offer excellent opportunities to get together with other psychology faculty to learn about course content updates, exchange ideas and experiences, discover new classroom demonstrations, consider issues, discuss problems, and even create a mutual support network that can help you find new ways to evaluate and improve your teaching. For more information about these conferences, visit their Web sites, and for news of additional conferences that might be announced, visit the conference update page on the Web site of the Society for the Teaching of Psychology at http://teachpsych.lemoyne.edu/teachpsych/div/conferences.html.

grams, support, and other resources offered by an organization called Teaching of Psychology in the Secondary Schools (TOPSS), which has a Web site available at http://www.apa.org/ed/topss/homepage.html.

Books and Journals

Ours is certainly not the only source of written material on the teaching of psychology, or about the teaching enterprise in general. Publishers such as APA Books, Lawrence Erlbaum Associates, and Jossey-Bass offer a wide variety of books and journals for teachers of psychology (see Table 8.4). Contact them to add your name to their mailing list, and you will be able to stay up to date on their latest publications. Other journals and newsletters, such as *College Teaching*, *The Teaching Professor*, and *The National Teaching and Learning Forum*, are not specific to the teaching of psychology, but can nevertheless be of considerable value, especially to new teachers.

SOME FINAL COMMENTS

Most institutions and instructors use student ratings as a major source of teaching evaluation, and those ratings can indeed be reliable and valid for drawing conclusions about teaching quality. As is the case in measuring other complex concepts, however, the assessment of teaching should be approached using multiple sources of information, including observations and evaluations from faculty colleagues and expert consultants. "No single source of data—including student rating data—provides sufficient information to make a valid judgment about overall teaching effectiveness" (Cashin, 1995, p. 1). Accordingly, we have suggested that if you combine your own reflections about and analysis of your teaching skills with feedback from students, peers, and instructional specialists, you will not only have a more complete picture of your teaching as it is today, but you will be better able to improve your teaching effectiveness in the future. Investing the time and energy required to collect all this feedback will pay huge dividends, both in terms of your comfort in the classroom and in terms of the summative evaluations likely to be used in promotion and tenure decisions. Further, remember that the process of evaluating your teaching never ends. Even the most experienced instructors, including those who have received local, regional, and national teaching awards and other kudos from students and colleagues, are always striving to improve and fine-tune their teaching skills. We hope that you will do the same.

TABLE 8.4

A Sampling of Books and Journals on the Teaching of Psychology

Bronstein, P., & Quina, K. (Eds.). (2004). *Teaching gender and multicultural awareness: Resources for the psychology classroom.* Washington, DC: APA Books.

Davis, S. F., & Buskist, W. (Eds.). (2002). *The teaching of psychology: Essays in honor of Wilbert J. McKeachie and Charles L. Brewer.* Mahwah, NJ: Lawrence Erlbaum Associates.

Forsyth, D. R. (2003). *The professor's guide to teaching: Psychological principles and practices.* Washington, DC: APA Books.

Griggs, R. A. (Ed.). (2002). *Handbook for teaching introductory psychology: With an emphasis on assessment* (Vol. III). Mahwah, NJ: Lawrence Erlbaum Associates.

Hartley, J., & McKeachie, W. J. (Eds.). (1989). *Teaching psychology: A handbook of readings from The Teaching of Psychology.* Mahwah, NJ: Lawrence Erlbaum Associates.

Hebl, M. R., Brewer, C. L., & Benjamin, L. T., Jr. (Eds.). (2000). *Handbook for teaching introductory psychology.* Mahwah, NJ: Lawrence Erlbaum Associates.

McKeachie, W. J. (Ed.). (2001). *McKeachie's teaching tips: Strategies, research, and theory for college and university teachers* (11th ed). Boston: Houghton-Mifflin.

Sternberg, R. J. (Ed.). (1998). *Teaching introductory psychology: Survival tips from the experts.* Washington, DC: APA Books.

Teaching of Psychology, the Journal of the Society for the Teaching of Psychology, published by Lawrence Erlbaum Associates (visit the STP Web site or http://www.erlbaum.com/index.htm for subscription information).

Ware, M., & Johnson, R. (Eds.). (2000). *Handbook of demonstrations and activities in the teaching of psychology: Vol. 1. Introductory, statistics, research methods, and history* (2nd ed.). Mahwah, NJ: Lawrence Erlbaum Associates.

Ware, M., & Johnson, R. (Eds.). (2000). *Handbook of demonstrations and activities in the teaching of psychology: Vol. 2. Physiological-comparative, perception, learning, cognitive, and developmental* (2nd ed.). Mahwah, NJ: Lawrence Erlbaum Associates.

Ware, M., & Johnson, R. (Eds.). (2000). *Handbook of demonstrations and activities in the teaching of psychology: Vol. 3. Personality, abnormal, clinical-counseling, and social* (2nd ed.). Mahwah, NJ: Lawrence Erlbaum Associates.

Whitbourne, S. K., & Cavanaugh, J. C. (Eds.). (2003). *Integrating aging topics into psychology: A practical guide for teaching undergraduates.* Washington, DC: APA Books.

Woods, P. J. (Ed.). (1988). *Is psychology for them? A guide to undergraduate advising.* Washington, DC: APA Books.

You can also search for other books, journals, and journal articles on the teaching of psychology by visiting Questia at http://www.questia.com/Index.jsp?CRID=teaching_psychology&OFFID=se1

Note. In addition to providing valuable information on the teaching of psychology, books and journals like these help newer teachers realize that all teachers face the same problems and issues, and that some solutions and resolutions work better than others.

Chapter 9

Integrating Teaching
Into Your Academic Life

Balancing Teaching, Research, and Service
Dealing With Teaching Anxiety
Some Final Comments

Has reading this book left you wondering how you will find the time to deal with all that teaching entails while still meeting the other obligations that you face as a member of the psychology department, let alone a member of your family? If so, welcome to the club. The truth is that, no matter how much time you plan to devote to teaching responsibilities, it will be less than you need. Especially at the beginning of your teaching career, it always takes longer than you think to plan class sessions, meet with students (or answer their e-mail), grade exams or papers, set up and administer record-keeping systems, accommodate students with special needs, and the like. Don't despair. Your first term of teaching psychology will probably take more time than any subsequent one, given equivalent course loads. This is because as you gain experience and build your arsenal of teaching materials, methods, and systems, the teaching process will become progressively easier and less time-consuming—although it will never be effortless or quick. You will always have to find ways of balancing the effort to teach effectively with all your other academic efforts—such as writing; conducting research; going to departmental, college, and campus committee meetings; engaging in service activities; attending conferences; preparing grant proposals; and on and on (King, 2002a).

In fact, when we think of the realities of teaching psychology in most departments, we are reminded of the sign we have seen in the offices of more than one psychology professor: "When you are up to your ass in alligators, it is difficult to remember that your original goal was to drain the swamp." We hope that some of the advice and ideas offered in this book will help you to keep the alligators at bay and to enjoy your teaching as much as we enjoy ours. In this final chapter, we offer some suggestions to help you better perform the academic balancing act your job might require, and to minimize the stress of doing so.

BALANCING TEACHING, RESEARCH, AND SERVICE

In virtually every psychology department, faculty are expected to engage in at least two of the following three academic activities: teaching, research, and service. As described in Chapter 1, if you are employed at a 2-year institution or a 4-year liberal arts college, your two main responsibilities will most likely be teaching and service. At some colleges and at virtually all universities, you will also be expected to conduct and publish research. The tension created by the simultaneous demands of teaching, research, and service is quite real, simply because—unless you have found a way to circumvent physical laws governing time and space—you can't be in two places at once. If you are in a committee meeting, you can't be working on your perception lecture. If you are running an experiment in your lab, you can't be meeting with students in your office. Still, this does not mean that your interest in and pursuit of teaching, research, and service goals are incompatible or inherently conflicting (Loui, 2003).

The trick lies in finding time to pursue all your goals, and in letting your activities in each domain inform and enhance your activities in the others (Loui, 2003). For example, if you are running a psychology research program, you can use the results of your work to illustrate lectures in your research area. Examples from your lab can also illuminate your lectures in other courses that deal with principles of scientific research, experimental design, and research ethics. Conversely, writing a lecture based on your work or answering a question posed by a student in class might well trigger a train of thought that leads to an important development in your research. The skills you develop as a teacher are likely to improve your ability to make effective presentations at research conferences, and to make service contributions ranging from expressing yourself at committee meetings to informing the public about the nature of your work.

The mutually supportive elements of teaching, research, and service apply even in psychology departments where the clearest expectations and the most visible rewards are for conducting research and attracting research grants. As evidence for this assertion, consider the fact that many well-known researchers in psychology are also stellar teachers. These people use their own research, and their intimate knowledge of the research of others, to enliven their courses and offer their undergraduate and graduate students an insider's glimpse of what is going on at the cutting edge of progress in psychology. Even though some psychology professors at major research universities say that they would rather do research than teach, the vast majority of psychology faculty in general—about 90% of all college and university faculty—feel that teaching is an important part of their job (Boyer, 1990).

So if you hear colleagues complaining about their teaching load, or about their students, remember that it does not necessarily mean that they don't enjoy teaching. Like students, faculty complain a lot, and teaching is an easy thing to complain about, especially in a research-oriented department. Even if teaching is truly not a revered activity in your department, don't be fooled into thinking that it doesn't count in your institution (Kemp & O'Keefe, 2003). If you have a genuine interest in teaching, and in becoming a better teacher, don't be afraid to pursue that interest. Many graduate students and young faculty members at research universities are reluctant to talk about their desire to teach psychology, and if you are in this category, keep your ears open, find out which of your colleagues are known for effective teaching, and ask them to help you along as you develop your courses and your teaching style. Find out, too, if your institution participates in the Preparing Future Faculty program. It is sponsored by the Pew Trusts and the Association of Graduate Schools and offers graduate students and faculty opportunities to teach, and to learn about teaching, that they might not otherwise have (Kennedy, 1997).

Some Time-Saving Tips for More Efficient Teaching

Some of the most important advice your mentors are likely to give will involve basic rules for making efficient use of the time you have available for teaching-related activities. For example:

1. Keep everything. Even if you do not plan to create one of the teaching portfolios we discussed in Chapter 8, don't discard grade rosters, exams, quizzes, papers, student correspondence, the results of student evaluations, or anything else related to a course for at least 2 years, and perhaps longer. Having these materials handy can save you a lot of time and trouble when a student asks to see a hand-scored paper from last term, or claims that there was an arithmetical error on a final grade.

2. As noted in Chapter 4, make notes about how each class session went, not only in terms of what worked and what didn't, but also whether you were ahead of or behind the schedule listed in the syllabus. Spend a few minutes after each class marking up your lecture notes to remind yourself of what to do, and what not to do, the next time you present that material, run that activity, or the like. Mark your notes to indicate how much material you actually covered during each class, so you can compare it to what you had planned to cover. These few minutes of reflection can help you to reshape your plans, avoid mistakes, fix problems, and thus save time when you start planning the next version of the course. To help in this regard, create a folder for each class session and use it to store the notes, overhead transparencies, and other materials that you used, or plan to use, for that session. (If you prefer to gather this material by course rather than by session, we suggest using a large three-ring binder for each one.) If you are as obsessive-compulsive as we are, you might even use each folder's inside cover to create a reminder list of all the handouts, videos, books, demonstration equipment, CD-ROMs, computer disks, and other things you will need for that session. These folders can also be used to file newspaper articles, notes on good examples or interesting applications of concepts, and any other information you might encounter that will help you to update and freshen each class session the next time it comes around.

3. Create your own versions of the teaching forms we described in Chapter 6 for dealing with student excuses, complaints about test items, and the like. Developing form-driven routines for handling these matters will not only save you time, but will also reduce the number of ad hoc decisions you will have to make each time you teach.

4. Build a directory of useful phone numbers, e-mail addresses, and Web sites that will help you refer students to various kinds of

help, to campus services and facilities, and to sources of additional course-related information. As noted in Chapter 6, having this material handy—and keeping copies of it at home as well as at the office and in your briefcase—can make discussions and e-mail exchanges with students more efficient for you and more valuable for them.

5. Finally, don't try to reinvent the wheel. Whatever you encounter in your courses—whether it is students calling you at midnight or dogs mating in your classroom—has probably already happened to other teachers. When you have found a mentor in your department, don't hesitate to consult with him or her on a regular basis—especially if it is your first year of teaching—to describe the teaching problems and challenges you are dealing with, and to ask for advice on what to do.

DEALING WITH TEACHING ANXIETY

For many psychology faculty, the stress of academic life stems not just from the constant effort needed to balance teaching, research, and service activities, but also from anxiety about teaching itself. After all, classroom teaching is a form of public speaking, and fear of public speaking is quite a common affliction. In one small-scale survey, 87% of psychology faculty reported at least some anxiety associated with teaching, and 28% described their anxiety as very to extremely severe. These respondents' fear was related to standing in front of a class, to the prospect of being unable to answer students' questions, and to the possibility that students would make hostile comments (Gardner & Leak, 1994). Our long experience in helping graduate students prepare to teach psychology leads us to believe that the figures cited in this survey are probably accurate. If they are, it means that a lot of psychology faculty experience anxiety in the classroom that is severe enough to disrupt their performance as teachers, even after years of teaching.

Some Possible Signs of Teaching Anxiety

Some signs of teaching anxiety, such as a quavering voice, are obviously fear-related, but others appear as problematic teacher behaviors that are all too easily misinterpreted by students as evidence of incompetence, laziness, aggressiveness, or disinterest. These more subtle signs of disruptive anxiety in the classroom can appear as:

1. *Confused thinking*, especially when responding to students' questions. As anxiety interferes with access to the information they need to answer a question, some teachers end up giving long, rambling, confused, and confusing answers. For others, anxiety might motivate hostile, sarcastic, or condescending responses that tend to discourage future questions.

2. *Avoidance tactics.* Some teachers who find dealing with students to be uncomfortable show it by being "too busy" to talk to students after class, failing to show up for scheduled office hours, or restricting student–faculty contact to e-mail exchanges. Those for whom lecturing is a frightening exercise might rely heavily on anything and everything they can think of to fill class time without having to lecture. This might include showing large numbers of videos, inviting lots of guest lecturers, and scheduling student presentations as often as possible.

3. *Poorly organized, or overly organized, lectures.* For some teachers, the mere thought of facing the next class is so threatening that they avoid planning their lectures until the last minute, if at all. The result is class sessions that are uncomfortable for the teacher, and excruciatingly boring for the students. Other teachers seek to deal with their anxiety by preparing meticulously for every class, including writing dense, detailed lecture notes that they end up reading, like a speech, to students who spend the class period doing little more than taking dictation.

4. *Development of overly rigid or overly lenient relationships with students.* Some teachers whose anxiety focuses on the possibility that students will be dissatisfied with their course or will pose challenges to their authority try either to intimidate students or to be so permissive as to remove any grounds for complaint. For those in the first category, the list of class rules and regulations they include in their syllabus (see chapter 2) might be excessive. For example, we know of one psychology teacher who backs up his ban on the recording of his lectures with the threat of prosecution under provisions in his state's criminal code against unauthorized privacy violations. At the other extreme are anxious teachers who will do anything to curry favor with students. Their exams are easy, their course requirements are flexible (we know a teacher whose students are allowed to vote on how many exams to have), they will raise a student's score or grade at the first sign of complaint (without regard for capricious grading), and they might even reveal exam questions ahead of time in response to students' badgering.

5. *The appearance of "multiple personality."* Anxiety about teaching can cause a person who is normally calm, relaxed, and gracious in most situations to become defensive, hostile, and rigid in class. Part of this transformation might even include paranoid thinking; we have heard normally level-headed, rational professors express concerns that students are out to make them look foolish.

Ten Scary Myths About Teaching

We hope that the goal-setting exercises, course planning suggestions, classroom management tactics, and student–faculty relationship skills that we have discussed in previous chapters will make it easier for you to feel relaxed and confident as you teach. If you need some extra help to combat jittery feelings before and during classes, you might want to hone your relaxation skills by consulting one of several standard relaxation training resources (e.g., Bernstein, Borkovec, & Hazlett-Stevens, 2000; J. C. Smith, 2000). Remember, too, that what you tell yourself about teaching—and about yourself as a teacher— can also have a significant effect on your comfort level while teaching. Even if you are well-prepared for class and skilled at relaxation, you might still upset yourself with thoughts about not really being ready to teach, about not knowing enough psychology to be teaching it, about being a fraud or a phony, and the like. These irrational, self-defeating thoughts can interfere with effective teaching not only by distracting you during class, but also by raising your anxiety enough to disrupt your performance (Ellis, 1962).

We know how frightening these thoughts can be, because—like most other psychology teachers at the beginning of their careers— we suffered with these self-doubts ourselves. In fact, no one who cares about effective teaching can step in front of a psychology class for the first time without wondering how it can be that they are really the teacher! Fortunately, like your teaching skills, your self-confidence will grow with experience, especially if you can learn to think realistically and rationally about your role as a teacher. We think that the best way to keep yourself calm in the classroom, whether things are going well or not, is to recognize—and be ready to counter—10 myths about teaching that tend to make it far more stressful and anxiety-provoking than it has to be. Here they are:

1. *I should always stay in the "teacher" role while I am teaching, even if it means suppressing my spontaneous human responses.* Try-

ing to be emotionless, or unflappable, or detached, or to enact any other behavior you feel goes with the "teacher" role can actually add an extra burden to your job in the classroom. Don't expect yourself to be superhuman. If those two mating dogs do enter your classroom, don't try to ignore them. It is fine to be astonished and amused, along with your students. In short, combating the "teacher role" myth is as easy as letting your own personality come through to your students. Many teachers don't do this because of the myth described next.

2. *If I come out of the "teacher" role, I will lose the respect of my students.* This myth is a variant on the more widely held dysfunctional belief that if you let someone get to know you, they will discover how inadequate you are. It also carries the presumption that students are against you from the beginning and are constantly probing for weaknesses to attack. We think that the tendency for people to build walls around themselves for protection against emotional pain is as problematic in the classroom as it is in other areas of life. As noted in Chapter 6, the vast majority of your students want you to succeed and will support you if you simply show them that you care about them and about teaching. It will be easier to begin to reveal your real self in class if you deal with the next myth.

3. *As an all-knowing teacher, I should never allow myself to appear uncertain or uninformed, or to admit that I am wrong.* No one can ever know everything there is to know about psychology. Your students don't expect you to be omniscient, so why expect it of yourself? As described in Chapter 4, there is nothing wrong with letting your students know that, like them, you are a fallible human being. They won't mind your being imperfect, but they won't like it if you insist on posturing, "vagueing-it-up" when uncertain, or otherwise faking it in class. Remember, it is OK to put on a show, but don't put on an act.

4. *My students must respect me because I am their teacher.* Many teachers expect unwavering respect at all times from all of their students, and become very upset at any hint that their students are less than totally obsequious. In our view, these teachers' dismay, anger, and other negative reactions are a waste of emotional energy. Although we do believe that students should be respectful, we know from long experience that teachers don't always receive respect, at least not from every student. This fact of teaching life might not be desirable, but getting upset about it is not likely to

help you to deal with the few problem students you might encounter. As described in Chapter 6, handling classroom incivilities is much easier and less stressful if you can remember not to take them personally. Stay calm, deal with the problem in class and perhaps in private after class, but don't jump to the conclusion that any disrespect from even one student is evidence of your lack of teaching ability.

5. *My students should always be interested in what I have to say.* It would be ideal if all our students were interested in everything we say and do in every class, but this is simply not always the case. In fact, it has been suggested that only about 20% of our students are paying full attention to us at any given moment (Cameron, 1990). We all have a tendency to let our attention drift during a colloquium or other presentation, so when you see a few students losing focus during class it does not mean you are failing. Even if you see a lot of students losing focus during class, there is no need to panic. Use the information as a cue that it might be time to insert that demonstration or active learning exercise you had been planning, or to ask the class a question. It might also serve as a reminder to rework your lecture, or that section of your lecture, to make it more interesting the next time around. You might also encounter students who for some reason remain disengaged from your course material no matter how well you present it. If their bored expressions or other signs of disinterest bother you, discuss the situation with them outside of class (see chapter 6). Perhaps they have no interest in any of their classes, or maybe they are forced to take yours to fulfill an unwelcome requirement. In any case, remember that, sometimes, there is a mismatch between a student's goals and yours, and if this happens, there is no need to get upset about it or question your teaching ability.

6. *My students must learn everything I teach.* It would be great to see all your students achieve high test scores and to know that they will retain what they learned in your course for years to come. Unfortunately, not even the smartest and most motivated students will learn and remember everything you teach. Even if you were the best teacher in the world, some of your students will do better than others. Some will do poorly on tests and most will forget much, or even most, of your carefully presented course material within days of the final exam. In short, no matter how hard you work at organizing and presenting your courses, and no matter how reliable and valid your quizzes and exams, some of your stu-

dents might not do as well as you, and they, had hoped. You don't have to be happy about such outcomes, but you should recognize they are inevitable in some cases, and that they do not always, or entirely, reflect on your teaching ability. Sometimes, and to some extent, poor student performance reflects lack of motivation or ability on the part of the student. If you have done all you can to teach well, to assist students who need help, and to evaluate their performance fairly, don't worry too much about the appearance of a bell-shaped curve on your grade distribution.

7. *Students are basically lazy, dull, unmotivated cheaters interested only in grades.* Teachers who behave in accordance with this myth—perhaps predicting on the first day of class that no one will do their reading on time or will all be downloading their term papers from the Internet—are likely to create an adversarial classroom atmosphere that makes teaching unnecessarily stressful for everyone concerned. You can eliminate this source of teaching stress by recognizing that although some students are lazy, some are untrustworthy, some are not very bright, and some don't care about learning, most of them do not fit this profile. (Even if they all did fit the profile, you might not be able to reform them, and we don't think it is your job to try.) Assume the best about your students and then deal with the problem cases as they identify themselves to you through their behavior.

8. *My lectures should cover all the assigned readings in my course.* Unless they don't require much reading, teachers who are governed by this myth find themselves rushing their lectures in an attempt to cover as much of the assigned reading material as possible. The result can be a hectic classroom experience that neither the teacher nor the students enjoy or benefit from. As described in Chapter 3, we believe that students can and should be expected to take some responsibility for independent learning, so don't feel guilty about not covering all the assigned material in class. We find it enjoyable to present a reasonable amount of material at a relatively relaxed pace, and in enough depth to stimulate students' interest in reading the textbook for themselves, and perhaps in taking additional psychology courses.

9. *This is my students' only class, or at least their only important class.* Many psychology faculty tend to overestimate the importance of their course in students' lives. In doing so, these teachers forget that some or even most of their students are not psychology majors and, in any case, must meet the reading and writing re-

quirements of several other courses, too. So, even if your course in, say, abnormal psychology is their most important course in some cosmic sense, your students still have to figure out how to meet your demands as well as those of other instructors. This fact is worth remembering when drawing up your required reading list, making writing assignments, and the like. If students' lack of class preparation, missed deadlines, or requests for extensions are a source of stress for you, perhaps a partial solution lies in a re-examination of how realistic your expectations are. We are not in favor of "dumbing down" courses or expecting the minimum from students, but we don't think there is any point in adding to the stress of teaching by trying to do too much. In our view, you can make your teaching less stressful, and ultimately more effective, if you adopt ambitious, but realistic goals.

10. *I am in competition with my teaching colleagues*. This myth might ultimately be the most anxiety-provoking one of all. Taking a competitive approach to teaching, and worrying about where you are in terms of teaching excellence, is not likely to be very productive either in terms of improving your teaching skills or minimizing teaching anxiety. In fact, a competitive attitude perpetuates anxiety by isolating you from the help you might need to teach better and to make teaching more fun. If you can reject the competition myth, you will find it far easier to take advantage of the many sources of teaching assistance and advice we have outlined throughout this book.

In summary, teaching can be less stressful and more fun if you focus not only on what you put into your lectures and how carefully you organize your courses, but also on being realistic about your teaching. Ease up on yourself, don't take the problems of teaching too seriously, and don't let yourself be governed by the self-defeating myths that can make teaching psychology seem to be a frightening prospect.

SOME FINAL COMMENTS

In Chapter 1 we offered a list of basic principles for effective teaching. Like us, you probably found them all to be worthy, but in the crush of all else that impinges on your academic life, you might find it hard to keep them in mind when planning courses, writing lectures, and dealing with students. So to remind yourself of how you want to conduct the teaching aspects of your academic career, why not post a copy of those principles in a prominent spot in your office, and perhaps even in your study at home? They can serve as useful guides when contemplating the many teaching decisions you will be making in the years to come.

We hope that this book will help you to make teaching one of the most rewarding aspects of your academic life. We hope, too, that you will continue to read and learn all you can about teaching, that you will try innovative techniques in your classrooms, and that you will do what you can to pass on what you have learned to those new teachers who, with sweaty palms and hopeful hearts, will follow in your footsteps. We wish you all the best, professor.

References

Allen, M. (2000). Teaching non-traditional students. *APS Observer, 13*(7), 16–17, 21, 23.

American Psychological Association. (2002). Ethical standards of psychologists and code of conduct. *American Psychologist, 57*, 1060–1073.

Andersen, J. (1986). Instructor nonverbal communication: Listening to our silent messages. In J. Civikly (Ed.), *Communicating in college classrooms: New directions for teaching and learning* (No. 26; pp. 41–69). San Francisco: Jossey-Bass.

Anderson, J. (1999). Faculty responsibility for promoting conflict-free college classrooms. *New Directions in Teaching and Learning, 77*, 69–76.

Anderson, J. (2001). Tailoring assessment to student learning styles: A model for diverse populations. *American Association for Higher Education Bulletin, 53*, 3–7.

Anderson, J. R. (2000). *Learning and memory: An integrated approach.* New York: John Wiley & Sons.

Angell, R. (1928). *The campus: A study of contemporary undergraduate life in the American university.* East Norwalk, CT: Appleton-Century-Crofts.

Angelo, T., & Cross, K. P. (1993). *Classroom assessment techniques: A handbook for college teachers* (2nd ed.). San Francisco: Jossey-Bass.

Appleby, D. (2001). The covert curriculum. *Significant Difference: Newsletter of the Council of Teachers of Undergraduate Psychology, 10*, 1, 3.

Aronson, E. (1978). *The jigsaw classroom.* Thousand Oaks, CA: Sage.

Ashcroft, K., & Foreman-Peck, L. (1994). *Managing teaching and learning in further and higher education.* London: Falmer.

Askew, P. (1998, January). University of Illinois, "Who's Coming to College Seminar." Urbana, IL.

Astin, A. (1990). *The Black undergraduate: Current status and trends in the characteristics of freshmen.* Los Angeles: Higher Education Research Institute, Graduate School of Education, University of California.

Astin, A. (1993). *What matters in college? Four critical years revisited.* San Francisco: Jossey-Bass.

Astin, A., Parrott, S., Korn, W., & Sax, L. (1997). *The American freshmen: Thirty year trend.* Los Angeles: Higher Education Research Institute, Graduate School of Education and Information Studies, University of California.

Astin, A. W., Banta, T. W., Cross, K. P., El-Khawas, E., Ewell, P. T., Hutchings, P., et al. (2003). *9 principles of good practice for assessing student learning.* Washington,

DC: American Association for Higher Education. Retrieved November 24, 2003, from http://www.aahe.org/assessment/principl.htm

Ausubel, D. (1968). *Educational psychology: A cognitive view.* New York: Holt, Rinehart, & Winston.

Ausubel, D. (2000). *The acquisition and retention of knowledge.* London: Kluwer Academic.

Ausubel, D., Novak, J., & Hanesian, H. (1978). *Educational psychology: A cognitive view* (2nd ed.). New York: Holt, Rinehart, & Winston.

Bailey, J. (2002). Remembering 100 student names: Beginning an introductory psychology course with a demonstration of memory. *Association for University Regional Campuses of Ohio, 8,* 176–185.

Bailey, J. (2003, January). *The quiet student: Methods for ending the silence.* Presentation at the 25th Annual National Institute on the Teaching of Psychology, St. Petersburg Beach, FL.

Baker, L., & Lombardi, B. (1985). Students' lecture notes and their relation to test performance. *Teaching of Psychology, 12,* 28–32.

Balch, W. (1989). Item order affects performance on multiple-choice exams. *Teaching of Psychology, 16,* 75–77.

Barrick, K. (1998, March). *Creating a syllabus.* Presentation to University of Illinois, Urbana-Champaign Faculty, Urbana, IL.

Bayer, A., & Braxton, J. (1998). The normative structure of community college teaching. *Journal of Higher Education, 69,* 187–202.

Bayly, M., & Spiker, M. (2003, January). *The much maligned pop quiz: How to improve its image and simultaneously benefit the student.* Paper presented at the 25th National Institute on the Teaching of Psychology, St. Petersburg, FL.

Beard, R., & Hartley, J. (1984). *Teaching and learning in higher education* (4th ed.). London: Harper and Row.

Beard, R., & Senior, I. (1980). *Motivating students.* London: Routledge & Kegan Paul.

Bergin, D. (1999). Influences on classroom interest. *Educational Psychologist, 34,* 87–98.

Bernstein, D. A. (1983). Dealing with teaching anxiety. *Journal of the National Association of Colleges and Teachers of Agriculture, 27,* 4–7.

Bernstein, D. A. (1993). Excuses, excuses. *APS Observer, 6,* 4.

Bernstein, D. A., Borkovec, T. D., & Hazlett-Stevens, H. (2000). *New directions in progressive relaxation training: A guidebook for helping professionals* (2nd ed.). New York: Praeger.

Bernstein, D. A., & Nash, P. (2005). *Essentials of Psychology,* (2nd ed.). Boston: Houghton Mifflin.

Bernstein, D. A., Penner, L., Clarke-Stewart, A., & Roy, E. (2003). *Psychology, 6th edition.* Boston: Houghton Mifflin.

Bernstein, D. J., Jonson, J., & Smith, K. L. (2000). An examination of the implementation of peer review of teaching. *New Directions for Teaching and Learning, 83,* 73–85.

Billson, J., & Tiberius, R. (1998). Effective social arrangements for teaching and learning. In K. Feldman & M. Paulsen (Eds.), *Teaching and learning in the college classroom* (2nd ed., pp. 561–576). Boston: Pearson Custom Publishing.

Bjork, R. A. (1979). An information-processing analysis of college teaching. *Educational Psychologist, 14,* 15–23.

Bjork, R. A. (1999). Assessing our competence: Heuristics and illusions. In D. Gopher & A. Koriat (Eds). *Attention and performance XVII. Cognitive regulation of performance: Interaction of theory and application* (pp. 435–459). Cambridge: MIT Press.

Bleske-Rechek, A. (2001). Obedience, conformity, and social roles: Active learning in a large introductory psychology class. *Teaching of Psychology, 28,* 260–262.

Bloom, B. S., Englehart, M. D., Furst, E. J., Hill, W. H., & Krathwohl, D. R. (1956). *Taxonomy of educational objectives: The classification of educational goals. Handbook 1: Cognitive Domain.* New York: David McKay.

Boehrer, J., & Linsky, M. (1990). Teaching with cases: Learning to question. In M. D. Svinicki (Ed.), *The changing faces of college teaching: New directions for teaching and learning* (pp. 41–57). San Francisco: Jossey-Bass.

Boice, R. (1996). *First-order principles for college teachers: Ten basic ways to improve the teaching process.* Boston, MA: Anker.

Boice, R. (1998). Classroom incivilities. In K. Feldman & M. Paulsen (Eds.), *Teaching and learning in the college classroom* (2nd ed., pp. 347–369). Boston: Pearson Custom Publishing.

Boice, R. (1998). New faculty as teachers. In K. Feldman & M. Paulsen (Eds.), *Teaching and learning in the college classroom* (2nd ed., pp. 241–255). Boston: Pearson Custom Publishing.

Bonwell, C., & Eison, J. (1991). *Active learning: Creating excitement in the classroom. ASHE-ERIC Higher Education Report No. 1.* Washington, DC: The George Washington University School of Education and Human Development.

Bowers, W. (1964). *Student dishonesty and its control in college.* New York: Bureau of Applied Social Research, Columbia University.

Boyd, D. (2003). Using textbooks effectively: Getting students to read them. *American Psychological Society Observer, 16,* 25–26, 32–33.

Boyer, E. L. (1990). *Scholarship Reconsidered: Priorities of the professoriate.* Princeton, NJ: The Carnegie Foundation for the Advancement of Teaching.

Braskamp, L., & Ory, J. (1994). *Assessing faculty work: Enhancing individual and institutional performance.* Boston: Jossey-Bass.

Brelsford, J. W. (1993). Physics education in a virtual environment. In *Proceedings of the 37th Annual Meeting of the Human Factors and Ergonomics Society.* Santa Monica, CA: Human Factors.

Bringle, R., & Duffy, D. (1998). *With service in mind: Concepts and models for service-learning in psychology.* Washington, DC: AAHE.

Bronstein, P., & Quina, K. (1988). *Teaching a psychology of people: Resources for gender and sociocultural awareness.* Washington, DC: American Psychological Association.

Brooke, C. (1999). Feelings from the back row: Negotiating sensitive issues in large classes. *New Directions in Teaching and Learning, 77,* 23–33.

Brookfield, S. (1996). Brookfield's questions. *The National Teaching & Learning Forum, 5,* 8.

Brookfield, S. (1990). *The skillful teacher.* San Francisco: Jossey-Bass

Brookfield, S., & Preskill, S. (1999). *Discussion as a way of teaching: Tools and techniques for democratic classrooms.* San Francisco: Jossey-Bass.

Brooks, D., Nolan, D., & Gallagher, S. (2000). *Web-teaching* (2nd ed.). Retrieved March, 2003 from http://dwb.unl.edu/Book/Contentsw.html

Brothen, T., & Wambach, C. (2001). Effective student use of computerized quizzes. *Teaching of Psychology, 28,* 292–294.

Brown, G., & Atkins, M. (1988). *Effective teaching in higher education.* New York: Methuen.

Brown, N. (2000). *Creating high performance classroom groups.* New York: Falmer.

Buskist, W., & Saville, B. (2001). Rapport-building: Creating positive emotional contexts for enhancing teaching and learning. *APS Observer, 14,* 12–13, 19.

Buskist, W., Tears, R., Davis, S. F., & Rodrigue, K. M. (2002). The teaching of psychology course: Prevalence and content. *Teaching of Psychology, 29*, 140–142.

Cambridge, B. (2001). Fostering the scholarship of teaching and learning: Communities of practice. In D. Lieberman & C. Wehlburg (Eds.), *To improve the academy* (pp. 3–16). Bolton, MA: Anker.

Cameron, P. (1990). At a lecture—only 12% listen. In R. Adler & N. Towne (Eds.), *Looking out: Looking in* (6th ed., p. 251). Fort Worth, TX: Holt, Rinehart and Winston.

Cannon, R., & Newble, D. (2000). *A handbook for teachers in universities and college: A guide to improving teaching methods.* Sterling, VA: Stylus Publishing, L.L.C.

Carbone, E. (1999). Students behaving badly in large classes. *New Directions in Teaching and Learning, 77*, 35–43.

Caron, M. D., Whitbourne, S. K., & Halgin, R. P. (1992). Fraudulent excuse making among college students. *Teaching of Psychology, 19*, 90–93.

Carson, B. (1999). Bad news in the service of good teaching: Students remember ineffective professors. *Journal on Excellence in College Teaching, 10*, 91–105.

Cashin, W. (1988). *Student ratings of teaching: A summary of research* (Idea Paper No. 20). Manhattan: Kansas State University, Division of Continuing Education. (ERIC Document Reproduction Service No. ED 302 567)

Cashin, W. (1995). *Student ratings of teaching: The research revisited* (Idea Paper No. 32). Manhattan: Kansas State University, Center for Faculty Evaluation and Development.

Cashin, W. (1999). Student ratings of teaching: Uses and misuses. In P. Seldin (Ed.), *Changing practices in evaluating teaching: A practical guide to improved faculty performance and promotion/tenure decisions* (pp. 25–44). Bolton, MA: Anker.

Cashin, W., & McKnight, P. (1989). Improving discussion. In M. G. Weimer (Ed.), *Teaching large classes well: New directions for teaching and learning* (No. 32; pp. 27–49). San Francisco: Jossey-Bass.

Center for Teaching Excellence (formerly Office of Instructional Resources), University of Illinois. (1999, February). University of Illinois Faculty Retreat, Urbana, IL.

Centra, J. (1993). *Reflective faculty evaluation: Enhancing teaching and determining faculty effectiveness.* San Francisco: Jossey-Bass.

Centra, J., & Gaubatz, N. (2000). Is there gender bias in student evaluations of teaching? *Journal of Higher Education, 70*(1), 17–33.

Cerbin, W. (2000). Investigating student learning in a problem-based psychology course. In P. Hutchings (Ed.), *Opening lines: Approaches to the scholarship of teaching and learning* (pp. 11–21). Menlo Park, CA: Carnegie Foundation for the Advancement of Teaching.

Cerbin, W. (2001). The course portfolio. *American Psychological Society Observer, 14*, 16–17, 30–31.

Chesler, M. (2003, January). Teaching well in the diverse/multicultural classroom. *AAHE Bulletin.com.* Retrieved February, 2003 from http://aahebulletin.com/member/articles/sociology.asp

Chickering, A., & Gamson, Z. (1987). Seven principles for good practice in undergraduate education. *AAHE Bulletin, 39*(7), 3–7.

Chickering, A., & Gamson, Z. (1991). Applying the seven principles for good practice in undergraduate education. *New Directions for Teaching and Learning, 47*, 1–69.

Chism, N., & Bickford, D. (Eds.). (2002). *The importance of physical space in creating supportive learning environments: New directions for teaching and learning* (No. 92; pp. 1–97). San Francisco: Jossey-Bass.

Chu, J. (1994). Active learning in epidemiology and biostatistics. *Teaching and Learning in Medicine, 6*, 191–193.

Clegg, V. (1994). Tips for tests and test giving. In K. Pritchard & R. McLaran Sawyer (Eds.), *Handbook of college teaching* (pp. 423–437). Westport, CT: Greenwood.

Coffman, S. (2003). Ten strategies for getting students to take responsibility for their learning. *College Teaching, 51*, 2–4.

Cohen, P., & McKeachie, W. (1980). The role of colleagues in the evaluation of college teaching. *Improving College and University Teaching, 28*, 147–153.

Collins, K. (2003, January). *Students with Disabilities at UIUC*. Presentation to University of Illinois, Urbana-Champaign EOL 490 class, Urbana, IL.

Condon, J. (1986). The ethnocentric classroom. In J. Civikly (Ed.), *Communicating in classrooms: New directions in teaching and learning* (No. 26; pp. 11–20). San Francisco: Jossey-Bass.

Connor-Greene, P. (2000). Making connections: Evaluating the effectiveness of journal writing in enhancing student learning. *Teaching of Psychology, 27*, 44–46.

Cooper, J., Robinson, P., & McKinney, M. (1994). Cooperative learning in the classroom. In D. Halpern (Ed.), *Changing college classrooms: New teaching and learning strategies for an increasingly complex world* (pp. 74–92). San Francisco: Jossey-Bass.

Cooper, M. (2003) *The big dummy's guide to service-learning*. Florida International University. Retrieved September, 2003 from www.fiu.edu/~time4chg/Library/bigdummy.html

Cramer, R. (1999). Large classes, intimate possibilities. *The National Teaching and Learning Forum, 8*, 5–6.

Curzan, A., & Damour, L. (2000). *First day to final grade: A graduate student's guide to teaching*. Ann Arbor: University of Michigan Press.

Cyrs, T. E. (1994). *Essential skills for college teaching. An instructional systems approach* (3rd ed.). Las Cruces, NM: Center for Educational Development-New Mexico State University.

Daniel, D. B., & Broida, J. (in press). Using Web-based quizzing to improve exam performance: Lessons learned. *Teaching of Psychology*.

Davis, B. G. (1993). *Tools for teaching*. San Francisco: Jossey-Bass.

Davis, S., Grover, C., Becker, A., & McGregor, L. (1992). Academic dishonesty: Prevalence, determinants, techniques, and punishments. *Teaching of Psychology, 19*, 16–20.

Davis, S., & Ludvigson, H. (1995). Additional data on academic dishonesty and a proposal for remediation. *Teaching of Psychology, 22*, 119–121.

DeAngelis, T. (2003). Higher-ed movement aims to elevate teaching. *Monitor on Psychology, 34*, 54.

Desrochers, C. (2000). Establishing expectations for our students. *The National Teaching and Learning Forum, 10*, 4–6.

Dey, E., Astin, A., & Korn, W. (1991). *The American freshman: Twenty-five year trends, 1966–1990*. Los Angeles: Higher Education Research Institute, Graduate School of Education, University of California.

DeZure, D. (1999). Evaluating teaching through peer classroom observation. In P. Seldin (Ed.), *Changing practices in evaluating teaching: A practical guide to improved faculty performance and promotion/tenure decisions* (pp. 70–96). Bolton, MA: Anker.

Diekhoff, G., LaBeff, E., Clark, R., Williams, L., Francis, B., & Haines, V. (1996). College cheating: Ten years later. *Research in Higher Education, 37*, 487–502.

Dinham, S. (1996). What college teachers need to know. In R. Menges & M. Weimer (Eds), *Teaching on solid ground* (pp. 297–313). San Francisco: Jossey-Bass.

Does Diversity Make a Difference? Three Research Studies on Diversity in College Classrooms. Washington, DC: American Council on Education and American

Association of University Professors, 2000. May be obtained from www.acenet.edu or www.aaup.org

Dweck, C. (1986). Motivational processes affecting learning. *American Psychologist, 41*, 1040–1048.

Dweck, C., & Leggett, E. (1988). A social-cognitive approach to motivation and personality. *Psychological Review, 95*, 256–273.

Ebel, R. (1965). *Measuring educational achievement*. Englewood Cliffs, NJ: Prentice Hall.

Eble, K. (1983). *Aims of college teaching*. Boston: Jossey-Bass.

Eble, K. (1988). *The craft of teaching* (2nd ed.). San Francisco: Jossey-Bass.

Edgerton, R., Hutchings, P., & Quinlan, K. (1991). *The teaching portfolio: Capturing the scholarship in teaching*. Washington, DC: American Association for Higher Education.

Eggleston, T., & Smith, G. (2001, January). *Creating community in the classroom: Ice breakers and creative closures*. Poster at the 23rd National Institute on the Teaching of Psychology, St. Petersburg Beach, FL.

Eggleston, T., & Smith, G. (2002). Parting ways: Ending your course. *APS Observer, 15*(3), 15–16, 29–30.

Ellis, A. (1962). *Reason and emotion in psychotherapy*. New York: Lyle Stuart.

Emmer, E., Everston, C., & Anderson, T. (1979). *The first week of class ... and the rest of the year*. Paper presented at the meeting of the American Educational Research Association, San Francisco, April 1979. ERIC Document Reproduction Service No. ED 175 861.

Enos, S., & Troppe, M. (1996). Service-learning in the curriculum. In B. Jacoby (Ed.), *Service-learning in higher education: Concepts and practices* (pp. 156–181). San Francisco: Jossey-Bass.

Eppler, M., & Harju, B. (1997). Achievement motivation goals in relation to academic performance in traditional and nontraditional college students. *Research in Higher Education, 38*, 557–572.

Erickson, B., & Strommer, D. (1991). *Teaching college freshmen*. San Francisco: Jossey-Bass.

Ericksen, S. (1974). *Motivation for learning*. Ann Arbor: University of Michigan Press.

Ewen, W. (1989). Teaching using discussions. In R. Neff & M. Weimer (Eds.), *Classroom communication: Collected readings for effective discussion and questioning* (pp. 21–26). Madison, WI: Magna.

Feldman, K. (1998). Identifying exemplary teachers and teaching: Evidence from student ratings. In K. Feldman & M. Paulsen (Eds.), *Teaching and learning in the college classroom* (2nd ed., pp. 391–414). Boston: Pearson Custom Publishing.

Fisch, L. (2001). Discussions: Seven guiding principles. *National Teaching and Learning Forum, 11*, 6.

Fisher, B. (1996). Using journals in social psychology class: Helping students apply course concepts to life experiences. *Teaching Sociology, 24*, 157–165.

Fiske, E. B. (2001). *Learning in deed: The power of service-learning for American schools*. Battle Creek, MI: W. K. Kellogg Foundation.

Flood, B. J., & Moll, B. J. (1990). *The professor business: A teaching primer for faculty*. Medford, NJ: Learned Information, Inc.

Forsyth, D. (2003). *The professor's guide to teaching: Psychological principles and practices*. Washington, DC: American Psychological Association.

Forsyth, D., & McMillan, J. (1991). Practical proposals for motivating students. In R. Menges & M. Svinicki (Eds.), *New directions for teaching and learning* (No. 45; pp. 53–65). San Francisco: Jossey-Bass.

Friedman, P., Rodriguez, F., & McComb, J. (2001). Why students do and do not attend classes: Myths and realities. *Teaching of Psychology, 49*, 124–133.

Fritschner, L. (2000). Inside the undergraduate college classroom: Faculty and students differ on the meaning of student participation. *The Journal of Higher Education, 71*, 343–362.

Fullilove, R., & Treisman, P. (1990). Mathematics achievement among African American undergraduates at the University of California, Berkeley: An evaluation of the mathematics workshop program. *Journal of Negro Education, 59*, 463–478.

Gardner, L. E., & Leak, G. K. (1994). Characteristics and correlates of teaching anxiety among college psychology teachers. *Teaching of Psychology, 21*(1), 28–32.

Gaultney, J., & Cann, A. (2001). Grade expectations. *Teaching of Psychology, 28*, 84–87.

Gauss, C. (1930). *Life in college.* New York: Scribner's.

Genereux, R., & McLeod, B. (1995). Circumstances surrounding cheating: A questionnaire study of college students. *Research in Higher Education, 36*, 687–704.

Gibbs, G. (1992). Control and independence. In G. Gibbs & A. Jenkins (Eds.), *Teaching large classes in higher education: How to maintain quality with reduced resources* (pp. 37–62). London: Kogan Page.

Gibbs, G., & Jenkins, A. (Eds.). (1992). *Teaching large classes in higher education: How to maintain quality with reduced resources.* London: Kogan Page.

Gillmore, G. M., & Greenwald, A. G. (1994). *The effects of course demands and grading leniency on student ratings of instruction* (Report No. 94–4). Seattle: University of Washington, Office of Educational Assessment.

Golde, C. M., & Dore, T. M. (2001). *At cross purposes: What the experiences of today's doctoral students reveal about doctoral education.* Pew Charitable Trusts (available online at http://www.wcer.wisc.edu/phd-survey/report%20final.pdf).

Gonzalez, V., & Lopez, E. (2001). The age of incivility: Countering disruptive behavior in the classroom. *AAHE Bulletin, 53*(8), 3–6.

Goodwin, S., Sharp, G., Cloutier, E., Diamond, N., & Dalgaard, K. (1981). *Effective classroom questioning.* Urbana-Champaign: University of Illinois, Urbana-Champaign, Center for Teaching Excellence (formerly Office of Instructional Resources).

Goss, S. (1983). Student perceptions and classroom management (Doctoral dissertation). *Dissertation Abstracts International, 46–01*, 105.

Goss, S. (1995). Dealing with problem students in the classroom. *APS Observer, 8*, 26–27, 29.

Graham, M., Monday, J., & O'Brien, K. (1994). Cheating at small colleges: An examination of student and faculty attitudes and behaviors. *Journal of College Student Development, 35*, 255–260.

Grant, H., & Dweck, C. S. (2003). Clarifying achievement goals and their impact. *Journal of Personality and Social Psychology, 85*, 541–553.

Greenwald, A. G. (1997). Validity concerns and usefulness of student ratings of instruction. *American Psychologist, 52*, 1182–1186.

Greenwald, A. G., & Gillmore, G. M. (1997a). Grading leniency is a removable contaminant of student ratings. *American Psychologist, 52*, 1209–1217.

Greenwald, A. G., & Gillmore, G. M. (1997b). No pain, no gain: The importance of measuring course workload in student ratings of instruction. *Journal of Educational Psychology, 89*, 743–751.

Gronlund, N., & Linn, R. (1990). *Measurement and evaluation in teaching* (6th ed.). New York: Macmillan.

Hake, R. (1998). Interactive-engagement vs. traditional methods: A six-thousand-student survey of mechanics test data for introductory physics courses. *American Journal of Physics, 66*, 64–74.

Halpern, D. (2000). *Sex differences in cognitive abilities* (3rd ed.). Mahwah, NJ: Lawrence Erlbaum Associates.

Halpern, D. (2002). Teaching for critical thinking: A four-part model to enhance thinking skills. In S. Davis & W. Buskist (Eds.), *The teaching of psychology: Essays in honor of Wilbert J. McKeachie and Charles L. Brewer* (pp. 91–105). Mahwah, NJ: Lawrence Erlbaum Associates.

Halpern, D. (2003). *Thought & knowledge: An introduction to critical thinking* (4th ed.). Mahwah, NJ: Lawrence Erlbaum Associates.

Halpern, D. F., & Hakel, M. D. (2003, July–August). Applying the science of learning to the university and beyond: Teaching for long term retention and transfer. *Change*, 36–41.

Hansen, E. (1998). Essential demographics of today's college students. *AAHE Bulletin, 51*, 3–5.

Hardy, M. (2001, January). *Extra credit: Gifts for the gifted?* Paper presented at the 23rd National Institute on the Teaching of Psychology, St. Petersburg Beach, FL.

Hardy, M., & Schaen, E. (2000). Integrating the classroom and community service: Everyone benefits. *Teaching of Psychology, 27*, 47–49.

Hemmings, B., & Battersby, D. (1990). The textbook selection checklist. In M. Weimer & R. A. Neff (Eds.), *Teaching college: Collected readings for the new instructor* (pp. 47–48). Madison, WI: Magna.

Hendersen, R. (2002a, June). *Introductory psychology forum: Case studies for increasing student engagement.* Presentation to 2nd annual Summer National Institute on the Teaching of Psychology, St. Petersburg Beach, FL.

Hendersen, R. (2002b, June). *Responding to failure: A survival guide.* Distributed at the 2nd Annual Summer National Institute on the Teaching of Psychology, St. Petersburg Beach, FL.

Hendersen, R. W. (2003). Good examples make better cases: Enhancing interaction in large classes. In H. L. Klein (Ed.), *Interactive innovative teaching and training: Case method and other techniques* (pp. 241–248). Needham, MA: World Association for Case Method Research and Application.

Hettich, P. (1990). Journal writing: Old fare or nouvelle cuisine? *Teaching of Psychology, 17*, 36–39.

Heuberger, B., Gerber, D., & Anderson, R. (1999). Strength through cultural diversity: Developing and teaching a diversity course. *College Teaching, 47*(3), 107–113.

Heward, W. L. (1997) Four validated instruction strategies. *Behavior and Social Issues, 7*, 43–51.

Higher Education Research Institute. (2002). *The American freshman: National norms for fall 2001.* Retrieved December 22, 2003, from http://www.gseis.ucla.edu/heri/yfcy/yfcy_findings.html

Hilton, H. (1986). *The executive memory guide.* New York: Simon & Schuster.

Hilton, J. (2003, January). *You can run but you cannot hide: What every teacher needs to know about copyright.* Presented at the 25th Annual National Institute on the Teaching of Psychology, St. Petersburg Beach, FL.

Holland, H. (1965). *The spiral after-effect.* Oxford, England: Pergamon.

Huber, M., & Morreale, S. (2002). Situating the scholarship of teaching and learning: A cross-disciplinary conversation. In M. Huber & S. Morreale. (Eds.), *Disciplinary Styles in the Scholarship of Teaching and Learning: Exploring Common Ground.* Retrieved February, 2003 from www.carnegiefoundation.org/elibrary/docs/situating.htm

Hutchings, P., Bjork, C., & Babb, M. (Eds.). (2002). *An annotated bibliography of the scholarship of teaching and learning in higher education, revised and updated, Fall 2002.* Menlo Park, CA: Carnegie Foundation for the Advancement of Teaching.

(Retrieved March, 2003 from http://www.carnegiefoundation.org/elibrary/index.htm#highered)

Jacobs, L., & Chase, C. (1992). *Developing and using tests effectively.* San Francisco: Jossey-Bass.

Jendrek, M. (1989). Faculty reactions to academic dishonesty. *Journal of College Student Development, 30,* 401–406.

Jendrek, M. (1992). Students' reactions to academic dishonesty. *Journal of College Student Development, 33,* 260–273.

Jenkins, A. (1992). Active learning in structured lecture. In G. Gibbs & A. Jenkins (Eds.), *Teaching large classes in higher education: How to maintain quality with reduced resources* (pp. 63–77). London: Kogan Page.

Johnson, D., Johnson, R., & Smith, K. (1991). *Cooperative learning: Increasing college faculty instructional productivity* (ASHE-ERIC Higher Education Rep. No. 4). Washington, DC: The George Washington University, School of Education and Human Development.

Johnson, D., Johnson, R., & Smith, K. (1996). *Academic controversy: Enriching college instruction through intellectual conflict* (ASHE-ERIC Higher Education Rep. Vol. 25, No. 3). Washington, DC: The George Washington University, School of Education and Human Development.

Johnson, D., Johnson, R., & Smith, K. (1998a). Research on cooperative learning. In K. Feldman & M. Paulsen (Eds.), *Teaching and learning in college classrooms* (2nd ed., pp. 467–483). Boston: Pearson Custom Publishers.

Johnson, D., Johnson, R., & Smith, K. (1998b). Cooperative learning returns to college: What evidence is there that it works? *Change, 30,* 26–35.

Johnson, D., Johnson, R., & Smith, K. (2000). Constructive controversy: The educative power of intellectual conflict. *Change, 32,* 28–37.

Johnson, G. R. (1995). *First steps to excellence in college teaching* (3rd ed.). Madison, WI: Magna Publications.

Junn, E. (1994). Experiential approaches to enhancing cultural awareness. In D. Halpern (Ed.), *Changing College Classrooms* (pp. 128–164). San Francisco: Jossey-Bass.

Keith-Spiegel, P., Wittig, A., Perkins, D., Balogh, D., & Whitley, B. (1993). *The ethics of teaching: A casebook.* Muncie, IN: Ball State University.

Keller, F., & Sherman, J. (1974). *The Keller plan handbook.* Menlo Park, CA: Benjamin.

Kellum, K., Carr, J., & Dozier, C. (2001). Response-card instruction and student learning in a college classroom. *Teaching of Psychology, 28*(2), 101–104.

Kemp, P., & O'Keefe, R. (2003). Improving teaching effectiveness: Some examples from a program for the enhancement of teaching. *College Teaching, 51,* 111–114.

Kennedy, D. (1997). *Academic duty.* Cambridge, MA: Harvard University Press.

Kerr, M. P., & Payne, S. J. (1994). Learning to use a spreadsheet by doing and by watching. *Interacting With Computers, 6,* 3–22.

King, R. (2002a). Managing teaching loads: And finding time for reflection and renewal. *APS Observer, 15,* 13–14, 35–36.

King, R. (2002b, January). *Portfolio development: Using authentic learning assignments in psychology courses.* Poster presented at the 22nd Annual Institute on the Teaching of Psychology, St. Petersburg Beach, FL.

Knapper, C., & Wright, W. (2001). Using portfolios to document good teaching: Premises, purposes, practices. *New Directions of Teaching and Learning, 88,* 19–29.

Korn, J. (2003, July). Writing a philosophy of teaching. *Excellence in Teaching, 5,* PSYCHTEACHER@list.Kennesaw.edu

Kounin, J. (1977) *Discipline and group management in classrooms*. Huntington, New York: Robert E. Krieger Publishing Company.

Kuhlenschmidt, S., & Layne, L. (1999). Strategies for dealing with difficult behavior. *New Directions in Teaching and Learning, 77*, 45–57.

Kulik, C., Kulik, J., & Bangert-Drowns, R. (1990). Effectiveness of mastery learning programs: A meta-analysis. *Review of Educational Research, 60*, 265–299.

Kulik, J. A., Kulik, C., & Cohen, P. A. (1979). A meta-analysis of outcome studies of Keller's personalized system of instruction. *American Psychologist, 34*, 307–318.

Lambert, L. M., Tice, S. L., & Featherstone, P. H. (Eds.). (1996). *University teaching: A guide for graduate students*. Syracuse, NY: Syracuse University Press.

Leamnson, R. (1999). *Thinking about teaching and learning: Developing habits of learning with first year college and university students*. Sterling, VA: Stylus.

Leonard, J., Mitchell, K., Meyers, S., & Love, J. (2002). Using case studies in introductory psychology. *Teaching of Psychology, 29*, 142–144.

Levy, G., & Peters, W. (2002). Undergraduates' views of best college courses. *Teaching of Psychology, 29*, 46–48.

Linn, R., & Gronlund, N. (2000). *Measurement and assessment in teaching* (8th ed.). Upper Saddle River, NJ: Merrill.

Loui, M. (2003, April). *What do professors do all day and why do they do it?* Presentation, University of Illinois, Urbana-Champaign.

Lowman, J. (1987). Giving students feedback. In M. Weimer (Ed.), *Teaching large classes well. New Directions for Teaching and Learning* (No. 32; pp. 71–83). San Francisco: Jossey-Bass

Lowman, J. (1995). *Mastering the techniques of teaching* (2nd ed.). San Francisco: Jossey-Bass.

Lowman, J. (1998). What constitutes masterful teaching. In K. Feldman & M. Paulsen (Eds.), *Teaching and learning in the college classroom*, (2nd ed., pp. 503–513). Boston: Pearson Custom Publishing.

Lusk, M., & Conklin, L. (2002). Collaborative testing to promote learning. *Journal of Nursing Education, 42*, 121–124.

MacGregor, J. (1990). Collaborative learning: Shared inquiry as a process of reform. In M. D. Svinicki (Ed.), *Changing faces of college teaching: New Directions for Teaching and Learning* (No. 42; pp. 19–30). San Francisco: Jossey-Bass.

MacGregor, J. (2000). Restructuring large classes to create communities of learners. In J. MacGregor, J. Cooper, K. Smith, & P. Robinson (Eds.), Strategies for energizing large classes: From small groups to learning communities. *New Directions for Teaching and Learning, 81*, 47–61.

Magnan, B. (1990). *147 practical tips for teaching professors*. Madison, WI: Magna.

Maier, M., & Panitz, T. (1996). End on a high note: Better endings for classes and courses. *College Teaching, 44*, 145–148.

Mann, R. D., Arnold, S., Binder J., Cytrynbaum, S., Newman, B., Ringwald, B., & Rosenwein, R. (1970). *The college classroom: Conflict, change, and learning*. New York: Wiley.

Maramark, S., & Maline, M. (1993). *Issues in education: Academic dishonesty among college students*. Washington, DC: U.S. Department of Education, Office of Research.

Marchese, T. (1997). Service-Learning in the Disciplines: An interview with monograph series editors Robert Bringle and Edward Zlotkowski. *AAHE Bulletin, 49*(7), 3–6.

Marin, P. (2000). The educational possibility of multi-racial/multi-ethnic college classrooms. In *Does diversity make a difference? Three research studies on diversity in college classrooms*. Washington, DC: American Council on Education and American Association of University Professors.

Marincovich, M. (1999). Using student feedback to improve teaching. In P. Seldin (Ed.), *Changing practices in evaluating teaching: A practical guide to improved faculty performance and promotion/tenure decisions* (pp. 45–69). Bolton MA: Anker.

Markie, P. J. (1994). *A professor's duties: Ethical issues in college teaching.* Lanham, MD: Rowman and Littlefield.

Marsh, H. (1987). Students' evaluations of university teaching: Research findings, methodological issues, and directions for future research. *International Journal of Educational Research, 11,* 253–388.

Marsh, H., & Bailey, M. (1993). Multidimensional students' evaluations of teaching effectiveness: A profile analysis. *Journal of Higher Education, 69,* 1–18.

Marsh, H., & Dunkin, M. (1997). Students' evaluations of university teaching: A multidimensional perspective. In R. Perry & J. Smart (Eds.), *Effective teaching in higher education: Research and practice* (pp. 241–320). New York: Agathon.

Marsh, H., & Roche, E. (2000). Effects of grading leniency and low workload on students' evaluation of teaching: Popular myth, bias, validity or innocent bystander? *Journal of Educational Psychology, 92,* 202–228.

Marsh, H., & Roche, L. (1997). Making students' evaluations of teaching effectiveness effective: The critical issues of validity, bias and utility. *American Psychologist, 52,* 1187–1197.

May, K., & Loyd, B. (1993). Academic dishonesty: The honor system and students' attitudes. *Journal of College Student Development, 34,* 125–129.

Mayer, S., & Sutton, K. (1996). *Personality: An integrative approach.* New York: Macmillan.

McCabe, D. (1993). Faculty responses to academic dishonesty: The influence of student honor codes. *Research in Higher Education, 34,* 647–658.

McCabe, D., & Bowers, W. (1994). Academic dishonesty among males in college: A 30 year perspective. *Journal of College Student Development, 35,* 5–10.

McCabe, D., & Trevino, L. (1993). Academic dishonesty. *Journal of Higher Education, 64,* 522–538.

McCabe, D., & Trevino, L. (1997). Individual and contextual influences on academic dishonesty: A multicampus investigation. *Research in Higher Education, 38,* 379–396.

McGlynn, A. (2001). *Successful beginnings for college teaching: Engaging your students from the first day.* Madison, WI: Atwood.

McKeachie, W. J. (1986). Teaching psychology: Research and experience. In V. Makosky (Ed.), *The G. Stanley Hall Lecture Series, 6,* 165–191.

McKeachie, W. J. (1997a). Good teaching makes a difference—And we know what it is. In R. P. Perry & J. C. Smart (Eds.), *Effective teaching in higher education: Research and practice* (pp. 396–411). New York: Agathon.

McKeachie, W. J. (1997b). Student ratings: The validity of use. *American Psychologist, 52,* 1218–1225.

McKeachie, W. J. (1999). *Teaching tips: Strategies, research, and theory for college and university teachers* (10th ed.). Boston: Houghton Mifflin.

McKeachie, W. J. (Ed.). (2001). *McKeachie's teaching tips: Strategies, research, and theory for college and university teachers* (11th ed.). Boston: Houghton-Mifflin.

McKeachie, W. J. (2002). *Teaching tips: Strategies, research, and theory for college and university teachers* (12th ed.). Boston: Houghton Mifflin.

McKeage, K. (2001). Office hours as you like them: Integrating real-time chats into the course media mix. *College Teaching, 49,* 32–37.

McKinney, K. (1999). Encouraging student motivation. *The Teaching Professor, 13,* 4.

McKinney, K. (2001). The teacher with the most negative impact on me. *The National Teaching and Learning Forum, 10,* 7–8.

McKinney, K. (2003, January). *Research methods for doing the Scholarship of Teaching and Learning*. University of Illinois Faculty Retreat presentation, Urbana, IL.

Meagher, L. D., & Devine, T. G. (1993). *Handbook on college teaching*. Durango, CO: Hollowbrook.

Menges, R., & Weimer, M. (1996). *Teaching on solid ground: Using scholarship to improve practice*. San Francisco: Jossey-Bass.

Mervis, J. (2001). Student survey highlights mismatch of training, goals. *Science, 291*, 408–409.

Mester, C., & Tauber, R. (2000). Acting lessons for teachers: Using performance skills in the classroom. *APS Observer, 13*, 12–13, 25.

Meyers, C., & Jones, T. (1993). *Promoting active learning: Strategies for the college classroom*. San Francisco: Jossey-Bass.

Miller, J., & Chamberlin, M. (2000). Women are teachers, men are professors: A study of student perceptions. *Teaching Sociology, 28*, 283–298.

Millis, B., & Cottell, P. (1998). *Cooperative learning for higher education faculty*. Phoenix, AZ: Oryx Press.

Mitchell, N., & Melton, S. (2003). Collaborative testing: An innovative approach to test taking. *Nurse Educator, 28*, 95–97.

Molden, D., & Dweck, C. S. (2000). Meaning and motivation. In C. Sansone & J. Harackiewicz (Eds.), *Intrinsic and extrinsic motivation: The search for optimal motivation and performance* (pp. 131–159). San Diego, CA: Academic Press.

Moore, R. (2003). Attendance and performance: How important is it for students to attend class? *Journal of College Science Teaching, 32*, 367–371.

Moran, D. R. (2000, June). *Is active learning for me?* Poster presented at APS Pre-convention Teaching Institute, Denver, CO.

Murray, B. (2000). Learning from real life. *APA Monitor, 31*, 71–72.

Murray, H. (1997) Effective teaching behaviors in the college classroom. In R. Perry & J. Smart (Eds.), *Effective teaching in higher education: Research and practice* (pp. 171–204). New York: Agathon.

National Center for Education Statistics. (1999). *Statistical Analysis Report, August 1999. An Institutional Perspective on Students with Disabilities in Postsecondary Education*. Washington, DC: United States Department of Education, Office of Educational Research and Improvement. NCES 1999-046.

National Center for Education Statistics. (2001). *Digest of Education Statistics, 2000*. Washington, DC: United States Department of Education, Office of Educational Research and Improvement. NCES 2001-034.

National Service-Learning Clearinghouse. (2003). *What is service-learning?* Retrieved August 7, 2003, from http://www.servicelearning.org/article/archive/35/

Neff, R., & Weimer, M. (1989). *Classroom communication: Collected readings for effective discussion and questioning*. Madison, WI: Magna.

Nilson, L. (2003). Improving student peer feedback. *College Teaching, 51*(1), 34–38.

Norcross, J., & Dooley, H. (1993). Faculty use and justification of extra credit: No middle ground? *Teaching of Psychology, 20*, 240–242.

Nummedal, S., Benson, J., & Chew, S. (2002). Disciplinary styles in the scholarship of teaching and learning: A view from psychology. In M. Huber & S. Morreale (Eds.), *Introduction to disciplinary styles in the scholarship of teaching and learning: Exploring common ground* (pp. 163–179). Menlo Park, CA: Carnegie Foundation for the Advancement of Teaching.

Ory, J. (2003). The final exam. *American Psychological Society Observer, 16*, 23–24, 34–35.

Ory, J., & Ryan, K. (1993). *Tips for improving testing and grading*. Newbury Park, CA: Sage Publications.

Palmisano, M., & Herrmann, D. (1991). The facilitation of memory performance. *Bulletin of the Psychonomic Society, 29,* 557–559.

Parkes, J., & Harris, M. (2002). The purposes of a syllabus. *College Teaching, 5,* 55–61.

Pastorino, E. (1999). Students with academic difficulty: Prevention and assistance. *APS Observer, 12,* 10–11, 26.

Pauk, W. (2001). *How to study in college* (7th ed.). Boston: Houghton-Mifflin.

Perlman, B., & McCann, L. (1996). *Recruiting good college faculty: Practical advice for a successful search.* Bolton, MA: Anker.

Prieto, L., & Meyers, S. (2001). *The teaching assistant training handbook: How to prepare TAs for their responsibilities.* Stillwater, OK: New Forums Press.

Rickard, H. C., Rogers, R., Ellis, N. R., & Beidleman, W. B. (1988). Some retention, but not enough. *Teaching of Psychology, 15,* 151–153.

Rodriguez-Farrar, H. (2003). *The teaching portfolio.* (The Harriet W. Sheridan Center for Teaching and Learning at Brown University.) Retrieved September, 2003 from http://www.brown.edu/Administration/Sheridan_Center/publications/teacport.html

Royce, D. D. (2000). *Teaching tips for college and university instructors: A practical guide.* Saddle River, NJ: Prentice Hall.

Ruhl, K. L., Hughes, C. A., & Schloss, P. J. (1987). Using the pause procedure to enhance lecture recall. *Teacher Education and Special Education, 10,* 4–18.

Ruscio, J. (2001). Administering quizzes at random to increase students' reading. *Teaching of Psychology, 28*(3), 204–206.

Ruskin, R. (1974). *The personalized system of instruction: An educational alternative* (ERIC/Higher Education Research Rep. No. 5). Washington, DC: American Association for Higher Education.

Sahadeo, D., & Davis, W. (1988). Review—Don't repeat. *College Teaching, 36*(3), 111–113.

Sanders, J., & Wiseman, R. (1994). The effects of verbal and nonverbal teacher immediacy on perceived cognitive, affective, and behavioral learning in the multicultural classroom. In K. Feldman & M. Paulsen (Eds.), *Teaching and learning in the college classroom* (2nd ed., pp. 623–636). Boston: Pearson Custom Publishing.

Sanders, L. (2001). Improving assessment in university classrooms. *College Teaching, 49,* 62–645.

Satterlee, J., & Lau, P. (2003, March). *Reading for meaning: Techniques for encouraging active reading.* Presentation at CTEN Teaching Workshop Series, University of Illinois, Champaign, IL.

Sawyer, R. M., Prichard, K. W., & Hostetler, K. D. (2001). *The art and politics of college teaching: A practical guide for the beginning professor* (2nd ed.). New York: Peter Lang Publishing.

Sax, L., Astin, A., Korn, W., & Mahoney, K. (1999). *The American freshman: National norms for Fall 1999.* Los Angeles: Higher Education Research Institute, Graduate School of Education and Information Studies, University of California.

Sax, L., Astin, A., Korn, W., & Mahoney, K. (2000). *The American Freshman: National Norms for Fall 2000.* Los Angeles: Higher Education Research Institute, Graduate School of Education and Information Studies, University of California.

Sax, L., Bryant, A., & Gilmartin, S. (2003). *A longitudinal investigation of emotional health among first-year college students: Comparisons of men and women.* Los Angeles: Higher Education Research Institute, Graduate School of Education and Information Studies, University of California.

Scholl–Buckwald, S. (1985). The first meeting of the class. In J. Katz (Ed.), *Teaching as though students mattered: New directions for teaching and learning* (No. 21; pp. 13–21). San Francisco: Jossey-Bass.

Schwartz, M. (1986). An experimental investigation of bad karma and its relationship to the grades of college students. *Journal of Polymorphous Perversity, 3*, 9–12.

Scott, S. (1997). Accommodating college students with learning disabilities: How much is enough? *Innovative Higher Education, 22*, 85–99.

Seldin, P. (1991). *The teaching portfolio: A practical guide to improved performance and promotion/tenure decisions.* Bolton, MA: Anker.

Seldin, P. (1999a). Current practices—Good and bad—Nationally. In P. Seldin (Ed.), *Changing practices in evaluating teaching: A practical guide to improved faculty performance and promotion/tenure decisions* (pp. 1–24). Bolton, MA: Anker.

Seldin, P. (1999b). Self-evaluation: What works? What doesn't? In P. Seldin (Ed.), *Changing practices in evaluating teaching: A practical guide to improved faculty performance and promotion/tenure decisions* (pp. 97–115). Bolton, MA: Anker.

Seward, L. (2002). A time for inclusion. *AAHE Bulletin, 54*, 3–6.

Shapiro, N. Z., & Anderson, R. H. (1985). *Toward an ethics and etiquette for electronic mail.* Santa Monica, CA: Rand Corporation.

Shimoff, E., & Catania, A. (2001). Effects of recording attendance on grades in introductory psychology. *Teaching of Psychology, 28*, 192–195.

Shore, B., Foster, S., Knapper, C., Nadeau, G., Neill, N., & Sim, V. (1986). *The teaching dossier: A guide to its preparation and use.* Ottawa: Canadian Association of University Teachers.

Shulman, L. (2003, January). *Lamarck's Revenge: Teaching and Learning Among the Scholarships.* University of Illinois Faculty Retreat presentation, Urbana, IL.

Silberman, M. (1996). *Active learning: 101 strategies to teach any subject.* Boston: Allyn & Bacon.

Silverman, R., & Welty, W. (1990). Teaching with cases. *Journal on Excellence in College Teaching, 1*, 88–97.

Skinner, B. F. (1954). The science of learning and the art of teaching. *Harvard Educational Review, 24*, 86–97.

Skinner, B. F. (1968). *The technology of teaching.* New York: Appleton-Century-Crofts.

Sleigh, M., & Ritzer, D. (2001). Encouraging student attendance. *APS Observer, 14*, 19–20, 32–33.

Sleigh, M., Ritzer, D., & Casey, M. (2002). Student versus faculty perceptions of missing class. *Teaching of Psychology, 29*, 53–56.

Smith, B., & MacGregor, J. (1998). What is collaborative learning? In K. Feldman & M. Paulsen (Eds.), *Teaching and learning in college classrooms.* (2nd ed., pp. 585–596). Boston: Pearson Custom Publishing.

Smith, J. C. (Ed.). (2000). *ABC relaxation training: A practical guide for health professionals.* New York: Springer.

Smith, K. (2000). Going deeper: Formal small-group learning in large classes. In J. MacGregor, J. Cooper, K. Smith, & P. Robinson (Eds.), Strategies for energizing large classes: From small groups to learning communities. *New Directions for Teaching and Learning, 81*, 25–46.

Sojka, J., Gupta, A., & Deiter-Schmelz, D. (2002). Student and faculty perceptions of student evaluations of teaching: A study of similarities and differences. *College Teaching, 50*, 44–49.

Steffens, H. (1987). Journals in the teaching of history. In T. Fulwiler (Ed.), *The journal book* (pp. 219–226). Portsmouth, NH: Boynton/Cook.

Stevens, R. (2003). *Test review PowerPoint presentation based upon Jeopardy!* Retrieved October, 2003 from www.ulm.edu/~stevens/review_page.htm

Stevenson, M. (1989). Creating a connected classroom: Two projects that work! *Teaching of Psychology, 16*, 212–214.

Suskie, L. (2000). *Fair assessment practices* (American Association for Higher Education Bulletin). Retrieved March, 2003 from http://www.aahebulletin.com/archive/may2.asp

Svinicki, M. (1998). Helping students understand grades. *College Teaching, 46,* 101–105.

Svinicki, M., Hagen, A., & Meyer, D. (1996). How research on learning strengthens instruction. In R. Menges & M. Weimer (Eds.), *Teaching on solid ground: Using scholarship to improve practice* (pp. 257–288). San Francisco: Jossey-Bass.

Teven, J., & McCroskey, J. (1996). The relationship of perceived teacher caring with student learning and teacher evaluation. *Communication Education, 46,* 1–9.

Tieberius, R., & Flak, E. (1999). Incivility in dyadic teaching and learning. *New Directions for Teaching and Learning, 77,* 3–12.

Timpson, W., & Bendel-Simso, P. (1996). *Concepts and choices for teaching: Meeting the challenges in higher education.* Madison, WI: Magna.

Tobin, K. (1987). The role of wait time in higher cognitive level learning. *Review of Educational Research, 57,* 69–95.

Tozer, S. (1992, August). *Effective lecturing.* Presentation to University of Illinois, Urbana–Champaign, Teaching Assistants Orientation.

Treisman, U. (1985). *A study of the mathematics performance of Black students at the University of California, Berkeley.* Unpublished doctoral dissertation, University of California, Berkeley.

Tufte, E. (2003, September). Powerpoint is evil. *Wired Magazine,* Retrieved October, 2003 from www.wired.com/wired/archive/11.09/ppt2.html

University of Illinois, Urbana-Champaign. (2003). *Code of policies and regulations applying to all students.* Retrieved March, 2003 from www.uiuc.edu/admin_manual/code

Upcraft, M. L. (1996). Teaching and today's college students. In R. Menges & M. Weimer (Eds.), *Teaching on solid ground: Using scholarship to improve practice* (pp. 21–41). San Francisco: Jossey-Bass.

Wade, C. (1988, April). *Thinking critically about critical thinking in psychology.* Paper presented at the annual meeting of the Western Psychological Association, San Francisco, CA.

Walck, C. (1997). A teaching life. *Journal of Management Education, 21,* 473–482.

Walvoord, B., & Anderson, V. J. (1998). *Effective grading: A tool for learning and assessment.* San Francisco: Jossey-Bass.

Ward, A., & Jenkins, A. (1992). The problems of learning and teaching in large classes. In G. Gibbs & A. Jenkins (Eds.), *Teaching large classes in higher education: How to maintain quality with reduced resources* (pp. 23–36). London: Kogan Page.

Watkins, D. (1994). Student evaluations of teaching effectiveness: A cross-cultural perspective. *Research in Higher Education, 35,* 251–266.

Weimer, M. (1988). Reading your way to better teaching. *College Teaching, 36(2),* 48–51.

Weimer, M. (1989). Research summary: Professors part of the problem? In R. Neff & M. Weimer (Eds.), *Classroom communication: Collected readings for effective discussion and questioning* (pp. 67–71). Madison, WI: Magna.

Weimer, M. (1996). *Improving your classroom teaching.* Newbury Park, CA: Sage. (Volume 1 of a ten-volume series collectively titled *Survival Skills for Scholars.*)

Weimer, M., & Lenze, L. (1997). Instructional interventions: A review of the literature on efforts to improve instruction. In R. Perry & J. Smart (Eds.), *Effective teaching in higher education: Research and practice* (pp. 205–240). New York: Agathon.

Weimer, M. G. (Ed.). (1987). *Teaching large classes well: New directions for teaching and learning.* San Francisco: Jossey-Bass.

Wilson, V. (1999). From "zzz's" to "A's": Using rubrics to improve student presentations. *The Teaching Professor, 13*, 3.

Zakrajsek, T. (1998). Developing effective lectures. *APS Observer, 11*, 24–26.

Zlokovich, M. (2001). Grading for optimal student learning. *APS Observer, 14*, 12–13, 20–21.

Zubizarreta, J. (1999). Evaluating teaching through portfolios. In P. Seldin (Ed.), *Changing practices in evaluating teaching: A practical guide to improved faculty performance and promotion/tenure decisions* (pp. 162–181). Bolton, MA: Anker.

Author Index

Subject Index

Note: Page number followed by *f* indicates figure, *t* indicates table.